D0916343

THE MAKING OF A SECRET AGENT

Frank H. D. Pickersgill, 1939

THE MAKING OF A SECRET AGENT

Letters of 1934-1943
Written by Frank Pickersgill

and Edited with a Memoir
by George H. Ford

McClelland and Stewart

Copyright © 1978 McClelland and Stewart Limited

All rights reserved
ISBN: 0-7710-7005-5

McClelland and Stewart Limited
The Canadian Publishers
25 Hollinger Road
Toronto, Ontario
M4B 3G2

Canadian Cataloguing in Publication Data

Pickersgill, Frank, H. D., 1915-1944.
  The making of a secret agent

First ed. published in 1948 under title: The Pickersgill letters.

ISBN 0-7710-7005-5

1. Pickersgill, Frank, H. D., 1915-1944. 2. Spies – Canada – Biography. 3. Spies – France – Biography. 4. World War, 1939-1945 – Secret service. I. Ford, George H. 1914- II. Title.

FC581.P5A4 1978   940.54′86′710924   C77-001826-2
F1034.P5A4 1978

Printed and bound in Canada

To Sara Pickersgill
(1877-1961)

"Speeding and soaring he comes the Atlantic sighting
and there is no Joshua can brake his flight nor
any clutch of ours can hold this precious night."
(Earle Birney,
Dusk on English Bay, 1941,
The Collected Poems of Earle Birney, 1975).

CONTENTS

ILLUSTRATIONS

PREFACE

The extraordinary degree of interest in the work of World War II secret agents has resulted in the production of a whole bookshelf of writings on this subject during the past ten or fifteen years. These books include some lively narratives about the exploits of individual agents as well as sober histories of the intelligence organizations under which the agents served. One of the most notable of such books has been the story of a Canadian from Winnipeg, Sir William Stephenson, who played an invaluable role in the success of Allied intelligence operations in Europe and America. Stephenson's story is told in *A Man Called Intrepid*, a best seller by William Stevenson, first published in 1976.

The present book is about another Canadian from Winnipeg, of a later generation than Stephenson's, who also played a role in that war. Several pages in *A Man Called Intrepid* are, in fact, devoted to celebrating his wartime exploits as a secret agent. This was Frank Pickersgill whose earlier career had begun as a student at Manitoba and Toronto. In 1938 he had gone to France for further studies, and when war broke out he stayed on there as a free-lance journalist. In the summer of 1940 he was captured and interned by the Germans. After a dramatic escape from prison, two years later, Pickersgill made his way to England where he joined the Canadian army and underwent training to become a secret agent. In 1943 he was parachuted back into German-occupied France, was captured, and later executed at Buchenwald in September, 1944. As such, the story of this young Canadian belongs on the same book-shelf with other accounts of agents and their organizations. On this level it is a story of adventure, adventure which ended in sacrifice (for want of a less hackneyed phrase).

I should nevertheless like to claim for the present book one or two differences from others. One is that this is the story of a man. Although the book about William Stephenson is called *A Man Called Intrepid* it is not, whatever its other virtues, really about a man. It focuses instead on large-scale events like the sinking of the *Bismarck* and summit meetings between Church-ill and Roosevelt. Stephenson himself remains, perhaps neces-sarily, a shadowy figure. Whereas in the story of Frank Pickers-gill, while the big events are there and are seen as profoundly affecting his life and thinking, the focus is on one individual, a highly colourful and distinctly original individual, and on how the world of the 1930s and 1940s looked to him. The story is hence more personal and immediate.

The other difference is suggested by the title, *The Making of a Secret Agent*. The key word here is *Making*, because the interest that Pickersgill's story has for the reader is not limited to his adventures as an agent but to how and why he grew to choose that role. The making wasn't restricted, that is, to the six months in 1942-1943 devoted to training in parachute jumping and how to blow up power stations with dynamite. Instead, the making involved a lifetime, albeit a relatively short lifetime (he was twenty-nine years old when he died). The real drama resides in changes and developments in his attitudes more than in exciting incidents such as his sawing his way out of prison with a saw smuggled to him in a loaf of bread.

The character of the man who stood up under Nazi torture in 1943 and encouraged others to stand up to it had been developed for many years before he volunteered for service as an agent. Character, as George Eliot reminds us, is "a shap-ing and an unfolding." For Frank Pickersgill, the making in-volved the shaping forces of family and friends and the whole community of a mid-western Canadian capital at Winnipeg. It also involved omnivorous reading and hard tussling with issues stimulated by this reading, especially religious issues as illustrated in the letters he wrote as a graduate student in Toronto. He had an unusual capacity to assimilate current ideas; one of his French friends described his mind as "merveilleusement assimilateur." His letters show the impact on a first class mind of such currents as Barthianism, French syndicalism, Catholicism, and Existentialism.

And the making also involved, obviously, his responses to events such as the Munich crisis of 1938, the invasion of Poland in 1939, and to political developments such as the decline and resurrection of democracy in France, and especially the rise to power of Hitler's Germany in the 1930s, which Pickersgill, like many of his generation, at first regarded with an indulgent benevolence.

The ingredients are here, that is, for a novel of development, a *Bildungsroman*, in which adventures of a mind and spirit are complemented later by adventures on the plane of physical action. It is a typical tale of groping one's way through the stages of growing up, characteristic of all generations, but with a special dimension, in this instance, provided by unusually tumultuous times.

The most striking illustration of Pickersgill's development is his radical about-face in his attitudes towards the war and his own role vis-à-vis that conflict. Having lost his father early in life as a result of World War I, and coming to maturity in a decade in which the young were to repudiate war as a grand illusion, Pickersgill was determined, and in this he was typical of most of his generation in the west, not to be seduced by bugle calls in 1939. Reinforcing this set of attitudes was his early developed dislike for military establishments and his awareness of the absurdities of regimentation and red tape. With his highly developed sense of the absurd, one could predict that had he lived, Pickersgill would have enjoyed Joseph Heller's *Catch 22* with its funny exposures of the mechanical qualities of military establishments – although he might have remarked then that Heller had chosen the wrong war as the subject for his novel. It deserves mention, in passing, that his own military career included at least one Heller-style incident when a letter was sent from the War Office in London to Captain Frank Pickersgill (addressed care of his brother). "Dear Pickersgill" the writer began, and he then went on to offer his felicitations to Pickersgill for having been mentioned in despatches (the certificate of this award was enclosed). It was signed by a Colonel, who concluded by saying: "Accept our sincere congratulations." This letter was dated April 4, 1946, almost two years after Captain Frank Pickersgill had died at Buchenwald. The Colonel's signature is illegible, but readers of *Catch 22* will be sure his name must have been that of the master of military form-letter writers, Colonel Cathcart.

In view of these irreverent attitudes of his during the 1930s, and his general commitment to an isolationist stance, the development into the Captain Pickersgill of 1942 is a fascinating record of his capacity to change his mind. This capacity marks the whole life and is a crucial component of the making process.

ii

In its original form, this book took shape shortly after the end of World War II. As a friend of Frank Pickersgill, I approached his brother Jack to ask whether he and his family would favour my trying to put together a book about Frank which was then to consist, predominantly, of an edited selection from the letters he had written to friends and family during his lifetime. Like most men who take to writing as a profession, Frank Pickersgill had been an enthusiastic letter-writer, and it was a tribute to the high regard his recipients had for his letters that over two hundred and sixty of them were still available for me to choose from at that date. Such letters, it seemed to me, framed with interspersed narratives and commentaries, could give a vivid and intimate portrait of a brilliant young man's development through a crucial nine or ten year period of our century, 1934-1943.

His family gave this proposal its blessings, and Jack Pickersgill, in particular, provided enthusiastic co-operation by supplying me with all materials then available about his brother's life and career. The resulting book was published in 1948 by Ryerson Press in Toronto. Its full title was: *The Pickersgill Letters: Written by Frank Pickersgill During the Period 1934-1943 and Edited with a Memoir by George H. Ford.*

The book was excellently received and soon sold out. Never having been reprinted, *The Pickersgill Letters* has become something of a collector's item, and much sought-after copies have been selling for about thirty dollars in second-hand bookshops. Given this continuing demand today, the obvious thing for an interested publisher to do would be simply to reprint the book unchanged. For me this was a tempting prospect, involving no effort whatever on my part, but on thinking about it further, I realized (and Jack Pickersgill fully agreed) that merely to reprint would be an evasion of responsibility. In thirty years a great deal of fresh information has come to light that was unavailable in 1948, especially about the last four years of his life. What was called for now had to be essentially a new book, one that would incorporate the qualities of the original version, such as they were, into a more complete story.

The present version includes unchanged all the letters in *The Pickersgill Letters*; in fact some five new letters, not available in 1948, have been added. The central core of the book is hence as it was. Some of the narratives linking each group of letters are likewise unchanged (Part II for example), but most narratives have been enlarged and extensively revised. The major changes involve the period 1940-1944, from the time of his internment until his death. For part of this crucial period, his letters can still carry some of the narrative, but overall they are scanty. In 1940 and 1941 after his internment, there is only one letter plus a post-card for each of both years. In 1942 there are nine letters, mostly short, and in 1943, up to June, the same. For the remaining crucially important fifteen months there are, of course, no letters whatever. In *A Man Called Intrepid* (page 232) it is stated that Pickersgill kept a diary about his experiences during those final fifteen months after being parachuted into France in June, 1943, but as far as I know, no trained secret agent would be foolish enough to keep a diary while in the field, or, if imprisoned, would he have the chance to keep one. Certainly no record of Pickersgill's having kept one has come to light. The only evidence we have, from his own hand, during this period, is a brief inscription he scrawled on a prison wall, in July, 1943, recording, like Kilroy, his existence.

His experiences during this late period have therefore had to be reconstructed without the aid of his lively letters, and, instead, have been based on assorted records, many of which have only recently come to light. As a result, three whole chapters in the present book are devoted to filling in the story that took up only a page and a half of *The Pickersgill Letters*. The latter parts of *The Making of a Secret Agent* could, as a result, be perhaps more appropriately styled a biography or history rather than a memoir, but I prefer to retain *Memoir*, a less pretentious term, to categorize my part in the production. In the Preface to *The Pickersgill Letters* I cited a charitable remark by Dr. Johnson about the role of an expositor. It is worth quoting again: "It is impossible for an expositor not to write too little for some, and too much for others."

iii

Dr. Johnson's observation about two kinds of readers has additional special applications here. In putting the book together I've been aware that some readers will have been friends of Frank Pickersgill, for he had a gift of making many friends in many lands. For them the book will have, I hope, special evocative qualities. Rereading his letters and the anecdotes about him, I was myself reminded of another brilliant young man who died in his twenties, Arthur Hallam, who continued to be a vital presence in the minds of his contemporaries, including Gladstone and Tennyson, for the rest of their lives. In the 1860s Tennyson revisited a valley in the Pyrenees, a place he had enjoyed seeing with Hallam thirty-two years earlier, and the sound of a mountain stream there brought his friend back to mind:

> And all along the valley, by rock and cave and tree,
> The voice of the dead was a living voice to me.

For readers who were friends of Frank Pickersgill the "living voice" is to be heard on page after page of what follows.

But this book is by no means simply a memorial for friends and relations. Instead it is aimed at the much larger group of readers who did not have the good fortune to have heard that distinctive voice of his. The book offers such readers a chance to discover that voice and, overall, to get to know a lovable and vibrant person and to share his growing up.

Some of these readers will be of a generation that was profoundly affected by the lamentable spectacle of Vietnam, and for them the later stages of Pickersgill's life as a secret agent may legitimately lead to their asking: How was it that in an earlier generation, an amiable fun-loving student of Classics should have deliberately chosen to fight and die as he did? The answer can be worked out, I trust, in the chapters that follow. Here one observation might be ventured. One of Hitler's assumptions about the Nazi take-over in Europe was that the typical thought-ridden, oscillating intellectual of the 1930s would remain a pushover for his police forces in the 1940s. It was one of several miscalculations made by Hitler, and one of his gravest. In M.R.D. Foot's history of agents who, like Pickersgill, fought back in the 1940s, there is a short statement describing the power of the Nazi police organizations that puts the matter prosaically but effectively:

> The Gestapo . . . was responsible for arresting agents. It overlapped with the *Sicherheitsdienst* (SD), the party security service. Between them these two sections came to run the private and public lives of several scores of millions of people, and the principal gain from the victory of 1945 is that they no longer do so.

My chief debt in preparing this book is once again to Jack Pickersgill. Since his brother's death he has accumulated extensive files of materials, some of which he was able to obtain because of his high position in the government of Canada, and others were contributed simply by his brother's friends. He has shared all of these items with me and given me complete *carte blanche* to draw from them as I saw fit. His supporting hand throughout has been invaluable for me. Friends of Frank Pickersgill also have been helpful, most recently Whitmore Hicks in France, Albert Fyfe in the United States, and Mary Lile Benham in Canada. Overall I am most indebted to Kay Moore Gimpel whose comments and recollections I have frequently cited. I also wish to thank Stanley Jackson, of the National Film Board of Canada, for supplying me with some materials collected earlier when it had been proposed to do a film version of the Pickersgill story. Thanks should also be paid to McKenzie Porter for permission to quote from an interview with Yeo-Thomas which he published in the December 2, 1961 issue of *Maclean's*.

G.H.F., Rochester, New York, September, 1977.

Part I

MANITOBA: 1915-1936
(to age 21)

A French friend who was with him a few days before his death in 1944 relates that Frank Pickersgill talked then with warm enthusiasm of Canada, the home which he had not seen for six years. Although his sympathies had become international, his roots were still Canadian. His family had been settled in Canada for generations. On his mother's side he was of United Empire Loyalist stock, but feeling that the story of one's eighteenth-century Tory ancestors (like the story of descent from the Mayflower Pilgrims) had become tarnished through time, he refused to take his Loyalist connection too seriously. In fact he treated it as a skeleton to be kept locked in the family cupboard.

Before the first Great War, the Pickersgill family had moved west from Ontario and settled on a farm near Ashern, Manitoba. Frank H. D. Pickersgill was born on May 28, 1915, in the city of Winnipeg, but his boyhood was passed on the Ashern farm. Of his early rural background he was much more proud than of his Loyalist ancestry. Farm life, he felt, develops both independence and conservatism (two elements of his character which were later to be in conflict), and although he left the farm in early boyhood, this background afterwards coloured his thinking about the political questions of his time, often forcing him to test urban and industrial theory in the light of the realities of farm life, especially of the prairie droughts of the 1930s.

Of the first Great War he was of course too young to remember anything, but its aftermath had far-reaching effects on his life. His father, Frank Allan Pickersgill, who had served overseas in the 16th Canadian Scottish from 1916-1918, never recovered from the disabilities of service and died at the age of forty-one when Frank was five years old. His mother, who had formerly been a nurse, had to take on the task of bringing up her family of five children, of whom Frank was the youngest. Frank's affection for his mother later in life was always heightened by his remembrance of her strength and cheerful self-reliance during those early years at Ashern. Their farm was not located in the rich prairie country in the southern part of the province but in the bush land between the lakes. It is poor land, and to bring up a large family there required courage and resourcefulness, the pioneer virtues at their best. Mrs. Pickersgill combined these with unfailing good humour. By moving to Winnipeg when all her children were at the university, she kept the family together as a unit until 1936 when her four sons had graduated, and her daughter, Elizabeth, was engaged as a dietician in the Winnipeg General Hospital.

In these early years Frank attended a typical rural one-room school-house and also received special tutoring at home in French and other subjects from his oldest brother, Jack. An early snapshot shows him proudly holding a calf with which he had won a prize in an Agricultural Fair. The calf and other country pleasures had to be abandoned on the occasion of the Pickersgills' moving to Winnipeg, when Frank was eleven years of age. Although he subsequently became more attached to Paris as a place in which to live, he always spoke of Winnipeg as his particular home. Its free-and-easy social atmosphere remained for him, something of a reference point. The free-and-easy quality of the city derived, in part, from its ethnic diversity resulting from the vast tide of European immigrants which had poured into Manitoba in the 1920s. Although the population of Winnipeg in 1931 was only 220,000, more foreign language newspapers were published there than in New York city. And for English language newspapers of that period, there was the notoriously colourful *Free Press*, under the direction of J. W. Dafoe, whose editorial perspectives took in not only problems of the prairie wheat crop but the clouded horizons generated by events in Europe and Asia. Despite the depression and the drought, despite Blue Laws, and despite interminably long winters cold enough to test the endurance of an Eskimo, Winnipeg in the 1930s was a lively city in which to grow up. It has been flatteringly likened, in that particular decade at least, to Edinburgh in the early nineteenth century. This comparison to another northern capital is not so altogether incongruous as it might seem in view of the prominent role played by Scotsmen in every walk of Winnipeg life at that time.

Because Frank had just turned fifteen when he completed his course at a Winnipeg high school, his family decided that he was too young to enter university. For part of the following year he attended business college and after that worked in a meat-packing plant, the Harris Abattoir. Frank never completely succeeded in adjusting his sense of smell to the odours of meat-packing, so he was more than delighted when the year was over and he could commence his studies at university.

During 1931-1936, the years of the depth of the depression, Frank was a student at the University of Manitoba. At this period he was affected only indirectly by the various crises which were to culminate in 1939. Events in Manchuria, Ethiopia, and Spain, which were later to seem of vast importance to him, were then only distant rumblings, not loud enough to distract him from his own orbit. Like many young men of the 1930s, he had soaked up the war-disillusioned books of Sassoon, C. E. Montague, Hemingway, Remarque, Beverley Nichols and others, and had concluded that 1914-1918 had been a great mistake and that its recurrence must be prevented – in some way. He was also aware that the lack of stability and security in his time seemed to set its seal against a planned career. But beyond such passing considerations, like most of us, he went his own road. He had five years in which to pick up the basic ingredients of a liberal education, to make friends, to sharpen his wits, and above all to develop his own strongly-marked individualism. In their way, these five years were fair seed time enough.

As an undergraduate he lived, of course, at home. Not many Winnipeg families in the 1930s could consider sending their sons or daughters back east to the relatively expensive dormitory living at McGill or Queen's University. In Frank's case, if compensation were needed, it was provided by the very liveliness of his own household. His undergraduate friends came to know that household well as a result of frequent parties on Sunday evenings to which they were invited by the whole Pickersgill family. No liquor was served; it wasn't needed as would be immediately evident to any latecomer opening the front door and confronting scenes of uproarious hilarity. Instead of liquor Mrs. Pickersgill and Elizabeth prepared great pots of coffee, and there were mounds of sandwiches (with their crusts on). Crazy games were played. In the basement one of the favourites was revolving ping pong, a fiendish game in which the players had to rush from one end of the table to the other to retrieve shots. One visitor recalled playing it when she was six months pregnant in front of a group of spectators who, as she reports, were "helpless with laughter as I ballooned around squeezing my six-months pregnant bulk between table and wall, and everyone shouting at me to speed it up!" Upstairs there would be word games which provoked similar shoutings. A Platitude Prize was offered every week for anyone who could come up with an appropriately silly bromide. Frank, early on, began to star in this game. His contribution one week was incontestably the winner, when he observed, with a straight face: "I always think St. Bernards are such *large* dogs." Looking back on these gatherings in 1977, Mary Lile Benham offers a useful reminder of other aspects of these Pickersgill open house gatherings: "Of course as well as crazy games there was always conversation – real conversation. We worried away at all the issues of the day – including that manifesto from the Oxford undergraduates who affirmed they would never fight in a war. We Saved the World – as University students always have. It was Important to be Earnest as well as to frolic."

Frank's first two years were passed at United College (where his brother, Jack, was lecturing in History), and the last three at the university itself. In both institutions he was a well-known figure. He was a big youth, over six feet tall, and powerfully built. During the summer vacations he used to throw himself energetically into the job of making roads in the bush country around Lake of the Woods, incidentally reading Plato at night and cursing mosquitoes night and day – all with equal vigour. His excellent physique was to stand him in good stead when he took parachute training in England many years later.

He had also at this time the big youth's jerky and rather awkward movements, accentuated in his case by ear trouble which left him somewhat deaf and may have affected his sense of balance. Students would grin amiably as they watched him lurching with great strides across the Fort Garry campus, his arms flailing the air as he talked. Indoors, his youthful lack of co-ordination often resulted in broken tea-cups and a scattering of furniture, at which he himself learned to laugh more emphatically than anyone else. Incidents of this sort seemed to happen to him daily. Everyone loved to tell of the occasion when Frank went out to crank his brother's car while it was parked in front of the house. He had left it in reverse gear, and so, of course, it went plunging backwards up the street, with Frank shouting frantically and holding on to its bumper, trying in vain to bring it to a halt before it finally crashed into the fence of a nearby park.

Frank seemed to enjoy all such incidents himself, but as he once admitted, he felt self-conscious and unhappy about many of them. Hence, upon first acquaintance, he seemed shy and ill-at-ease. His friend, Brock King, first saw him on a Sunday evening in 1932, when he had been invited to the Pickersgill home by Jack. In the background he observed Frank hovering around and noted that "he kept appearing in the living room or flitting through the dining room, looking meekly sort of sideways."

After two or three meetings, however, Frank's shyness and meek appearance would vanish and he would launch into loud, hilarious discussions, during which he made hosts of good friends. His laughter was contagious. He had an eye for the absurdities of pretentious professors, or embarrassing incidents, or literary twaddle. In the university library, for example, he found an anthology called *Canadian Singers and Their Songs*. It consisted, as the title suggests, of blundering poetasters' verses, the Edgar Guests of the Maple Leaf School. These Frank would memorize and then recite them, with exaggerated emphasis, over the morning coffee cups in the Snack Room, until everyone was in gales of laughter. His own laughter was never the sly snigger of the little pseudo-intellectual; it was abdominal, clear and hearty, like the laugh of Stephen Leacock, another Canadian who hated shams.

Reminiscing about him in 1977, a friend commented: "If there are angels, I'm sure Frank keeps some of them in stitches."

Naturally, among some of those who did not know him, his awareness of absurdities was not entirely appreciated. G. K. Chesterton has remarked that to be always serious is hardly a test of human virtue. Monkeys are unfailingly serious. The test of humanity is to know what are the things about which to be properly serious, and what are the things about which not to be serious. To some of his fellow-students, of course, Frank failed to be serious about what seemed to them to be important. Although he had a brilliant academic record and won scholarships every year, he refused to consider formal grades of any importance. Although he had many close friends, he was not in the slightest interested in organized friendship societies. Although he shared enthusiastically in many student gatherings, he laughed heartily at the artificially generated "pep-rallies" imported from Hollywood. The same principle applied even in religion. His letters show how deeply religious he was to become, but he nevertheless found the S. C. M. (Student

Christian Movement) oppressive and painfully self-righteous. While he was at United College, a former Methodist institution, he announced that he was going to draw up a group of his own to be called the S. H. M., the Student Heathen Movement!

In short, as an undergraduate, Frank Pickersgill was the genuine student of the non-conformist stamp which gives a university its colour and its *raison d'être*. In an editorial he contributed to an undergraduate magazine, *'Toba*, which he founded (April, 1935) he mildly expressed a tenet of his iconoclasm:

> We are only on this earth for a very short time, and our main business here is leading a life which is valuable and happy, and this cannot be done very satisfactorily merely by sticking grimly to one's task and never taking one's eyes off the road which leads onward and upward to financial success. Those who cannot pause and look around them in their struggling, when asked what their aim is, can only say '*to get There*.' And when asked where '*There*' is they are at a loss for an answer.

One comic-epic incident in which he starred may bring out some of these characteristics. Because the University was located in the municipality of Fort Garry, some miles south of the city, the students needed transportation to get to classes. Frank ran a kind of taxi service for a gang of his friends, using an old car of his brother, Jack's. One day with his carload of passengers, he was stopped by a municipal policeman, who had been lurking behind a billboard to track down speeding student's cars. Frank was of course given a ticket. Although all his passengers wanted to pool their resources and pay the fine, Frank insisted that he had not been speeding and that he was going to fight the case. And fight he did. A lawyer was engaged in the cause of justice, James Coyne (it was the first case in which he appeared in court). Families of passengers were consulted concerning exact times of departure; Professors of Mathematics, after having painstakingly measured distances of the highway, prepared elaborate statistics to demonstrate that the alleged speed was erroneous, and Lloyd Wheeler, a Professor of English, volunteered to testify as a character witness. The whole affair became a *cause célèbre*. The little municipal courthouse in which the case was tried before an astonished magistrate was jammed with students; indeed the crowd flowed out into the grounds outside. All passengers were called to the witness stand, and the high point, according to one of them (Mary Lile Benham) occurred when a blonde student passenger took the stand. This was Margaret Ann Bjornson.

> She was a scream – dressed as though she were the defendant in a breach-of-promise suit – all in black – looking great, with the blonde hair and blue eyes. She sat in the witness chair with black-stockinged legs crossed provocatively – vamping the magistrate for all she was worth (and that was a good deal!) Yet we lost the case. Justice did not triumph. Poor Jack Pickersgill ended up as usual paying for Frank's follies, as I remember it.

In reality the effort had not been altogether in vain; the over-zealous policeman was replaced, shortly after the trial.

It has been indicated that when he was older, Frank's main interest centred in politics and religion, but during his five years at Manitoba, he was primarily interested in literature. He majored in classics and modern languages, and read prodigiously in these fields. Stanley Jackson, who became one of his closest friends, remarked that the first time he saw Frank he thought he must be something of a fake. One Friday afternoon in the library, when week-end books were being taken out, Jackson incredulously listened to him requesting the librarian, in his loud voice, for books in German, French, English, Latin and Greek. Jackson was convinced that the request must be a mere stunt! He found, later, that it was genuine enough, and that the books were actually read over the week-end.

Some of the university people he knew at Manitoba were later to become eminent in Canada and elsewhere. In his classes in Greek under Skuli Johnson, a distinctive fellow-student was Marshall McLuhan. And in the year before Frank graduated, he came to know E. K. Brown, the brilliant young chairman of the English Department. Another member of the English Department with whom he developed especially close ties was Lloyd Wheeler, who had built a cottage at the Lake of the Woods on the same stretch of lakefront where Jack Pickersgill had also built a cottage, at a top of the hill, which came to be known as "Highbrow."

During the summer vacations, Frank's language studies were continued to some extent. In 1934 he had a summer in Europe, which is described in the first group of his letters, and the following summer, while working at the Lake of the Woods, he was a guest at a cottage of Mlle Celine Ballu, of the University French Department, with whom he talked French.

Mlle Ballu regarded him as her favourite "nephew," and he in turn, in his letters, speaks often of her mature good sense and wise perception. One instance of the latter occurs in a comment she made upon Frank when recommending him for a scholarship:

> I personally have witnessed Frank Pickersgill twice act in emergencies that demanded utter disregard of physical fear. He judged what to do without thought of his personal danger or hope of reward ahead; but 'it was the thing to do.' ... Furthermore, he is unafraid to face the truth and tell it.

This recommendation was written in 1935, before his other friends thought of him in terms of physical courage. On the plane of ideas, his vehemence was obvious enough, and there were many things which put him into a state of what he called "high dudgeon." With people, however, he was gentle and mild in manner. Most of his friends had the impression that in spite of his fierce energy and bigness he was essentially one of the meek.

A snapshot on the next page shows him during the summer he passed with Mlle Ballu. There is an amusing passage in one of his letters describing his activities:

Lake of the Woods, 1935

Wood-gathering and cutting has been our main diversion. I have been wielding the Swedish saw fair like Gargantua, putting Lloyd and Stan to shame with my activity. I must be in a lot better condition than I was because I have been working twice as hard and feel like a million dollars – although I'm not sleeping too well yet. The night before last I was bitten by a rattlesnake and had to have an operation at the Misericordia Hospital, which I was late for and couldn't get to, hard as I tried. The result was that I nearly jumped out of bed, groaned, gnashed my teeth and scared the guts out of Mlle.

J. W. Pickersgill, Lake of the Woods

Mlle Celine Ballu

The account of his nightmare is scarcely exaggerated. In fact, on nights when Frank's nocturnal groaning and threshing about had roused the entire cottage household, his hostess would reach over the partition with a broomstick and poke at him exclaiming: "Fwank! Fwank! for heaven's sake stop dweaming!"

He seemed to have an excess of energy, even in sleep.

Part II

FIRST IMPRESSIONS OF EUROPE: 1934
(age 19)

A typical ambition among North American university students of Frank's generation was to spend at least one summer vacation in Europe. The usual procedure was to work one's way across the Atlantic on a cattle-boat, and then to tour as economically as possible, usually by bicycle.

Frank managed such an expedition in the summer of 1934. Accompanied by a friend, Brock King, he cycled through England, France, and Germany, and was certainly economical. At the end of his tour, he succeeded in selling his bicycle to an English bus driver for the price of a cup of tea.

The following group of letters, in which he describes the trip, appear here not only because they are youthful and entertaining in their own right (he was nineteen at the time), but because these first impressions are sometimes so markedly at variance with his more mature impressions. Four years later, when he returned to Europe, he was appalled to think back to the summer of 1934 when he had happily chanted Nazi songs and had admired the Germany of Hitler and disliked the France which Blum had developed. There was, in reality, nothing at which to be appalled. His early impressions were simply typical of the average North American visitor's first reaction to Europe.

One further difference should be noted for it also throws light on his subsequent development. In this early group of letters, he writes almost exclusively of European scenery, of curious characters, of small adventures such as the amusing account of his first imbibing of heady Munich beer. His later letters from Europe are usually devoid of all such comments, and, instead, ideas of war, politics and religion then become predominant. The change is in part an indication of maturity, but it is also a sign of the times.

*   *   *

Dear Margaret:
Well I got here safely yesterday, on my nineteenth birthday, at two in the afternoon. Was I ever glad to get off the beastly boat! I am afraid I am a confirmed landlubber; I loathe not being able to walk more than 150 yards in one direction. The "Manchester Producer" is a little tub which tosses a good deal and our quarters were in the forecastle where this is most effective. I was horribly seasick for three days.

The work I suppose is not hard, but it is hell trying to pull up heavy bales of hay, and trying to water impatient and thirsty and stupid cattle when you are seasick. Also, the food was inexpressibly awful. All I ate in the whole ten days was the dozen oranges, the dozen apples and the cookies I brought along, a few potatoes and some pickles. It is very difficult doing strenuous manual labour when you are weak with hunger. The cook was a loathsome specimen, who wouldn't even take pity on one of the men who when sick one time had lost his false teeth over the rail, much less pay any attention to the rest of us. I now know what an insult it is to call a man "son of a seacook." My mates were all excellent fellows. Among these were two Lancashire lads who were very amusing. After living for ten days with a lot of North-country men and (by contrast) a few southerners, I am proud that my name is Pickersgill – a good old Yorkshire handle. They seem to be as a class about the finest lot I know – enduring and cheerful and very intelligent (ahem!). . . .

Well, I must confess I left the boat with mixed feelings: they were an awfully good crowd and we had had jolly times in the forecastle together. I feel lonely and depressed in this horrible town. I am awaiting with eagerness the letter which will tell me to go to Wolverhampton to stay with Jack's friends there. If I have to stay here after tonight, I must go hungry and without a bed: my money will run out, and not having a decently permanent address till I get to Wolverhampton I cannot send for more till I get there.

I suppose you will be in Jasper when you get this letter. I do hope you like it. What I saw of the English countryside between Liverpool and Manchester makes me think that I shall enjoy our trip thoroughly. I am eager to get started on it.

The family wired me to the boat to tell me about the scholarships. You can imagine how excited and pleased I was. I really didn't expect an Isbister: my marks at spring were not so good – I barely made an *A*. Thanks for your congratulations.

Well, I must go out and finish arranging my affairs. I have about a ten-mile tram-ride ahead of me, the prospect of which does not please me.

Goodbye – and write soon,

Yours,
Frank

To HELEN MAGILL (Winnipeg)
Penn Vicarage, Wolverhampton, Staffordshire,
June 4, 1934

Dearest Helen:

I have been having a marvellous time. I have played a lot of tennis and my tennis is remarkably good for this early in the season. I have been going to numerous tennis parties with Sylvia and Philip. These have been faintly amusing, although it does become rather a bore explaining to people that we don't live like hairy apes in Canada. After they express surprise at the "enterprising spirit" of one who would come across the Atlantic at less than first class accommodation, they say – "Of course, you do get down to fundamentals and live closer to nature OUT THERE, don't you," and then I painfully explain that we actually live more luxuriously in many ways in the aforementioned OUT THERE.

These people – always excepting the Hartills who are simply delightful – are a rather unimpressive lot, taken by and large. However, thanks to the vicarage, I am having a frightfully good time. Mrs. Hartill is a woman after my own heart, a very merry and a thoroughly good sport. She and I went on a picnic today to the Clee Hills in Shropshire. Shropshire, I think must have been Eden. It has to be seen to be believed. I never thought that trees and grass could be so green. We half lost our way, and went driving about in the Baby Morris all down little lanes which were much prettier than the main roads – and asking people the way, more to hear their accent (which is vaguely like Canadian) than to get any really sound information. (Their directions were always interspersed with unintelligible admonitions, such as "double back on yourself at Farmer Giles's barn" and so on.)

On the way home we came through Bridgenorth which has the added interest of being Market Blandings. (Are you a devotée of P. G. Wodehouse, and have you read the Emsworth stories?) We then passed by Blandings Castle (I don't know its real name) and it so tallied with the descriptions that I fully expected Lord Emsworth to dodder out from behind a tree. Oh – a break while I tell you a limerick I made up:

> An amazing young lady of Shropshire
> Took her Arab steed out for a gropshire,
> The nag jumped a ditch;
> In the ditch, she cried, "which
> Is my front and which back? I'm a scopshire.

(For clue see next page – you lazy thing!)
Clue: the other name for Shropshire is Salop.

Sylvia and Philip have been enjoying themselves hugely at the expense of my accent. They try to imitate it and the best they can make of it is a sort of cross between an Irish brogue and broad lowland Scotch – which as I have pointed out, is not very flattering.

Well, my dearest, I must go to bed . . . Give my greetings to your family.

Love,
Frank

P.S. I realized after I finished the letter last night that I had more to say which I had previously forgotten. I actually met one of those refained people which grows only in England. She was perfectly poisonous. (No shock absorbers and was frightfully taken aback because Sylvia appeared at a tennis party with ankle-high socks and otherwise bare legs.) Her name was, of course, Imogen – and she said "Good-bay" for Good-bye and "Hayow do you do." Sylvia takes her off marvellously. It was quite an experience – I never in my secret heart of hearts thought such a person existed.

To HELEN MAGILL
Youth Hostel Association House, London, England
June 11, 1934

Dearest Helen:

Well, we have been about five days on the road and have arrived here with comparatively few mishaps. I was delighted to get your letter. After meeting Brock, we hit for a pub and had a very long chat, and then made our way to Stratford-on-Avon. We were now Youth Hostel members, so we spent the night in the Hostel there. It is a fairly pleasant little town, though infested with jam and aluminum factories and souvenir vendors and Anne Hathaway's beastly cottage, but the country around about is really lovely. Well out of the Black Country, and much nicer than photos of the "English Countryside." Horse chestnuts, hawthornes (millions of them!), lilacs and laburnums were all blooming in profusion and the trees and grass so marvellously green. All the little streams and wooded ravines and hills look marvellous after flat Manitoba, too.

The Hostel-monger in Stratford was a poisonous creature who wouldn't let us get breakfast in the morning because we were about five minutes late in getting up. However, we saw *Much Ado* at the Theatre, which we both enjoyed tremendously. I think the new theatre is lovely both inside and out, although most English people think that it looks like a jam factory or something.

Oh by the way!! in the hotel (bed and brek) where we spent the first night on the road, the very loquacious landlady (note alliteration) told us in the morning before breakfast that she was simply ravishing – poor soul she wasn't trying to be funny. I caught Brock's eye and had to stuff a fried egg down my throat in haste.

In Oxford we looked up Bill Morton and Jerry Riddell. Jerry showed us about a bit. Brock rather hated Oxford – I definitely liked it. I think the difference is that I like England and Brock really doesn't and Oxford is in many ways the epitome of England.

After Oxford, we got to a little place called Flackwell Heath, where we were given royal welcome by the queen of Hostel-keepers, a frightfully kind, nice and amusing old lady of seventy-four years, and we stayed there for two nights. The neighbours, who had lived for a few years in Canada, had us over for the first evening (and it was actually pleasant and not in the least trying) and had a chat and a sing-song, in which we sang two Nazi songs in German. They were excellent and stirring pieces too. The nearer I get to Germany the more I come around to admire Hitler and Co. However more of that at a later date when I may know a little about it.

I came into London alone, coming through Eton where I saw the boys in their ridiculous clothes – their clothes make them all look like drawings by "Phiz"; and then went across the river to get a still closer view of Windsor Castle. Windsor isn't up to much: it looks just like the pictures. That of course is the disappointment of a lot of travelling. The really enjoyable part of travelling is seeing the country and the fields, and talking to strange people. Sight-seeing is just a bore in the main. It's usually what you come across by accident that interests you, not what you set out to see.

I got into town about two in the afternoon. Last night, I went to the Duchess Theatre to see Priestley's play "Laburnum Grove." It was marvellous comedy, a treat after "Faraway" and "Wonder Hero."

For heaven's sakes, warn me if my letters become clogged and boring, and I shall do my best to cut down on the number of words. I hope to get another letter from you pretty soon – it's marvellous getting them.

Well good-night and write often –

Love,
Frank

P.S. I have seen a *Daily Express* and read Beachcomber's column. He hasn't degenerated.

To HELEN MAGILL
Chateau d'Arry (Somme), France,
June 18, 1934

Dearest Helen:

I last wrote from London didn't I? I got quite to like London before I left. We left London on Saturday and crossed the channel at Folkestone-Boulogne. At last we were able to ride on the right side of the roads again. Our French turns out to be tolerably good: we can understand and make ourselves understood quite well. Brock has already taken to punning in French: ça c'est trop fort!

We cycled out from Boulogne for Paris and stopped at a little farming village for a meal (one loaf of bread and two litres of milk). We had it at a farm-house. It was great fun talking to the people and telling them all about Canada and how the French there talked differently from the French. As Brock remarked, it was really too quaint that the French actually did use words like "donner" and "trouver" and "n'est-ce pas?": that it wasn't just a myth.

By the time you get this I expect you will have left Minaki; I hope you have had a marvellous time.

Love,
Frank

To HELEN MAGILL

Hotel Modern Duplein, Paris XV,
June 22, 1934

Dearest Helen:

We managed to get safely into Paris yesterday afternoon. On the way, we spent a night in an inn in Abbeville, called L'Etoile du Jour. One very amusing thing about this pub was a sign on the door of the outdoor *cabinet*: "Prière de ne pas monter: veuillez vous asseoir." It set me roaring with laughter.

Here in Paris we passed through a hotel district that looked reasonably cheap and nasty. So we tried here, the first place, and got a double room for 50 francs! We jumped at it. It's an excellent jernt and the admirable proprietors treat us like long-lost uncles. About six little men, all looking exactly alike, dash about doing this or that for us. They are the proprietors. It's reminiscent of Alice in Wonderland, for some obscure reason. (Why do the French say "Alors" so much? And also "Ah oui," which I think is vaguely insulting – it sounds so like "Oh Yeah!")

I haven't seen much of Paris yet: still too tired. However, we walked about a bit this morning. We walked about the Tuileries, which is *hideous* (appalling statuary, and ghastlily ornate architecture) and along the Seine to Notre Dame. Notre Dame is splendid. It did something to me that some poetry and a very few pictures, and Mozart, do – almost made me weep. I don't know why it is, but I always feel twenty times more worshipful in a Roman Catholic church than in any other – even in the Church of the Holy Rosary in Winnipeg. But Notre Dame – in the inside! It seems miles to the roof, and the end wall is covered with the most wonderful stained glass. The carved figures and the statuary are frightfully impressive: the mediaeval artists might not have known much about anatomy, but they were artists – and I contend a damn sight more so than Raphael or even Titian ever could be.

The theatre program looks a bit bleak. However, *Péleas et Mélisande* (Debussy and Maeterlinck) is on at the Opéra Comique and we may go to that. I *loathe* and despise that opera, but there would be some point in going just for the sake of seeing an opera on the stage – a thing which I've never done. (I wish now I'd gone to *Otello* at Covent Garden: even Verdi is better than Debussy). The Opéra has *La Damnation de Faust*: that might be preferable, but, I think, more expensive.

We think we shall take the train to Strasbourg from here. Well my dearest, I must have something to eat, so I shall close abruptly. Write soon.

Love,
Frank

To HELEN MAGILL
Furstenfeldbrück, Bavaria,
July 1, 1934

Dearest Helen:
I am writing, lying on my stomach under the shade of some

pines beside the Ammer (or something) river. We are twenty-six kilometers from Munich where we are to meet Mrs. Jones and Frank.

The last two days in Paris were a definite bore. We got seats for *Faust* in the top-gallery and weren't allowed in because we didn't have dinner jackets. It was gala week or something in Paris, so it was almost impossible even to get a meal without a dinner jacket. Taken by and large – and it was about as by as it was large – I rather abominated Paris. It's so much just a money-making scheme on a large scale. No one will do anything without a tip. I was standing one afternoon at the wicket in the Métro Station and there was a line-up. A woman came up and asked me to buy her a ticket because she was in a hurry – and tried to tip me for it! Imagine a place where the people are so disobliging that one is expected to pay 50 centimes for a miscroscopic favour like that. It got me down, thoroughly.

We went to Strasbourg on Monday. In the evening, we went into a biergarten and spent a couple of hours drinking German lager. Strasbourg is a marvellous place – almost entirely German. The people aren't so hard-boiled looking, and they don't look as though they'd murder their mothers for tuppence the way the French do. Also, they're willing to give you information without robbing you of all you own for the favour.

The next day we crossed into Germany and found our financial arrangements had gone astray and that we'd have to cycle the 350 kilometers to Munich on mk 1.50 a day, or 37½c each, which is pretty good going. We have been living excellently on it though; three good (though not very varied) meals a day, and enough money left over to let us have a pint of beer in the evening. In fact tonight we have it worked out so well that we will be able to carouse on three pints each to "celebrate." It's great fun really, but it will have a rather tragic end if there is any difficulty about getting the money tomorrow in Munich. However, tomorrow can take care of itself and it's too pleasant here under these trees to think about money worries.

Germany's marvellous. We spend our nights out in the

woods under my little tent – and except for the fact that it's occasionally chilly and I'm infested with fleas (Brock, lucky devil, seems to be immune) – it's really delightful.

During the second day we crossed the Schwarzwald. The woods and mountains were the most glorious I've seen, prettier even than the Lake of the Woods, and much prettier than the Green Mountains. On the third day, we passed through a series of villages and towns which must have been transplanted from fairyland. They were magical places, with their shady, sleepy main squares (nearly all now called Adolf Hitlerplatz – which, however, doesn't seem to make much difference to their character), their baroque fountains and their pretty, gaily-coloured houses. The people are all so nice, too. We had one evening meal harassed by four drunken men who insisted that I *must* be of German descent. Finally I gave in and said all my people were German except for an obscure black-sheep of a maternal grandmother who had the bad luck to be Dutch. This they said did not matter as the Dutch were Germanic anyway. They went away satisfied.

– Continued July 2nd, evening, sitting in the windowsill of our Munich pension.

We are however, not bothered by the Nazi régime at all, in fact, but for the ubiquitous swastika, and the fact that numerous people salute Brock everyday (he is inadvertently wearing a khaki shirt). The people all seem very hopeful for the future, and most of them seem to approve highly of the régime. I really think it's a good thing, although I suppose it's a heretical sort of thing to say.

Yesterday we left Furstenfeldbrück, where I started this letter, and went on to a place about 12 kilometers from Munich. We went off the main road and into a wood. We came upon a simply delightful biergarten in the heart of the pine trees and decided that that was the place to have our proposed carousal. So we got permission to pitch our tent a little way off, and indulged in what amounts to two quarts of beer, and (should you see the family don't inadvertently breathe a word of this to mother – she would be horrified) we both got thoroughly plastered. My it was marvellous beer. I can't see how anyone could help liking it. But we had a hell of a time putting up our tent.

We got into Munich this morning and I got my money from the bank. I got your letter from Minaki yesterday. The mosquitoes are bad this year eh? You should have my fleas! Gee, they're troublesome. The worst of it is I (a) don't know how to say flea-powder in German and (b) don't know what kind of store sells it and can't find out because of reason (a). I do wish they would teach you something practical in the beastly German III classes at university.

We're fortunately very fond of wurst – but not so fond of oxen's-guts. We discovered something in a tin in a store in Ulm, called *Ochsenmaulsalat*. I made out the "Ochsen" and the "salat" and we decided to take a chance on the "maul." When we ate it the next day it turned out to be perfectly god-awful – and in the middle I remembered what "maul" meant. It does mean "guts." However we had stewed gooses' guts for dinner in Strasbourg and they were really quite excellent.

Well, my dearest, I must write home, and now to my flea-bites, so goodbye for a time.

Love,
Frank

To MARGARET BEATTIE
Pension Artmann, Munich, Germany,
July 3, 1934

My dear Margaret:
I had the most appalling dream the night before last. We were tenting out, near Munich, and we both had drunk too much beer.

It started: Brock and I were in among some stalls with cattle and we were frantically trying to escape some men who were in league with the Devil, and who were seeking our bodies and souls. Then Brock, the cattle and the men faded. I was walking in the twilight along a lonely street in Ulm (which we had passed through the previous night) and I saw the figure of a woman walking toward me. It was dressed as a nun, but when we met, it drew down its veil and stared at me with deep, glowing red eyes. We fought; long and hard all night – I can't remember whether the fight was physical or moral, but it ended in her defeat.

I knew that the Powers of Darkness would now be planning to avenge this deed, and so I had to make an escape. Brock again came into the dream: we escaped to the planet Uranus, where Brock had an uncle named Chaussée d'Antin (actually the name of a Métro Station at Paris which was involved in some long-forgotten difficulties), who wrote poetry.

Then followed a long and curious digression about Chaussée d'Antin. He had married a squaw and had begotten fifteen children – and then in a fit of temperament cast them all off and let them starve. He read us some of his poetry – I don't remember anything about it except that it was very weird and very beautiful and had a curious *golden* quality about it.

Then Brock and his uncle faded; I was again, I realized, in danger. So I went to a Justice of the Peace for protection. I was telling him my trouble. We were alone together in a room lighted by one candle. I was not looking at him, and suddenly I looked to the wall, and saw his shadow, reflected from the candle. It was twisted in a horrible shape, and had eyes – red burning eyes – that bored through me into my very soul. I uttered a long and shattering yell, which woke up both Brock and myself – and didn't dare go to sleep again for about half an hour, for fear that the dream would continue.

It was very horrible – and so vivid that I actually shuddered and broke into a cold chill when I was writing about it. It was the first supernatural dream I have had since I was a child and afraid of ghosts. I felt I must write about it: it was such a curious mixture of past and present events – and so frightfully vivid.

Yours,
Frank

To MARGARET BEATTIE
Hall, Schwaben, Germany,
July 18, 1934

My dear Margaret:

We met Frank Jones in Munich on Friday. We had a glorious carousal the night of our day of meeting. I prepared for it by having half a liter (a liter is a quart) of beer in the late afternoon and another half liter with my supper. Then Mrs. Jones, Frank and Brock and I, and two Americans whom the Joneses had met on the boat, all went to the Hofbraühaus. After we had consumed a quart there we were beginning to feel very merry. There were a number of youths singing defiantly at the next table, so we rivalled them by singing English songs and limericks at the top of our lungs. The contest ended amicably by our telling them we were from Canada, and all about ourselves. My German was amazingly fluent with all that beer inside me. Finally we all drank each others' healths, and they, saying "aufwiedersehn, Heil Hitler" left.

By this time we had consumed another quart and were about ready to leave. When we got up something started us laughing, then all three of us began, and we laughed uproariously until we reached the street and stopped for sheer exhaustion. Brock and I then made our way back to our diggings. The fresh air and the walk seemed to provide a finishing touch for both of us: Brock laughed all the way home, and I talked steadily. My voice grew thicker and thicker until finally I couldn't say any consonants at all. I walked all over the sidewalk, and my head swayed back and forth from side to side, and I know I had the most idiotic smirk on my face. We managed, however, to get in safely, although not very quietly.

The curious part was that I was entirely aware how sillily I was acting, and exactly what I was doing, but I couldn't control myself.

All three of us left Munich on Tuesday. Tomorrow we go to Heilbronn on the Neckar, where we expect to get mail. Our time in Germany is nearing its end. The summer seems nearly over and I had hardly realized it had begun! I have had a marvellous time and I expect to for five weeks more until we get on the boat. Then, perhaps, life will be a little more real and earnest.

We must forage for food – (as Brock neatly puts it – look up wurst) so goodbye for now.

Love to all,

Yours,
Frank

P.S. Brock has a message for you: HeLLo MArgarET – Brock.
P.P.S. Brock is on his last legs – that was his last one that he wrote with.

Part III

TORONTO: 1936-1938
(age 21-23)

"Historians seem to have forgotten the fact that men act from ideas. . . . About half the history now taught in schools and colleges is made windy and barren by this narrow notion of leaving out theological theories."

(G. K. Chesterton)

Because of his having arrived now at man's estate, and with his undergraduate career behind him, Frank Pickersgill will be referred to in the remainder of this narrative by his surname instead of by his Christian name.

While attending the University of Manitoba, Pickersgill had been assisted by I.O.D.E. bursaries and by scholarships. In 1936 he obtained further assistance by winning a Fellowship to Canada's leading school of graduate studies at the University of Toronto, where he completed his M.A. degree in Classical History two years later.

His responses to his move to the Toronto scene were various. At the University itself he was delighted by the excellence of the library, and he was impressed by a number of outstanding scholars under whom he studied, in particular by Dean Charles Cochrane, who was then completing his great book on St.

Augustine, *Christianity and Classical Culture*, and by Donald McDougall, Professor of History, who had hired Pickersgill to read books and articles aloud to him (he had been blinded in the first World War). These reading sessions were frequently followed by animated discussions and arguments about history and politics in the time of Cromwell and Charles I. And, at the Mediaeval Institute, he was to have the good fortune to take courses in religion and mediaeval philosophy under Jacques Maritain and Etienne Gilson.

Although his response to the University faculty and library was generally enthusiastic, his response to the city itself was altogether different. In fact, so irreverent were his vigorous comments on what seemed to him Toronto's stuffy Establishment, that when *The Pickersgill Letters* was published in 1948, a reviewer for one of the Toronto newspapers treated the book almost as if it deserved to have been burned.

One historical footnote may be required here for a later generation of readers. An American who recently read this chapter told me that he had great difficulty in recognising the city against which Pickersgill was venting his indignant reaction. For this American, as for thousands of others in the 1960s and 1970s, Toronto has become known as a fun city, ideal for a visitor to enjoy the cosmopolitan fare of its array of restaurants, its lively cultural events, and its sense of civic esprit. In the 1930s, however, these attributes were certainly not yet in evidence. It was a dour community, and, in general, tradition-bound and satisfied with established values. Pickersgill and his friends from Winnipeg contrived to make their own brand of fun in its midst, but, as his letters show, he continued to view the old-style Queen City as an outsider, unimpressed by its ways.

One Toronto student with whom he struck up a friendship, Albert Fyfe, recently recalled Pickersgill as the best conversationalist he had known in his lifetime. Fyfe and others used to meet him in one or other of the two public facilities situated near campus which Toronto offered as locations suitable for conversation. One was Murray's Coffee Shop on Bloor Street, where a cup of coffee, with endless free refills, cost ten cents. The other was a noisy establishment in the basement of the Park Plaza Hotel where beer was unceremoniously dispensed to hordes of thirsty male customers seated round beer-slopped tables, until the 11.00 P.M. closing time. There, despite the din, and perhaps aided by his slight deafness, Pickersgill would give full rein, as Fyfe says, to a whole gamut of conversation topics, "suggested, perhaps, by the most recent of his omnivorous reading." Pickersgill often found much amusement in this room's being designated, like all such Ontario establishments, with the name in large letters at the entrance: BEVERAGE ROOM. This sign used to provoke him into reciting a satirical poem by L. A. Mackay, one of his Classics professors at Toronto, which contrasted Quebec's simple term TAVERN with Ontario's euphemism:

> "Give us a name with a resonant boom,
> A respectable name like BEVERAGE ROOM!"

As Samuel Butler has noted, "embryo minds, like embryo bodies, pass through a number of strange metamorphoses before they adopt their final shape." Pickersgill's letters from Toronto illustrate a succession of strange and changing shapes as he probed his way among the various currents of thought in his day. Like many young men in the 1930s, he was hopeful that he could find final answers. These two years were, for him, a period of *Sturm und Drang*.

Yet, as the letters also show, Pickersgill's stay in Toronto had its light-hearted sides. Until going there, he had lived with his family, but he was thereafter a boarder or roomer. His experiences in assorted boarding houses were legion, and are often described in his letters. An incident which is not described should be mentioned here. He was notified that he was being considered for a post in a Canadian university and that the president would phone to arrange an interview. As he states in a letter, Pickersgill purchased a new suit in order to make a good impression during this interview. But he never had a chance to show it off. One morning he stumbled to his bedroom door to answer a knock, and lo, there was the president introducing himself and seeking admission without warning. The room was of the usual drab and tattered variety of Bloor Street and Spadina Avenue boarding house, but in addition, the floor was littered with beer bottles from the previous night's celebrations, the air was still heavy with smoke, and there were clothes and books and essays in all directions. The new suit was on a hanger suspended from the chandelier. The president did not prolong his inspection for Pickersgill was almost tongue-tied, and, as he predicted, the job did not materialize.

Several of the letters of this group refer to the gatherings for talk and beer and cards which constituted his principal form of evening's entertainment. Another favourite diversion was hunting up double-billed moving pictures. They were usually at inexpensive little places in the remoter suburbs of Toronto. Having a part-time job as a reader, he was economy-conscious, and therefore insisted that no matter how far he had to travel on the street-car, he saved money by attending these outlying theatres. Often, however, the double-bill would be so outrageously bad that he would be obliged to leave, after twenty minutes or so, vowing that he would never go again. But he always did.

These two years were filled with some good hard thinking, and good talk. His degree was taken in classics, with emphasis upon ancient history, but his thesis topic, significantly enough, was upon St. Augustine. During this Toronto period, his centre of interest was shifting from language and literature to religion and politics. A few of his more secular-minded friends were alienated by his passionate concern for theology. Dr. Elsa Lehmann who knew him well in Toronto, remarked that "many people found this a difficult and most perplexing phase of Frank's life, but it was an important one." The reader who has no concern whatever for theology may wish to skip over the theological letters (those addressed to Kay Sinclair), but he will miss, in the process, a vividly dramatic account of the impact, upon an outstanding young mind, of some of the principal trends of the religious thought of his time. I say "dramatic" because Frank Pickersgill was honestly groping his way from one conflicting stage of belief to another, retaining some tenets and discarding others as he moved.

Pickersgill had been brought up in a Presbyterian-United Church family, but he had not taken much interest in religion until he was twenty. At sixteen, he wrote what he called "A Poignant Poem" (with apologies to P. G. Wodehouse) on the subject of church-going:

> Churches! churches!
> Grim, relentless, sordid churches,
> Full of loathsomely meticulous parsons,
> Full of malevolent, baleful, staring elders,
> Crowded with vacuous, sightless congregations,
>   Churches!. . . .

It might be well to add here that many years later, while walking through a forest in Europe with Albert Fyfe, he suddenly blurted out, with characteristic vehemence: "Ugh! I just about vomited!" "Why?" asked Fyfe. "Because" said Pickersgill, "I just thought of some poetry I wrote as a youth. Gawd it was awful!"

One point which remained constant was his dislike of liberalized Protestantism. He disliked its air of compromise, its soft rounded edges, its failure to face the full implications of evil. He sought, rather, the sharper outlines, the harsher realism (as it seemed to him) of dogmatic religion. An early study of T. E. Hulme and of T. S. Eliot confirmed this bent of his mind. His first letter here indicates that before he left Winnipeg in 1936, he had become deeply interested in the Anglican High Church. At Toronto, two other forms of theology also attracted him. He studied, for a period, as has been mentioned, under the eminent Roman Catholic philosophers, Professors Maritain and Gilson, and at one time he was considering joining the Roman Catholic Church. It was to continue his study of mediaeval thought under M. Maritain's direction, that he eventually went to Paris. In Toronto, a further stage in his development occurred when he was living in Knox College residence and made some friends among one wing of the Presbyterian theology students there, especially Wilfred Butcher from Winnipeg. Through them, he became interested in Barthian neo-Calvinism. At this time he was fond of citing Donne's comment upon the search for truth:

On a huge hill
Cragged, and steep, Truth dwells, and he that will
Reach her, about must and about must go;
And what the hill's suddenness resists, win so.

It is obvious why this should have been one of his favourite passages.

"In our time" said Thomas Mann, "the destiny of man presents its meaning in political terms." These Toronto letters show an attempt to integrate religion with politics. Later, in France, Pickersgill's awareness of the more obviously immediate pressure of political questions led him to relinquish his concern for early Christian and mediaeval thought, upon which, at one time, he planned to lecture in Canada.

His last letter from Toronto reflects this change clearly. Although his intellectual interests there were primarily theological, he made most of his friends among a group he used to call "pagan." He shared rooms in what was labelled "the most cacophonous corner in Toronto" with two students of Economics from Winnipeg, William Buchanan and "Angus" Mac-Donald. Through them, he became fascinated with the economics of Thorstein Veblen, and more particularly with Veblen's literary disciple, the American novelist, John Dos Passos. The sour hardness of the *U.S.A.* trilogy suited him best in 1940, but even in internment camp later, he requested a copy to be sent to him.

By comparison with his later writings from Europe, these Toronto letters may seem immature, but there is a freshness and gusty enthusiasm here, and already some of his wonderful wisdom. They evoke a world of boisterous beer parties, of lots of solid, hard reading, of silly double-bill movies, of God and

John Knox and G. K. Chesterton. Underlying most of them is a warm pervasive laughter.

To GEORGE FORD (Montreal)
609 Home St., Winnipeg, Canada
June 8, 1936

Dear George:

Your letter was very welcome; just this morning I called your family to find your address. I'm still in a state of super-excitement over getting the Travelling Fellowship to the University of Toronto.

My reading during the past three weeks has been mainly Plato and Stephen Leacock. I bought a book of Leacock's for 15 cents called *Further Foolishness*, which is marvellous. MacDonald, Jackson and I eat lunch by the river bank and have readings from it every day.

Buchanan is in town and is as carefree and cavalier as ever. We argued about one thing and another (mainly religion) for four hours last night, and have agreed to meet and settle six points later in the week.

I am growing more and more depraved, I guess. Last week, I spent two hours with a parson, the Rector of All Saints'. He's the first parson I ever met that I really liked. We have many mutual likes and dislikes: detestation of Noel Coward, attraction to D. H. Lawrence (funny how he's accepted by orthodox Anglicans), and admiration of T. S. Eliot. I hope to see quite a lot of him this summer. He's an Anglo-Catholic, and explained the point of it to me. It seems to me to be very sound, and not based, as most people seem to think, on "dog." Its deviations from the Low Church are liturgical, of course, but on major points, such as celebration of the Sacraments. I am really involved in religion now; of course I've been coming to it in a vague sort of way for about two years. It seems to be the only hope for Occidental civilisation, because it solidly and staunchly contains the principles which make the civilisation worth while. Asses who think we can quietly revert either (a) to a nation-worshipping paganism or (b) to a belief in "humanity," are either soft-boiled idiots or fanatics. I consider that Catholic (I don't mean Roman) Christianity offers all that matters. Not only does it put reverence, awe and worship in the right place, towards Godhead, and not towards some ridiculous or depressing anthropomorphic concept, but also it realistically accepts the ineffectuality and wickedness of human beings, and besides offers a solution for the chaos and futilitarian aimlessness of a necessarily sinful existence. T. S. Eliot's poetry, from Prufrock to The Rock, is a marvellous study in the development of a mind which reached a climax of futilitarianism in the Waste Land and then developed away from it to a satisfactory position.

But anyway Thank God for pagans like you and Buchanan who are earnestly trying to reach a consistent and decent point of view. It's the Nazis and others of this world who are the despair of me.

Yours,
Pick

To GEORGE FORD
602 Spadina Ave., Toronto, Ont.,
Oct. 13, 1936

Dear George:

Well (I don't want to break the tradition; I begin all my letters with "well") I have established myself in an excellent room with chesterfield, a fireplace, paper flowers and Bill Buchanan. There is a photograph of the landlady over the mantelpiece which must be taken down soon or we shall both go crazy. MacDonald is living at Knox College, and stubbornly insists that he likes it. For the past week I have been suffering from a peculiar form of gut-trouble. I switch back and forth from constipaggers to the reverse at a high rate of speed. It's most disconcerting.

My courses are all arranged and I've started to work. I just avoided a bloody awful course in Latin Epigraphy, which means pottering around with Latin inscriptions. Ask Jackson about it. However I'm going to have a good year – because the men I'm working under are excellent and the library is so complete. I am taking a course in Aristotle with L. A. Mackay who is a very good man, and another with an energetic little bloke named Cochrane, in political thought and history in the third and fourth centuries A.D. It's going to be marvellous and all sorts of work. I'm now reading Gibbon whom I actually like! It's exactly the course I want as background. The third course will probably be St. Augustine or Plato, or maybe I'll relapse into Latin Epigraphy.

Toronto is certainly a very ugly city except for trees, a couple of ravines, Hart House and Knox College. I'm constantly astonished by its intense ugliness. And Americanised – it's far more uncivilised than Winnipeg. The advertisements and the newspapers show it. The popularity of the *Star* is clear proof that a million people *can* be wrong. The only thing that remotely resembles a newspaper is the *Mail and Empire*, and it's pro-Fascist.

I have been going to an Anglo-Catholic church up the street. It has a fairly large congregation and so can afford to do things properly. It's a very well conducted and beautiful service. The curate is a Trinity man and I think a good fellow – from his sermons. He appears to be one of these people who lean very much towards Socialism but haven't yet discovered how to reconcile it with Christianity and practical politics at once – like me.

Goombye,
Pick

To KAY SINCLAIR (Winnipeg)
602 Spadina Ave., Toronto, Ont.,
Nov. 12, 1936

Dear Kay:

I must tell you about a funny thing that happened last week. We went to the University C.C.F. club to hear Underhill on the English Labour Party. The club is made up largely of Victoria College Women who are about on a par with "the Wesley Woman" – you know the sort. There was a business meeting first which was the most god-awful shambles I have ever witnessed. But the crowning touch was after the speech when one particularly earnest-looking female gazed up at Underhill and asked: "Professor Underhill, in the next war, if there's general conscription and they tell you you've got to fight or they'll take you out and shoot you, what should a good socialist do?" Underhill, needless to say, was very sarcastic.

Re socialism – as you certainly realise, I am a strong conservative – probably stronger than you are – and a sturdy liberal individualist almost as much as you are. I am a conservative because I see that some things are permanent and cannot be changed: the sinfulness, and humour, and nobility and tragedy and bestiality and semidivinity of human beings from the moron to the genius – the Incarnation of God in Our Lord Jesus Christ. . . . I am an individualist in the sense that I don't think the individual is here for the State but the State for the individual, and that it is the prime privilege and duty of the individual to work out his salvation to the glory of God and through the merits and death of our Blessed Lord. This is not selfish or egocentric actually, because a man's salvation can only be worked out in society.

Of course the social order I wrote to you about would be branded as State Capitalism by Communists but I don't give a damn what name it's called.

I saw *Murder in the Cathedral* last week. It was splendid: It is really possible to have good poetic drama still! As poetry it is a climax to Eliot's career and is as dramatic as hell. The thing is he has done what no poet has done since the Elizabethans: fuse the drama and the poetry. In other attempts (e.g. Shelley, Browning, etc.), the drama goes along in shoddy blank verse and occasionally there are undramatic purple patches. With *Murder in the Cathedral* every line is significant and dramatic – and really, for that reason, poetry. The result is gripping theatre, and fine tragedy. Read it if you get the chance – but to appreciate it completely you have to see it done. I haven't read Auden's *The Dog Beneath the Skin* yet, but I gather it is fine dramatic poetry too. Maybe we're having a revival of the drama: I hope so. I saw *Bury the Dead* and also *Waiting for Lefty*. Lefty had dreadfully weak spots, but Odets certainly has a future as a good, if not a great, dramatist.

Well, after this confused epistle, goombye

Yours,
Frank

P.S. I notice a horribly didactic tone to parts of this letter. Please forgive – it seems to be in my nature.

To HELEN MAGILL (London, England)
602 Spadina Ave., Toronto,
Nov. 24, 1936

Dear Helen:

How are things over in England? Is everyone as thoroughly disgusted with the British Government as they ought to be? It's got to such a state that one couldn't be sure whether they wouldn't support Germany and Italy instead of France in the event of war. At any rate if the Conservative Party in England hasn't got Fascist sympathies regarding Spain, they're certainly behaving in a very curious manner.

It's getting sadder and sadder for anyone who, as I do, hates both Fascism and Communism. Fascism is in the long run less dangerous I think: I have enough faith in human nature to think you can't take in all the people all the time with bilge like that. But Communism is much more acceptable to an intellectually honest person, as its inconsistency is fairly far advanced in abstract metaphysics. The difference between an atheist and a theist is this: the theist believes in final causes, the atheist only in efficient causes. The atheist bound by the cause-and-effect chain, would if he were strictly logical make no effort to strive after what was either fated to happen or not to happen. Herein lies the inconsistency of the Communists. They, by their mechanistic dialectic, try to show that a rigid chain of cause-and-effect governs human society, and makes it inevitable that the communist state will eventually come into existence. Yet they propagandise to beat hell and fight and strive for this just like any benighted Christian believing in free will. If they were strictly honest they would say they are fated to propagandise and that others are fated to attack them: but that reduces the whole business to such a ridiculous game of puppets that nobody could work up any moral fervour without making an ass of himself. And actually the Communist at every turn behaves as though he and the rest of the world had some control over their own destiny. Most people take the theistic order for granted though they would deny its know-ability.

Outside of my work just now, I'm reading Baudelaire and C. Day Lewis. Day Lewis seems to me to be the best of the young revolutionary poets – as Stephen Spender is the best critic. I'm also reading Ezra Pound's early work and consider him no fraud but a real poet. Of course, in other respects he's an ass: a Social Crediter and, living in Italy now, he dates his articles from the Fascist revolution: "anno XII" etc. I think I'm becoming educated slowly: at any rate I'm more intelligent about philosophy, politics and poetry than I used to be and this surely must mean that I'm more of an adult.

I wish Jackson, Ford, you, Baby and Jane were in Toronto.

That would be admirable and make the place quite bearable.
You must stay over in Toronto on your way home if I'm still
here.

Love,
Frank

To GEORGE FORD

602 Spadina Ave., Toronto, Ont.
Dec. 2, 1936

Dear George:

Has the Senior Division improved any? It can't be any worse
than the collection of shoddy stick-in-the-muds they have here.
The average undergraduate here gets his first suit of tails at the
age of fourteen – which is a fair indication of his calibre. Most
of them come from the Eastern uppah clawsses: that group
who have formed themselves into an aristocracy which accepts
the cheapest aspects of English upper class life and combines it
with all the cheapness in American life. I have seen nothing
like it in Winnipeg: the "Gamma Phi" spirit is not comparable
because it's such a small minority. Here the rich have the town
by the ears.

These people don't justify their existence, much less their
position. The result is that the university, or more especially
University College is made up of what are politically hide-
bound Conservatives – and in every other way completely
rootless and traditionless (i.e., perfect Fascist material). A little
bit of political radicalism and cultural conservatism would be a
welcome sight to see. The radicals however are a sorry lot of
sentimental Student Christian Movement – CCFers who don't
really know what the score is. Most of them merely see the
socialist movement as an anti-war movement to save their own
skins. Skin-saving is an all too prevalent ideal in all political
parties down here. I don't know what will be in store for

Canada: this is supposed to be its intellectual centre and it's a saddening spectacle. The "intellectuals" fall into two classes: (1) the political radicals; (2) the head-in-the-sand arty folk. The former are too urban in outlook and environment, too unobservant, and too credulous; the latter are people who are trying to escape from themselves into a dream world of smart sayings, Van Gogh and "mawrvellous plays." No, there is more hope from Winnipeg. There, at least, there is no hide-bound conventionalism, and the arty people, if any, are scorned.

The latest intellectual titillation has been a Nancy Pyper play production which has been universally dubbed mawrvellous and which I carefully avoided seeing (anyway it cost a dollar). It's apparently social satire, of the sort which gives the wealthy a comfortable feeling that they are broad minded because they can laugh at themselves.

The newspapers are a fair indication of the docility of the place. A week and a half ago, the only decent paper (the *Mail and Empire*) died – bought by the *Globe*. The offspring is called the *Globe and Mail* and is worse than the evening papers. Buchanan and I cancelled our subscription when in the fourth number there was (without exaggeration) three-eighths of a column of news – and not a word about Spain! When Buchanan cancelled the subscription, he told the circulation department that we were seriously thinking of subscribing to the *Port Rowan News*, because it was less offensive. Imagine a city of over a million people which contentedly gets along without a newspaper. We are now taking the *Montreal Gazette*. It's the best newspaper in Canada, and we will have the added advantage of reading about the Fascist drive in the Province of Quebec at first hand. One of the more sinister aspects of this last is that it seems to be rousing a counter blast of Imperialist-Orange Fascism which should go over in this province with a bang. It's a subtler and more respectable vehicle for fascism than such fascist groups as Workers' Christian Movements and Patriotic Defence Leagues and such like (I hear some little pimp has started one of these in Winnipeg).

I don't know what to think about Canada and its future

(ahem) but I would be damned bitter if it weren't for MacDonald and Buchanan here who are as fresh breezes to a troubled soul (Ahem ahem).

My work is intensely interesting. I'm taking a course in what is really the breakdown of Paganism. Just now I feel lost in a forest, and it's going to be exciting finding my way out. So don't expect any brilliant generalisations about the rise of the Christian Empire from little F.H.D.P. till about next February. This is my first serious attempt to study history.

Goombye,
Pick

To GEORGE FORD
602 Spadina Ave., Toronto, Ont.,
Feb. 8, 1937

Dear George:

I just got a letter from Baby today, castigating me for my bad language. According to her a league has been formed. As I point out to Jackson, I resent the way you people treat my letters: I feel you are all CRITICS, not BOOSTERS. You object to them because they are obscene, or because they are political, or because they are too trivial, or else accuse me of being pontifical. But I'm not either Marx or Lawrence or J. M. Barrie or the Pope: I'm just my own little self, so what am I to do about it, but inflict my current thots on my eager public.

I've spent Saturday and today down at Eaton's at the most marvellous book-sale I've ever seen – without exception. I shall have to live for the rest of the winter on dry bread and milk to recoup my expenditures, as I poured out money like a drunken sailor and spent $15.20. Here is what I got (all new books and very good editions): the best English annotated edition of Aristotle's *De Anima*, the Cambridge text of Cicero's *De Officiis*; the Oxford text of Cicero's *Catilinian Orations*,

Belloc's *Shorter History of England*; Dryden's *Essay on Dramatic Poesy* and other prose; Bury's *Selected Essays*; Goethe's *Iphigenaeia auf Tauris*; Bosanquet's *Science and Philosophy*; Cross' *Epirus* (a study of Greek constitutional history); and six books by Santayana, seven volumes of Meredith, including his poetry and his essay on comedy; Blake's poems; another book of essays on theology; Chesterton's *Autobiography*. Doesn't that make you jealous? I now feel like a person who has been chastened after a debauch. When we were down at the book store, I discovered *Canadian Singers and their Songs*, and I read "God's Library" to MacDonald and Buchanan. They almost had hysterics, and we were just about ejected from the store.

Buchanan is annoying me at the moment by singing some particularly loathsome sentimental song in my ear. We are having a supper of milk and dry bread (cracked-wheat bread). Oh, say, if you have any spare time this winter, take Julien Benda's *Trahison des Clercs* from the library; it is very good indeed, I consider, and the most interesting diagnosis of the trouble with modern intellectuals that I have ever seen.

Do you know anything about Louis MacNeice? He's an up-and-coming young poet apparently, and I am engaged in reading his translation of Aeschylus's *Agamemnon*. In spots it is quite good, but there is the odd howler. In the original, there is a very moving choral passage describing Agamemnon sacrificing his daughter. Here is MacNeice's rendering of three lines:

"Her prayers and her cries of father,
Her life of a maiden,
Counted for nothing with those militarists."

Isn't that god-awful?

New boarding house gossip. Apparently the draggle-tail on the third floor can be purchased for a nominal fee. Who'd want to buy her I can't imagine as she weighs about 350 lbs., and she has pimples all over her face.

Regarding next year: I expect I shall be here next winter, so be sure to come down. I am applying to three or four American universities for fellowships, but I don't think there is a possibility of getting one this year.

I now have some wretched Latin prose to do which will doubtless waste my whole evening. God how I hate wasting my time over Greek and Latin prose. However, my teechrs tell me it's all for the best, so I guess I have to submit. It has its practical virtues anyway, as American colleges are terrifically impressed by Canadian training in Prose Composition.

Offer the olive branch to Jackson for me, and write occasionally, eh?

Goom,
Pick

P.S. Don't tell Jack that I spent $15.20 at one fell swoop or he'd probably burst a blood-vessel.

To MARGARET BEATTIE
602 Spadina Ave., Toronto, Ont.,
Feb. 16, 1937

Dear Margaret:

I've been so busy the past week, what with work, another essay, Andy's poker-beer party, and leading a couple of Presbyterian theologs down the primrose path (also via poker and beer), and reading to Mary Rogers, that I don't KNOW WHICH WAY TO TURN. And now I've got to go to the dentist's and have eleven fillings and one extraction. Isn't that appalling? It will cost me about fifteen dollars. So I now make two meals a day of milk and dry bread, and am again rolling my own. Well, anyway, I made a dollar at poker the other day, so if I can keep that up about every two weeks from now till the end of term, I should be able to pay my dentist's bill.

During my harum-scarum career of the past two weeks I've managed to find time to read most of Chesterton's

Autobiography. I think it is without doubt the best thing he wrote. It's very personal, and in places very moving, and always terribly funny of course.

I've committed myself to go over with MacDonald in half an hour and have a WORK-OUT (i.e., run around the track) at Hart House. It's a very boring sort of exercise, but what can you do when there is no snow to ski on, and the badminton courts are filled? However Bill and I get in some badminton, and are getting to be quite the sharks.

Good for Wampoles! I eat dry cracked-wheat bread, and it keeps me regular and FIT, so that I am in almost permanent high spirits. I'm really enjoying things, far more this term than I did last, although I don't quite know why, as I'm working harder, and not making so much whoopee. For one thing the weather has been simply marvellous the last few days: just like early summer, nobody wearing overcoats, and things like that. It's the most astonishing sort of February I've ever seen.

I want to thank you again for those superb cookies; they certainly were WORTH-WHILE (hint?)

Well ta-ta for now, Miss Buggy, and write soon.

Love,
Frank

To KAY SINCLAIR

602 Spadina Ave., Toronto, Ont.,
March 3, 1937

Dear Kay:

I've just been having a hell of a day, doing Greek Prose, which is damned difficult, and boring, and reading the Theodosian Code, which is a 900-page collection of Latin laws, and the most obscure Latin I've ever run into, and I cut my finger on my razor, and MacDonald cannot remember the rest of an obscene limerick about a Young Girl from Azores.

I don't know why you castigate me for my political views: they seem pretty well in accord with what you say in your letter. I have no objections to mixed constitutions, and I think that ultimately by far the most satisfactory solution would be a mixture of Socialism, co-operation and private ownership. (Of course, co-operation implies private ownership.) As I've told you before, I look to Scandinavia rather than Russia for a good solution: I think that in many ways our economic and geographical and political position is similar enough to Scandinavia to allow us to give our country an economic basis like theirs. Russia and Germany are extremes, but they are not opposite extremes. How different are they really? They both derive their philosophy from Hegel, to start with. This philosophy, whether garbled by Hitler, or deliberately turned upside down by Marx, is a horrible over-simplification. They both establish totalitarian states, with an oligarchic bureaucracy to govern them, and their Bureaux of Propaganda and the G.P.U. and Gestapo to keep up the right gush and put down the wrong. They both deny the rights of the individual personality, the Nazis expressly, the Communists by denying the existence of personality. They are both strongly Nationalist (the Russians now talk about the "Socialist Fatherland"). And I shouldn't be at all surprised to see the differences in economic arrangement gradually being ironed out over the next period of years.

In other words, when I suggest another way out, it is not a *via media* between Fascism and Communism, but something which veers sharply away from either. If I thought we really had private property and individual rights now, I should be content to make whatever minor adjustments were necessary to oil up the present system, and let it go at that. But very few people have private property, and fewer and fewer are having it; and the direction in which I would revolt would be towards extending private property, not taking it away altogether. In other words, towards co-operation and peasant proprietorship, rather than Socialism. It is not that I'm reactionary, nor is it that I'm ready to sit back and enjoy watching the world go to pot. I'd be willing to join a bloody revolution tomorrow, provided it were the right bloody revolution (and by right, I mean right, not Right). It's not because the C.C.F. is a gradualist party that I support it; but because it does seem to be headed in the right direction. I deplore gradualism as excessive; I wish it were more revolutionary. A revolution can be a very fine and noble thing, provided the thing fought for is fine and noble, but I'm damned if I can get worked up about Revolutionary Communism, when, apparently you're just revolting so that you can be part of the cosmic process.

I don't know whether I make my point clear; this arguing by letter is very difficult. In short, I don't like the *status quo*, and I think social change should be worked for, but I don't think there are only two directions in which to go.

Regarding theology: well, to start with, you probably realise that proofs positive are not forthcoming. There is no proof positive of the existence of a personal God, and yet you are willing to accept it as an article of faith, because it shows only common sense to believe in Him: there being odds of an infinite number of trillions to one that He does exist. St. Thomas's *ordo est in mundo* argument makes this apparent. Well, that is the basis of any discussion of the Incarnation: that it cannot be proven positively, nor did God mean it to be proven positively, as faith is a virtue, and if there were positive proof of the Incarnation, the virtue of faith would be taken away from us. This is not actually a sophistry: compare the phrase *passionate conviction* with the incongruity of the possible phrase *passionate knowledge*. Well, then, all that can be done is to show that everything points to the fact of the Incarnation, and then it is for you to take it or leave it.

I'll go into the philosophical and historical demonstrations later. This is all a ticklish problem and I can't help feeling that many of those who have glibly accepted Catholicism and Christianity in the past twenty years have really not given

enough thought to the question of the Incarnation.... I hope
that you can think yourself through it so as to come to the
Christian conclusion.

Yours,

Frank

To KAY SINCLAIR

602 Spadina Ave., Toronto, Ont.,

March 9, 1937

Dear Kay:

If you can possibly borrow, beg or steal Christopher
Dawson's *Inquiries Into Religion and Culture*, do so at your
earliest possible convenience, and read especially the last four
essays in the book. It is, I think, the most outstanding
exposition of the significance of the doctrine of the Incarnation
that I have ever read. Dawson is an English Roman Catholic,
professor in anthropology in some English university, and he
has a very wide range of culture.

He points out how actually the Incarnation bridges the gap
between flesh and spirit, and solves the problem which had
baffled the ancients, even including Plato and Aristotle. It's
obvious that you can't get away from matter, it's here, in spite
of what the subjective idealists say. The result is that you have
two sets of heresies: (a) Idealism, represented by Platonism,
Manicheism, Hegelianism, and (b) Materialism, represented by
Epicureanism, Montanism (Tertullian's heresy), and Marxism.
They both discredit life, the idealists by defying it, the
materialists by denying it. For if you postulate as the idealists,
and also the Buddhists, did, an irreconcilable dualism between
matter and spirit, you are obviously going to have a contempt
for the flesh which is matter, and a desire to escape from it,
into the Buddhist Nirvana, or the neo-Platonic *ecstasis*, but as
life is simply the spirit couched in matter, this means a disgust
with life and a corrosive sort of asceticism. On the other hand,

the materialists, by identifying spirit with matter, destroy life, because on this basis a stone obviously has as much life as I have, and thus as you can see all significance is eliminated from the term "life." In other words, both these sets of heresies are life-destroying. Now as a matter of fact the bridge over the gap was undiscovered by the ancients, nor could it have been bridged until the revelation of God showed the spiritual person of God united with the carnal spirit of Man in Christ. Christ's life was in a sense a sacrament, inasmuch as it overcame the dualism between flesh and spirit, and showed the flesh, redeemed, operating in co-operation with the spirit, forming a harmonious whole, instead of the conflicting dualism which is the only thing witnessed by men in their natural state. And this is the meaning of the Sacraments, also: they are spirit working through and with matter for, (and note St. Paul's words) the purpose of the "redemption of the *flesh*." How can you explain the fact that this painful dualism was always present even in the most saintly ancients, such as Socrates, and that it disappears in the lives of the Christian saints; how can you explain it except in terms of "the grace of Our Lord Jesus Christ," operating through prayer and sacraments. If this is true, it is only the Christian then who can have real *joie de vivre*, because he alone doesn't deviate into contempt for either one or the other of the two essential attributes of life, matter and spirit.

This evening I was at Trinity College and heard an Anglo-Catholic priest from Cincinnati. You should have been there. How he did shock that audience! He turns out to be an out-and-out Marxian Communist. Although I disagree with him, it was nevertheless refreshing to see a priest of the Church who was really hard-boiled in the good sense of the word, and who had his teeth so well into the roots of the social problem. It looks as if it is the dogmatic element of the Church which is really forward-looking. I've thought for some time, anyway, that dogma wasn't a hindrance to action, but a release for action.

I'm becoming more and more convinced that the Anglo-

Catholic movement is the beacon of Christendom – by their honesty and courage and radicalness, the Anglo-Catholics will, I think, save the Church and Christendom.

Well, it's 1.30, so I must away to my trundle. I do hope you can get ahold of this Dawson book. It's a magnificent apologetic for Christian dogma.

Don't get tied up in the Lessing net, whatever you do. Read it, but be careful. To reject dogma is to dispense with action. Because if you examine it deeply, every single moral act which you perform has a dogmatic sanction. Lessing's defiance of dogma is just an example of the gutting and gutless pseudo-liberalism, the gradual mortification of which is one of the few gratifying sights of the modern generation.

Yours,
Frank

To MARGARET BEATTIE

602 Spadina Ave., Toronto, Ont.,
March 14, 1937

Dear Margaret:

Whee, my hands are cold. I can just barely typewrite. I've been out in the country all day.

I went over to Trinity College a couple of nights last week to hear some lectures from an Episcopalian priest from Cincinnati – well, anyway, at one of the evenings Morley Callaghan was the chairman. He's *the* Canadian novelist, dontcha know. He's also an R.C. But what a speech he made. He got up and talked about how much he sympathised about this and that and talked about sitdown strikes and then quite suddenly switched to the Middle Ages and then to Fascism and Communism, and then just as suddenly to the infallibility of the Pope, and then began lamenting the fate of the laundresses of the United States. Apparently there is no minimum wage for laundresses in the U.S. and Roosevelt tried to inaugurate one which was thrown out by the Supreme Court. Callaghan went on at a great rate and talked almost with tears in his eyes about them, and referred tearfully to "those *poor* laundresses," and at that point MacDonald and I almost fell off our seats laughing. But what a poor timid naive little goof he is! Or maybe he was pulling the audience's joint and several legs.

I did very little work last week, as I kept going over to Trinity to hear this fire-eater from Cincinnati, but except for that I'm working fair like a beaver this term and getting a lot done, which is quite gratifying.

Have you seen the Plainsman? It is a "thoroughly excellent picture," and really captures the expansive spirit of the Western frontier in an authentic fashion. MacDonald and I traipsed miles out Queen St. to see it last night. Go to it at your earliest opportunity.

I always pronounce sloughs sloos.

I'm glad you're still full of beans. So am I. I'm running around the track, which in addition to my brown crusts keeps me fit as a fiddle. Well, Miss Buggy, I *must* get some work done. Write often.

Love,
Frank

To GEORGE FORD
602 Spadina Ave., Toronto, Ont.,
March 29, 1937

Dear George:

We had the most hideous Red-Dog poker game here the other evening, which lasted until a quarter after five in the morning. I ended up with a bet of six dollars on a very feeble hand, and luckily won, thus putting myself very slightly up. MacDonald and I have made a pact never to play the wretched game again. How went your paper on T. S. Eliot to the Culture Club? What a marvellous name, especially for a

working man's club! You have read Eliot's *After Strange Gods*
have you? My impression of it wasn't altogether favourable.
Eliot's Toryism has of course softened, but I still regard it as
the only queer thing in his ideological makeup. Every
intelligent person today is anxious for some species of social
reconstruction, and it seems obvious to me that the Labour
Party, imperfect as it is, is the only effective channel through
which a person with distributism or any other sensible social
ideals could work. At least the Labour Party isn't lending its
support to wholesale insidious pro-Fascist propaganda which
"the great British leaders" are dishing out. I sometimes suspect
Eliot's political sense; he seems so imbued with the Anglo-
Catholicism of the seventeenth century as to regard
seventeenth century royalism as an essential corollary, without
taking account of the fact that most of the twentieth century
Anglo-Catholics are staunch supporters of the Labour Party,
and that therefore, since there are some very clear-thinking
people among them, the ecclesiastical Right is not
incompatible with the political Left.

Anglo-Catholicism is still a revolutionary movement in this
country, but it has a strong centre in Trinity College. It is
interesting to observe that its Theological Faculty are far more
open-minded and intelligent than their stolid reactionary
brethren across the street at Wycliffe. I do not maintain that
the Church should support a program, but I do think the
clerics should be free to support political programs, even if
they are left wing. And, as a matter of fact, one real
condemnation of the stick-in-the muddish part of the Church is
not that it does not support a program, but that it *does*,
implicitly at any rate, and the program is reaction.

I have finished reading the new number of *New Frontier*. It's
the worst yet. Ask Jackson what he is doing reading the *New
Masses*, it's practically pure nonsense from start to finish.

Re our minor controversy on the subject of satire. True
scepticism (which generally leads to faith) should never be
confused with the "I'm from Missouri" attitude. St. Thomas
himself opened his monument to the Catholic faith with the

words: "It would seem that there is no God." The critical
spirit is absolutely essential to any sound faith. Our fault is that
we are under-critical. Even the much vaunted scepticism of the
twenties was built on a whole lot of pre-conceived notions
which hadn't been examined.

After this outburst, Goom, as Angus MacDonald is here to
drag me over for coffee.

Pick

P.S. With regard to our pact, it may interest you to know that
the "ink was scarcely dry" before this pact was shattered.
Pickersgill, the weak-minded poop, played Red-Dog the very
next night!

(Signed: Angus MacDonald)

To KAY SINCLAIR
Knox College, Toronto, Ont.,
May 15, 1937

Dear Kay:

Just a brief note to inclose something which I thought might
be of interest to you. These are rather full notes on Jacques
Maritain's book, *Three Reformers*. It is about the finest critique
of Protestantism I have ever seen. Reading Maritain is like a
personal revelation, really – refreshing and illuminating. I have
rarely been so captured by any writer. I also have Gilson's new
book. Maritain and Gilson are both on the staff of this
University.

I have read over that article of Laski's and have decided that
his attack on the curious woolliness of the Anglican Church is
quite justified. As you may have gathered, I am in a rather
dangerous position – of viewing Rome with longing. It is the
tone of authority, and of secure dogmatic foundations, which is
so satisfactory there. If only they had left out the infallibility of
the Pope, their edifice would have been so perfect and so

symmetrical. I don't think I shall ever become a Roman Catholic, because the doctrine of Papal Infallibility is too high a hurdle. I would, however, wish for a little of the Ultramontane spirit to enter the Anglican Church. All this disconnected jumble can only be straightened out by conversation, however. It may postpone my confirmation for awhile, though.

Yours,
Frank

To GEORGE FORD
Knox College, Toronto, Ont.,
June 14, 1937

Dear George:

Well, here I am twenty-two (since two weeks ago to be exact). Makes you think, doesn't it? It seems only yesterday that I was two.

McDougall, the blind professor I'm working for, is engaged now on a book, which makes it pretty soft for me. I just sit there, quietly reading Chesterton to myself, and about every half-hour he asks me to look up something for him. I get paid forty cents an hour for this. I'm consequently getting a lot of reading done. I have read a life of Charles Gore, that great Anglican bishop. He had a very good sense of humour, and a healthy hatred of prohibition. On being offered tea by a fanatically tee-totalling wife of a bishop, he said: "Thank you, but I never touch anything but alcoholic beverages!"

I am reading Maritain and Gilson, and that, with an ever-growing consciousness of the shambles which is being made of Anglicanism by heretics of every sort, and the fact that I read colossal quantities of material to McDougall on that debased secularisation of the Church which is known as the Henrican "Reformation," all this is involving me in serious "Romish

Tendencies." These divagations of mine may strike you, who are not directly concerned with religion, as rather arid argumentation, but I honestly and seriously believe that Christianity is the only thing that can save the world, and as Christianity itself can only be saved in and by the Church, it becomes pretty important to find out just how far the "true Church" extends. I would "go Roman" at once if the R.C. Church did not demand that I go farther than I – at present – am prepared to go, dogmatically. My summer's reading, discussion and prayers will be mainly concerned with the solution of this extremely thorny question.

I am rather concerned about the new interest in religion shown by that woman you mentioned. She talks about Grace as though it were a new brand of ice-cream. She should make sure she is not being unconsciously insincere about the whole business.

As you can see, my pursuit of the study of philosophy and theology is not from any abstract zeal for learning, but to aid in the solution of a very present personal problem.

I have a magnificent plan for Ph.D. study. The major course would be the early Renaissance viewed from the eminence of the thirteenth century. Which means that next year, as a preparation, I would be working to a large extent in mediaeval philosophy over at the Mediaeval Institute, quite possibly with Gilson! This year's work has been a splendid preparation for that.

Goom,
Pick

To KAY SINCLAIR
Knox College, Toronto, Ont.,
July 15, 1937

Dear Kay:

I enclose a rather detailed summary of Gilson's *Philosophy of St. Thomas Aquinas* which you will be interested in reading. Save these notes and I shall pick them up when I'm making my visit to Winnipeg.

I am reading Berdyaev's *Christianity and Class War.* It is about the best critique of Marx I have seen. Berdyaev is coming to interest my greatly. In fact there is a whole Russian Orthodox tradition, starting really with Dostoevsky, which is extraordinarily fruitful. I incline to think that Dostoevsky, rather than Marx, was the nineteenth century prophet of our time. However, I do wish somebody would standardise the spelling of his name.

Did you hear about Ezra Pound's social credit pamphlets? In one of them he said: "No one can possibly understand Gibbon's *Decline and Fall of the Roman Empire* who has not read Major Douglas on Social Credit." That would seem to eliminate, among others, Gibbon himself, as he had the misfortune to die at too early a date.

Yours,
Frank

To KAY SINCLAIR
606 Spadina Ave., Toronto, Ont.,
Dec. 5, 1937

Dear Kay:

I have moved again and am in a moderate place where I get a room and two meals a day for $5.50 a week.

I've just come out of hibernation and started writing people. I'm working quite hard this year for a change, and it is fascinating work. I take lectures from Gilson who is the best lecturer I have had.

Regarding the question of the truth of Christianity, I think you are approaching it from the wrong angle altogether. The problem is clearly Sin. Sin is the starting point of Greek philosophy, and its fruits were all prickly pears. Sin is the starting point of modern ideas of social reconstruction, in sin is it born and its fruits are the liquidation of the kulaks, and the concentration camp. Sin is also the starting point of Christian thought, but Christian thought is not born in sin, but in the Cross of Christ. Now this is no answer to your problems, of course, it is merely a hint as to what the answer is, as it has been found and elucidated by men who can talk more convincingly than I can, such as Dostoevsky, Augustine, Karl Barth, Pascal, Newman.

But I'm convinced that it is not the "proofs" that count in this business. Not even Dostoevsky, or St. Paul, will convert you: but they will make you see the problems more clearly, and by bearing such striking witness to the Cross of Christ they may very well put you in a position where the Faith will seize hold of you.

Well, I must go to work now. This letter may indicate a fairly considerable change in emphasis, if not in position. My arguments with Wilf Butcher this summer and fall have been epoch-making for me. By forcing me to sink deeper and deeper into dogmatic foundations of faith, it made me penetrate to the place where Catholicism and Protestantism find their fundamental parting-point. And thus I learned to understand and appreciate the terrible beauty of Protestantism in its purest form – in a person like Karl Barth, and to see how minutely, and yet how terrifically, I differed, in accepting the Catholic position in its purest form (Augustine and Pascal – not the Jesuit tradition). And thus I learned that there were considerably more important things than the rationale of the Faith as found in St. Thomas Aquinas or the New Testament apologetics, important and valuable as all these are.

Write soon. Don't neglect me as long as I have you, please. Remember, I had to move recently, and had a rather harassing fall up till then.

Yours,
Frank

To KAY SINCLAIR
97 Bedford Road, Toronto, Ont.,
February 22, 1938

Dear Kay:

I just spent forty dollars today. God, I feel awful. I had to
borrow it. But I decided to gamble on a new suit to impress
this university president with when he comes to Toronto and
interviews me. It is a good gamble as he is rumoured to be an
old woman and things like that impress him. I must discover
whether he uses his knife and fork – or just his fork – or just his
knife, and also learn how not to bolt my food.

I am really very excited about the business, as the job would
set me up perfectly. I discovered suddenly the other day that I
had grown up to a rather substantial extent in the past six
months – and as one of the manifestations, I am getting pretty
thoroughly fed up with irresponsibility and the student life etc.

If this job doesn't kick through I will likely go back to
Winnipeg and spend the summer working on Mr. Oastler's
farm with Buchanan at $25.00 a month and board, which
would be exceedingly pleasant. Another alternative is for
MacDonald and I to go up north and look for jobs in mines.
The third thing, if neither of us has any prospects for the
future, is that MacDonald and I may buzz off to the Old
Country if we can get a free passage over – but I don't think
there is much chance of that.

If I get out to Winnipeg I hope you'll be there. I am dying to
have a chance to chew the rag with you till all hours. You will
be surprised, I think, by a pretty decided change in my
position. It would be impossible for me to tell you the ins and
outs of it in a letter as it is too complicated, but I shall give
you the bare details now.

As you may have gathered from the slightly belligerent tone
of my letters before Christmas, I was busying myself most of
the time trying to think my way through numerous problems –
mainly religious. I had no idea where my enquiry was taking
me – except that I was finding guidance and help from Wilf

Butcher, and through him, from Karl Barth. Well, about three Sundays ago I went to Church, St. Thomas's, and heard a sermon on Faith. The sermon was not a bad sermon – I have put up with plenty of bad sermons which have had no effect on my attitude whatever – it was a very good, competent, reasonable, sane and typical Anglican sermon – representative of the best traditions of Anglican theology – that was just the trouble. A sermon on faith – which made rationalised faith out into a sort of mystical philosophy – and the Word of God wasn't even so much as mentioned from start to finish in the whole thing. The thing that struck me so forcibly was that this was the typical Anglican position – really the typical Catholic position. And this thing pretended to be the Church – the Body of Christ speaking the Word of God. Well I rebelled, and I rebelled against the whole service, until finally I had to get up and stroll out before it was half over. And what got so thoroughly in my hair was that the creature preaching that sermon – or Bishop Zilch of the Church in Spain who has been oppressing his flock for centuries – presumes to point to Niemöller in a German prison or Barth in exile – and says: "You are not of the Catholic Church." And I am forced to the conclusion which Luther expressed: "The Holy Catholic Church is there where the Word of God is *truly* preached and the sacraments are *truly* administered." – and such a definition cuts across all denominational or institutional boundaries. Of course the institutional organization is necessary to the efficient carrying on of the battle – but to assume that any specific type of ecclesiastical organization has a special divine sanction seems to me quite incongruous with the Cross and all it stands for. Have you read the Legend of the Grand Inquisitor – in the *Brothers Karamazoff*, on that score?

I shall, I expect, return to the church in which I was brought up, the United Church – without any illusions about it, but always recalling Luther's phrase; there is no danger of my deifying the good old United Church of Canada. I feel tremendously happy to have found my feet theologically. This letter may not sound much like a feet-finding sort of one, but my ideas are not as confused as the letter sounds. As you will realise – this implies a pretty thorough-going revolution in my whole position; I am anxious to discuss the whole thing with you in person as it is hopeless to try to go into all the ramifications of the thing in a letter. It must sound like a frightful *volte-face*. But I offer no apologies – except for past mud-slinging and past indecent lack of humility.

I do hope that you can get around to reading some of Barth – though you should be educated to him through Brunner, as Barth is so intransigent, and is very obscure unless you are already familiar with the ground on which he stands. I think Barth would excite you mightily – you might not agree, but you couldn't fail to be impressed with his greatness – or rather his timeliness – since as he says, he is a witness, not the founder of a school.

Have you read Veblen? He is magnificent – a Norwegian-American sociologist who died in 1929 – and whose critique of capitalist civilisation is more pertinent than that of Marx because he takes more factors into consideration. He is the apostle of a great deal of American leftism, rather than Marx. His work was buried in obscurity for years, probably due to the boom period, and as the truth of his statements is only now beginning to be felt his work is becoming better and better known, and his importance is being recognised. The best book is probably *Theory of the Leisure Class* which you have probably already read. Pardon this little lecture; Thorstein Veblen's a new enthusiasm of mine – and I thought possibly he might not have come your way.

I have moved very far to the Left – and definitely, this time, I think. My reasons for welcoming revolution are not quite the orthodox leftist reasons but I imagine they would be fairly acceptable – I don't think they are too bad.

Well, this letter has developed. It was intended to be about three-quarters of a page – as I *must* get to bed.

The boarding house is still good. The food is excellent, and I like the other boarders exceedingly well; we've all become very pally.

Goooooom-bye,

Yours,
Frank

Part IV

PARIS, MUNICH, WARSAW: 1938-1939
(Ages 23-24)

And we who have been brought up to think of 'Gallant Belgium'
As so much blague
Are now preparing again to essay good through evil
For the sake of Prague.

(Louis MacNeice)

After completing his M.A. at Toronto, Frank Pickersgill was offered the chance of a year's post-graduate study in Europe. The offer was made by his oldest brother, Jack, who managed effectively here, as on many other occasions, to combine the roles of brother and father for Frank. It was assumed that after completing this year, that is by September 1939, he would return to Canada and probably obtain employment in a Canadian university.

His principal headquarters in Europe was the Maison Canadienne, a students' residence of the University of Paris. About half the students living there were French; the others consisted of English Canadians and French Canadians. Pickersgill's preliminary objective was to improve his knowledge of the French language and he was afraid, at first, that he would talk English if he remained at the Maison. Instead, by great good fortune, he found that he made almost all his friends among a remarkable group of the French students. He was soon entirely at his ease with the language.

Pickersgill's determination to steep himself in the life of the country had one curious result which is occasionally reflected in these letters. Between the French students and the French Canadians there was a lack of sympathy not dissimilar to that often found between the English and English Canadians. Pickersgill had never had any real contact with French Canadians until, in Paris, he began to view them through French eyes, critical eyes that is. Three or four years later, when he met up with the Régiment de Maisonneuve in England, he realised, as he ruefully admitted, that his Parisian estimate of French Canada had been misguided and ill-informed.

In addition to his pursuit of formal studies at the Sorbonne, which were aimed to his writing a thesis on St. Augustine, he also spent a good deal of time, of course, in the give-and-take of café dialogue. A Canadian student, Gordon Wright, who met him in 1938, recalls his impressions of Pickersgill's talk at café tables in the Latin Quarter:

> He made a very deep impression on me through his keen intelligence, his rather sardonic sense of humour, his warm personality, and the tough integrity of his character. He struck me as a man who was looking for his place in life, who had not yet decided what to make of himself, but who was clearly marked for eminence. I always looked forward to our meetings ... for the talk ranged widely through French politics, history, the impending crisis in central Europe, with no holds barred.

In this first year in Paris, his principal friends were the Maison Canadienne crowd, in particular Robert Lapassade and Marc Maurette (who left the Maison shortly after Pickersgill arrived, but remained in Paris) and Jean Pouillon, Jean Varille, René Guimet and Henri Robillot who continued to live at the Maison. Maurette's sister, Fleurette, who later married Robillot, and the young woman who later married Pouillon, were also close friends.

These French friends speak highly not only of Pickersgill's language proficiency but of his thorough understanding of French esprit. Jean Varille, writing in 1948, summed him up as "un américain de 'bonne foi' merveilleusement assimilateur." And he adds (here I translate):

> I have never known an Anglo-Saxon who understood France and its people so well. He spoke French marvellously and even French slang, almost without a trace of accent. He had read enormously (one wonders where and when!) and he had a thorough understanding of the whole of modern French literature which he used to judge clearly and critically. When he became associated with the group of French students at the Maison, he came into contact, little by little, with French points of view and . . . he seemed thoroughly at home . . . We considered him as one of us, for his inclinations were the same as ours, and he conceived of 'liberty' and 'intelligence' as we did. His French culture was very considerable. It leaned more in the direction of the Voltairian tradition (left-wing republican, non conformist and revolutionary) than in the direction of the clerical tradition (the moral order and 'Action Française'). And what most astonished me, in my conversations with him, was how he ever had time, in so few years, to learn so many things about France.

For his part, Pickersgill said in a letter to Robillot (written in January 1939): "Why have I felt so instinctively and almost immediately at home with you, with Varille, with Guimet and with Pouillon? I have never been anywhere before where I felt at ease with people so quickly as here in Paris."

One result of his new French attachments was to lead to his gradual abandonment of academic work for the study of current political developments and for newspaper writing, a transition which can be followed in the subsequent letters.

A second and more obvious factor which brought about the change in direction was the international situation. Pickersgill was in Munich during the September crisis in 1938, and the impact of that event can be seen in his later newspaper articles and, more vividly, in his letters. The disillusionment which followed culminated in the bitterness of his feelings about Poland while he was there just before war broke out in 1939.

Earle Birney, the Canadian poet, has some fine lines describing the sense of an inevitable and dreadful dawn approaching to shatter the night of peace:

> Speeding and soaring he comes, the Atlantic sighting
> and there is no Joshua can brake his flight, nor
> any clutch of ours can hold this precious night.

Birney here was writing of Vancouver, a community remote from Europe. Pickersgill, of course, was at the centre of it and his awareness of the impending sunrise was consequently earlier and more acute than that of most of us.

Yet this precious night lasted its appointed time. The year between the Munich crisis and the outbreak of war was probably the happiest in Frank Pickersgill's life. In the summer of 1938, in pursuit of his studies, he visited Belgium where he lived in a monastery, and spent September in Germany improving his German as well as observing a country that seemed on the brink of war. In the winter of 1939, he visited Italy and the Spanish border, and, in the summer, to obtain materials for articles, he returned to Germany for two weeks, followed by a month in Poland where he lived with two Polish families and taught French to the children. As the Nazis began their invasion of Poland he added an unscheduled country to his travels, Roumania, to which he escaped just in time. From there he returned by train to Paris.

It is evident, during this happy year, that he enjoyed writing. But above all, he had found a new love, in a country rather than in a person, in which he was delighted to live. *Chacun a deux pays* ... but Pickersgill loathed *clichés* and would never let anyone get away with that time-worn observation.

To J. W. PICKERSGILL
Maison Canadienne, Paris,
July 22, 1938

Dear Mother and Jack:

Well I've got myself still further settled. I went out to see
Jacques Maritain last Sunday. He gave me a very interesting
suggestion. At Saulchoir in Belgium there is a Dominican
convent in which lives a certain Père Chenu, who is a friend of
Maritain's and quite a remarkable mediaevalist apparently.
Maritain suggested that I could go up there and spend two
weeks or a month in the monastery, reading under Chenu's
direction. It would be a very good idea, I think, from several
points of view. Among others, I would learn more French there
than at the Alliance Française, which I am finding rather
simple and a bit disappointing. So I don't think anything
would be lost if I were to leave the Alliance and go up to the
Belgian monastery.

My French is improving all the time. Mlle Ballu really must
have given me an extraordinarily good foundation down at the
lake that summer. I'm beginning to think in French now – in
ordinary conversation, but not when I'm alone; although I had
a bilingual dream the other night. The place where I do get
mixed up is at the bridge table. Plafond is a stupid game
anyway. I wish someone would introduce Culbertson contract
into the Canadian House. The only fun of bridge is bidding
slams.

The teachers at the Alliance Française are the most
extraordinary females I have ever laid eyes on. The average
old maid schoolteacher in Canada doesn't wear nail-polish and
bangs and attempt to flash sex-appeal – but these do, and the
effect is highly comic. Some of them seem to be quite good
things in spite of it.

Went to the Opera on Wednesday night with three
American lads to hear *Faust* – which was jolly well done – but
it's a childish thing, from the dramatic point of view; the music
nice though.

This city reminds me a bit of Winnipeg. I think it's the wide streets and the intelligent looking people on them – as well as the nonchalant way in which the pedestrians disregard traffic regulations.

Love,
Frank

To J. W. PICKERSGILL

Chartres, France,
July 30, 1938

Dear Mother and Jack:

The Alliance classes for the month finished on Thursday. I picked up a second hand bike for 195 francs, and am taking a little tour. Then tomorrow I'm going back to Paris. I'm going to go up to the Belgian monastery for about ten days, or longer if I like it. After that I don't know. Meredith Jones strongly advises me to spend a month in Germany to brush up my German as I'll have to do a lot of reading in German this winter. I could live cheaply *en pension* in some place like Frankfurt or Munich where I would have access to a library. What do you think of that, Jack?

Chartres is a marvellous place. It's a wonderful sight when you're riding along through the wheatfields of la Beauce, and suddenly that tremendous building looms up – apparently just sitting on the prairie – as you can't see any of the rest of the town which is down in the valley. It gives the most extraordinary impression – that building in the middle of the wheatfields.

I suppose it is because it is an agricultural centre that Chartres is almost untouched by the horrors of industrialism. I intend to return here – believe me. The cathedral itself is amazing. I agree with you Jack – that it beats Amiens. Amiens is finer architecturally, I think, but the windows at Chartres!

The whole town is hot stuff though – much better than for instance Rothenburg which is too self-consciously a show place. You feel that Chartres has a life of its own and isn't just a museum.

Gosh I like this country. I think it was a great mistake to come here in 1934. I was too adolescent to appreciate any of it. The idea of preferring Germany to France rather appals me now – and where I got the idea that the French people are unfriendly I can't figure out. They're just as friendly as the Germans and much more intelligent about it. Particularly the men. The women – except the young ones – are more inclined to view situations from a purely economic point of view.

Such appalling heat. I've been out in it wandering round this shadeless town all day and am well nigh done in. But my fanny is so stiff I can't sit down and my back so sunburned I can't lie down, so there you are.

Love,
Frank

To REV. W. F. BUTCHER (Newfoundland)

Maison Canadienne, Paris,
Aug 6, 1938

Dear Wilf:

I see you go in for Princess Elizabeth on your postage stamps too. If more than one person around the Maison Internationale sees those Newfoundland stamps I'm afraid blood will flow. I've never seen such fanatical stamp-collectors as these people – all Europeans apparently are just wild on the subject. They fairly froth at the mouth when they see an ordinary Canadian three cent stamp.

You will miss your friends there. Newfoundland is the sort of place that no one thinks of stopping off at or going to.

However, when you're there, you're practically at Yurrup: if you get holidays next summer, why don't you drop over? Pardon this Utopianism – it's probably just annoying. But frankly – I was thinking I was well fixed here and in a super-fortunate position – when I got your letter I couldn't avoid a pang that I was carrying on in a rather useless and butterfly fashion. Your letters and Buchanan's are the only ones that make me feel that way: your work and his seem to have a solidity which is sadly lacking in my career to date, and in moments of pessimism I think always will be. However I still think – when I'm saner – that some day I may be of use. If I could exert an influence on people there is something to be done in teaching – and I think I can on individuals.

Maritain suggested that I look up a Spaniard named Zubiri who lives out here in the Spanish house. He was a prof of philosophy at Madrid . . . an awfully nice chap, and we quickly discovered a common ground in an enthusiasm of Karl Barth. He has met Barth and heard him speak – described him as "un homme passionant" which is hard to translate – doesn't mean passionate – but rather one who inspired passionate enthusiasm in others.

Maritain is one of the most charming people I've ever met. One would never expect such an impression of sweetness (disgraceful word) from the writer of *Three Reformers*. He gives the impression of great spiritual depth – A neat example is the way in which Maritain has got himself thoroughly in Dutch with Catholics over here – and I think is being viewed now with a certain degree of suspicion in Rome – over the Spanish War (and also the Front Populaire here). He was not afraid – in fact was morally impelled – to come out with several strong condemnations of the general Catholic attitude of regarding the rebellion as a crusade and a Holy War – saying that this was straight blasphemy and a horrible travesty of Christianity. He was supported by the Dominicans here, and by two novelists Bernanos and Mauriac. The net result is that the Franco-ist papers in Spain actually call these people "Reds."

Well, cheerio for now, and write whenever you find the time. Thanks very much for your letter.

Yours,
Pick

To KAY SINCLAIR

Le Saulchoir, Belgium,
August 19, 1938

Dear Kay:

I just got your letter. I think I would very much like to read over those letters I wrote to you from Toronto. It would probably recall a lot to my mind. I'm appalled now when I think back over some of the things I thought and said as short a time ago as ten months – but to read the whole record would be a real revelation, as I think my letters to you have represented it better than the others.

Upon Maritain's advice, here I am in a Dominican monastery where I will be now until September 1st. I just got here half-an-hour ago. I'll be reading mediaeval philosophy pretty intensively here and under intelligent direction, and there will be plenty of opportunity to concentrate.

I've actually been getting quite a bit of work done, as well as learning French, after I left off the flat, stale and unprofitable task of taking courses at the Alliance Française. I was told the Alliance was almost indispensable for a decent knowledge of French, so enlisted for two weeks. They teach on the level of "The ink of my aunt is on the table while that of my third-cousin-once-removed is on the desk near the blackboard" sort of thing. (Perhaps it is significant that the first thing you learn in any foreign language is how to discuss your relations). The only way to learn the bloody language is to talk yourself blue in the face to any one who will put up with it, I've found that out.

This is the most off-hand and informal country I've ever seen – even more so than France. In France they have rules, but no one dreams of obeying them. (for traffic etc.) Here they don't even have rules. I must stop – I'm just about dead on my feet.

Yours,
Frank

To MRS. SARA PICKERSGILL (Ottawa)

Le Saulchoir, Belgium,
August 22, 1938

Dear Mother and Jack:

I think I'm going to like it here very much. The guests have all the freedom they want. There are only four guests now – myself – two rather unpleasant Jesuits from Lille (what the devil are they doing here? I thought they were mortal enemies of the Dominicans). Why is it that all Jesuits look unhealthy in an unpleasant way? That isn't true of these Dominicans who, in the main, are pretty good specimens physically – and a very cheerful and informal crowd. I've decided I don't like Jesuits. They remind me of Germans. The fourth guest is a little German refugee who is living in Paris. He's a very nice little goof and by no means an idiot though he looks like one.

Well I must go into town and buy some tooth-paste or my mouth will rot right away.

Love,
Frank

To MRS. SARA PICKERSGILL

Freiburg, Germany,
Sept. 2 1938

Dear Mother and Jack:

The trip Albert Fyfe and I intended to take was postponed until my return from Belgium. As a result, here we are now in the Black Forest, southern part, which I hadn't seen before. I'm going to come back here and live with a family and use the University library.

This is a most charming town externally. These south German towns are really marvellous. Things that would be grey or brown anywhere else are fine colours of pink, green, yellow or blue here – houses, mediaeval gates, everything – all are painted and there's nothing garish about it. It really isn't human. The Germans certainly excel in that sort of decoration. The streets are like a sort of stationary goldfish bowl.

The stay in the monastery was a huge success. I worked twelve or thirteen hours a day without any trouble, reading mainly mediaeval history. It was such a comfort having a library I could nose about in once more. I'm afraid I got thoroughly spoiled at Toronto. I certainly miss the University of Toronto library over here.

Mother, I certainly think if you're feeling up to it, you'd better come over here this winter. Things are really very cheap here. Now's your chance!

Sorry for the too long interval in my letters. I shall try to reform.

Love,
Frank

To MRS. SARA PICKERSGILL

Freiburg, Germany,
Sept. 13, 1938

Dear Mother and Jack:

I got your letters today advising me not to go to Germany until Sept. 15 – too late!

I'm now going to Munich for reasons which can wait to be explained, No – I'm not in trouble with the police – don't be alarmed! This country is more interesting than it was four years ago. However, France will look pretty good to me when I get back.

I've managed to hear most of the Reichsparteitag from Nürnberg over the radio – including speeches of Goering and Hitler. Goering yelled so that I could understand almost nothing – but I got nearly all of the Führer's oration. It was divided into three parts:

(1) The glorious history of the Party and the way it has reawakened the Folk.

(2) How the capitalistic-democracies have leagued with the Communists in a gigantic conspiracy to suppress Germany and the Party.

(3) How aforementioned capitalistic-democracies and Communists are encouraging Czechs to terrorize and suppress the poor Sudeten-Germans so that they will be afraid to demand their rights – and how if this terrorisation continues, the Czechs will learn to their cost that all Germany – Folk and Führer – are behind the Sudeten Germans.

There – I hope that is sufficiently objective and coldly truthful to pass the frontier. Do be bright enough to do a little through-the-lines-reading. This is the first chance I've had for quite a little while to let off steam, and I'd hate to think it was just a "burst of music down an unlistening street."

Had an amusing experience yesterday. I was walking

downtown and saw a middle-aged man with two kids in knee-pants and braces – the assembly looked typically South-German. As I passed, I was astonished to hear: "Et maintenant, mes enfants." I was well past, but turned around and rushed back and shook his hand telling him I wanted to talk a bit, I was so pleased to hear a French voice. He must have thought I was drunk or crazy – this outburst coming out with a good healthy Anglo-Saxon accent. Jack – if you think you're a Francophile you ought to see me *now*. You know the way somebody from Piddling-Duke, Kansas, allegedly behaves when he meets somebody from his home town in the African wilds? I felt much the same about this bird. I haven't the foggiest notion what his name was.

However, there's a very nice old chappy here – he runs a bakery – he has a wooden leg and represents SOUTH GERMANY AT ITS BEST – i.e., has colossal moustaches, shouts at you, and is very hearty.

The language is coming along as you may guess from my résumé of Hitler's speech. Speaking German wouldn't be bad if you didn't have to fit the phrases together like a jig-saw puzzle. I wonder if the German language is the explanation of the character or *vice versa* – or if they both spring from some hidden original source.

Well, cheerio – and here's hoping this gets through the censors – if any.

Love,
Frank

To REV. W. F. BUTCHER
Schellingstrasse 19, Munich,
Sept. 17, 1938

Dear Wilf:
I got your letter today, and in the same mail a cablegram

from Jack telling me to go to Switzerland. I cabled back that I wouldn't – adding reassuring words regarding my connection with the Consulate here through whom I'll hear some hours in advance if war breaks out. Switzerland is out of the question and I'd be starving in a week – it's an appallingly expensive country and I'd have to leave my German money here or spend it which would lose me vast sums.

But I think things will hold out here for a while longer. I am leaving Germany about Oct. 3 and most of . . . what I have to say will have to wait until after that date. The atmosphere of waiting to see which way the cat will jump is, needless to say, a trifle wearing – but I'm glad I'm here. Think of the story I'll have to tell my grandchildren!

I'm annoyed with my family for sending that cable. I had some bad moments today trying to decide whether I was morally obliged to leave the country to stop Mother worrying (she's not given to fussing about her brood – I don't know what's up – she knows I'm not a moron and can manage to keep my feet out of the fire). Finally decided that after all I HAVE MY OWN LIFE TO LEAD – as the super-dramatic movies put it.

Albert Fyfe left a week ago for Paris. While there he kept sending me post-cards with alarming reports of the state of "grandmother's health" and warning me to come back quickly to Paris as all feared the end was near. Why this excessive discretion I don't quite know – as everyone talks quite frankly about possibilities of war. The Germans try to be reassuring. They are convinced there won't be one of course because "Der Führer doesn't want war – he just wants to see that the Sudeten Germans get a square deal." However such naiveté is anything but reassuring. . . .

My present reading includes Thurneysen's *Dostojewski*, and *Das Wort Gottes und die Kirche*; Gogarten's *Politische Ethik* which I haven't yet started; Kierkegaard's *Die Krankheit zum Tode* which is exciting; Przywara's *Ringen des Gegenwart* and *Analogoia Entis*; Dorothy Sayers' *Unnatural Death* translated into German and P. G. Wodehouse's *Psmith Journalist*, untranslated. The German reading is really progressing, though I still maintain it's a repulsive language. Thurneysen writes too heavily with thick long, clause and phrase-clogged sentences – terrible reading but awfully good stuff. But more of these when I finish them.

Now I must go to bed. Write soon eh?

Yours,
Pick

To HELEN MAGILL (London, England)
Maison Canadienne, Paris,
September 26, 38

Dear Helen:

Today and tomorrow at any rate will decide whether it would be safe for you to come to France or not – I imagine though that if you were going to stay in Europe France would be as safe as England – I don't know what the hell is going to happen. That bastard is going to make another of his inflammatory speeches tonight. Jack cabled me to Germany telling me to visit Switzerland. I took it to mean get out of Germany. The consulate hinted broadly on Friday and I left Germany on Saturday.

But I'm beginning to wonder if he meant specifically Switzerland – as neutral territory. If there's a war my academic career is shot here anyway – There's no danger of getting interned or jailed or anything now, and after my three weeks in Germany I rather think I'd like to stay here in France for a bit anyway to see how the land lies.

My God – I don't think there'll be conscription in Canada this time, but Canada will probably be in there anyway. I've got to start working out my morals in the matter right away I guess. If I hadn't spent those three weeks in Germany I think I would C. O. the business as far as Canada was concerned. But having been there is the best anti-German war propaganda I've ever seen.

I have a curious feeling about the whole business – that Canada should stay out – of that I'm convinced – but that doesn't solve my personal problem in the matter.

What is so dreadfully disheartening is the thought that if France and England had made things plain two weeks ago and dictated terms to Hitler there'd be no danger now and no crisis, and the German newspapers would be busily having a go at Jews or the Church or something and the Germans would have forgotten about the existence of the Sudetens.

You have no idea how quickly public opinion can be changed in Germany. Three weeks ago people snapped their fingers at the possibility of war. All this last week in Munich everyone had become convinced that a war with Czechoslovakia was inevitable. Simply the dead weight of all the newspapers in Germany printing eight pages a day of atrocity stories horror stories, etc. – at least one inflammatory speech by a big shot or sob-interview with Sudeten "refugees" over the radio every night – all the thing of course becoming more intense all the time. It is so painfully obvious that they want the control of Czechoslovakia that one would wonder how the common people can possibly be taken in by the crusade-talk. Of course the present Godesberg plan gives the Germans all they want because it means in actual fact the control of Middle-Europe. So that if the Czechs give in now, the war, when it finally comes, will be so much worse than the one that might have to be fought now.

Even now I think the odds are against a war. The Germans are obviously scared to death at the prospect of a war with France and England – they're not gambling on winning a war against France and England but on scaring France and England out of the picture once again. I don't think even yet Hitler has gone so far with the Czech business not to back out if he has to – and I think he will even now if France and England make it perfectly plain that it's going to involve fighting them too.

God what a country. It was an interesting three weeks but about as depressing as any I've ever spent. The thing is so much worse now than four years ago that the place isn't recognisable – I heard the Nurnberg business – nearly all of it – over the radio. I'm glad I didn't see it in the flesh – I think I wouldn't have remained sane. It was bad enough over the radio. That was National-Socialism *en fete*. If it had been merely barbaric it wouldn't have been so bad. Honestly that nation is, I think, possessed by the devil – I see now what Dostoevsky meant in his novel. The inspiration behind their "culture" isn't merely subhuman or uncivilised. It's worse than that. In Munich I went to visit the exhibition of Nazi art at the New Museum of German Art – it is incredible the effect that stuff has on one. An absolutely unheard of unity of inspiration hangs over the place like a fog – and a sinister fog, because the pictures are really unpleasant. I felt an almost insane desire to grab an axe and go to work on the place. Of course the superficial objection to the exposition is that it reeks of sadism and homosexuality, but there's something lying behind that even which is much more sinister—maybe it's my imagination – but by Heavens I wish Dostoyevsky were alive to look at that stuff. And not only there. The thing hangs in the air of the country. Honest to God I feel superstitious. I imagine Italian Fascism must look like the incarnation of sunny health and sanity by comparison. When I saw the sloppy dirty cheery French customs officers at Kehl I could have hugged them. And then at Strasbourg the train filled up and I never would have dreamed that the crowded noisy disorder could be so glorious. I just sat in the corner of the carriage and grinned and giggled like a loony for about an hour. No wonder these people love their country.

The hateful thing about Germany is that in their off moments you like the people so much – that makes it all the worse when they get caught up in this grip of their religion. If they were always hateful or contemptible the country wouldn't be so depressing at all. It's not the people you are revolted at – but just this alien spiritual force which seems to have got hold of them. God this must sound like insane superstition. If my impressions were unique I would say I had projected my own feelings into the thing and had let my imagination run away with me – but they're by no means unique.

I had some interesting conversations with (a) a Benedictine Monk and (b) an ex-professor of English of the U. of Munich when I was there. The latter lost his job on three charges one of which I can't remember, the other two being (a) he said that the German script was in its origin not German, and (b) he said that Shakespeare was an individualist.

As you can see I've been turned into a first class subject for war propaganda. But I still think it would be suicidal for Canada to participate. And yet as I say that doesn't solve my own personal problem in the question – which would never have arisen, damn it all, if I hadn't gone and visited the bloody country. . . .

Love,
Frank

To HELEN MAGILL

Maison Canadienne, Paris,
October 1, 38

Dear Helen:

Well, France and England have thrown the wolf a bit of meat and staved off the attack for another day. One must feel terribly relieved and yet, as everyone here realises, the thing is going to have to be fought out some day. Maybe in six or seven years it'll be even more disastrous than it would have been now. Re pacifism, it is highly significant, I think, that the really pacifist paper in this crisis has been the *Action Française*.

The behaviour of the French people was magnificent, almost incredible. I'm glad to have come back – if this business had to be gone through I'm glad to have seen it. The calm and quiet way in which everyone took it on the chin – without any trace of war-psychosis or anti-German propaganda or sentiment was simply wonderful. Wednesday, the day the news came through that the German army was to be mobilised by two in the afternoon, the French Canadians staged a regular panic in the hall here over their bloody baggage. They were all leaving of course and thought they wouldn't get their baggage out and it'd be lost in the evacuation. Well (the house is half-full of French chaps you know) there were five or six French lads sitting around quietly eating breakfast and watching this performance – I've never felt so ashamed of my countrymen in my life before. Of course they had a right to worry about their baggage but they needn't have made such a fuss in front of those people who were looking forward to probable death – at any rate the ruin of their careers as they had planned them. It was like a death bed scene in which a couple of distant relatives start audibly complaining about the bore of having to put off Aunt Lizzy's cocktail party till after the funeral.

Well anyway now that they have given Hitler the Sudetenland the issues are clear. When the war comes it's perfectly apparent that it will be in defence of their own life and interests that France and England fight and not in the least in defence of a cause. And in the meantime the strength of the isolationist movement in Canada will develop and maybe keep us out. There's no longer any doubt in my mind. As a Frenchman or Englishman it would be of course "fight" – when the time comes – as a Canadian "Keep bloody well out and cook your own cabbages." England and France aren't going to go on any crusade – and I don't think it's up to Canada to. If it were to be a war of principles it'd be a different matter – but when it's certain to be one of interests – well frankly I would feel much more justified in volunteering in Spain – where there is a question of principle, than in flying to the colours when England calls – some time round about 1942–1945. God – if it were a question of collective security there would be an issue – but as it stands now, after the present Munich agreement – there is none.

Of course maybe the Germans may have got all they want –

but I doubt whether Chamberlain is enough of a fool sincerely to believe that. Maybe though the rearmament of Britain can now move along at a higher rate of speed than the German economic advance as a result of her possession of all the industrial area of Czechoslovakia. But I do know that people here, in spite of their horror regarding the war, are viewing the agreement with decidedly mixed feelings. I'm not at all sure that I wouldn't too if I were French or English. To say nothing of the fact that now England could probably sweep all the Dominions into it, and five years from now will certainly not get South Africa, probably not Canada, and very possibly not Australia – and it is well-known that in the last war the Dominions produced the best fighting material in the British armies. . . .

Love,
Frank

To J. W. PICKERSGILL

Paris,
October 8, 1938

Dear Jack:

I was very pleased indeed to get your letter. I have started to follow your advice and have already sent off the enclosed article to *Saturday Night*. I feel a little like the author of *My Twenty-four Hours in Russia*, but the thing is sufficiently impressionistic to be safe I think. I don't know whether it is any good or not but have the consolation, at any rate, that people will publish the awfullest bilge if it is topical. I am now finishing up something for the *Free Press* – in the nature of an interview with the English professor I met in Munich.

God I hope the stuff is decent. If it goes over, I'm afraid I'm not going to be entirely a star pupil at the University of Paris this winter. I've done nothing since getting your letter but sort out my German stuff and try to work out things.

Well, must go to lunch, and will post this on the way over. What is your candid opinion of French Canadians as individuals? Mine isn't very high at the moment though there are a couple of exceptions.

Well cheerio, and write soon.

Love,
Frank

To J. W. PICKERSGILL

Maison Canadienne, Paris,
November 1st, 1938

Dear Jack:

My work is going to be in later scholasticism. I'm working under Jean Vignaud of the Ecole des Hautes Etudes – a pupil of Gilson's and a "coming man." Haven't chosen a thesis subject yet. It will bear on the problem of the relation of faith to reason (ie., theology – philosophy) in later scholasticism – likely in the field of Nominalism. . . .

Re the political health of this country; like everybody else I've talked to, I'm rather "left behind" by the politics of after-Munich – aside from the obvious things such as the decided swing to the right indicated by the Radical-Socialist pow-wow at Marseilles. The French fellows I go around with out here – who tend to be Radical-Socialists or further left, and who are my age and who haven't yet done their military service – are thoroughly disheartened. They tend to think that working to prepare for a career of any sort isn't worth while because they've only got a couple of years at the most before there's either war or France goes Fascist and joins the anti-Komintern bloc. The fear of the latter would seem to me to be a fairly clear indication of a recognition of the passing of France into the rank of powers that toe the line.

M. Salque, whose sympathies tend to be Action Française, nevertheless is very bitter about the "peace" and is convinced that the war will have to be fought after a while – and that now the chances are it will be lost.

The most intelligent lad I know here (who doesn't live in the house but comes out two or three times a week – he works for a film studio in Paris) has decided that if peace lasts long enough for him to do it, he's going to make every possible effort to emigrate to Canada or the U.S. as soon as he has done his military service. His attitude is that he was prepared to break his head in September, but that now there isn't anything left worth fighting for. (From what Bessie tells me, his chances would be no better in Canada: apparently we were all ready to answer the bugle-call at the first summons).

This isn't a very intelligent answer to your question, but, as I said, I am left somewhat bewildered by the politics of the past month. When the air clears a bit I may be brighter. At the moment, I'm so involved in the annoying and absorbing business of registering properly that my mind registers blank for pretty well everything else.

I was over to see my German friends the night before last, and was appalled at the fact that once more I'm forgetting my German – and now I'm reading German all the time – more than French. When I first came back, I could speak without hesitation and with very few mistakes. Now I have to translate everything I say from French to German or from English to German or sometimes from both at once in my mind before I say it! There was a time when I thought I was pretty good at languages! I suppose maybe if I were talking English all the time instead of French, I wouldn't forget the German so quickly. At any rate I can read it now.

Well cheerio.

Love,
Frank

To ELIZABETH PICKERSGILL (Winnipeg)

Paris,
November 18, 1938

Dear Ducky:

I was elected treasurer of the Maison Canadienne! A group of people ganged up with intent to annoy me and staged a campaign which got me elected. Fortunately there's no treasure. All I have to do is sign my name to a problem in addition which is done once a month by somebody competent.

I suppose you know that I got an article published in *Saturday Night*. I wonder if the *Free Press* published the other thing. If they didn't they're rats not to send me back the manuscript. The *Saturday Night* one ought to pay fairly well.

I'm going to do some more as I hope to finance a trip to the Balkans that way. France should create a fair amount of interest the more she goes Fascist. I wish you could read French. There's a howlingly funny comic weekly – Leftist – which has simply excelled itself this week over the decree-laws. And has produced about the best criticism of them that I've seen. (Paper is called "The Chained Duck.")

People go on saying they'll fight before they give up colonies – but Hell – Chamberlain can betray France as easy as Czechoslovakia – and it's pretty obvious that European politics are now openly orientated towards Germany.

How do you like La Guardia installing an all-Jewish guard around the German consulate in New York? That's about the best story of the year. If somebody doesn't give that guy the Nobel Prize for something or other there's no justice. I haven't seen the protest from Germany. Or maybe they're coming to learn that their protests to U.S.A. are so many arrows shot into the air.

I become a stronger pro-American every day. Also pro-French. And anti-English . . .

Well, I must away to lunch, such as it will be. I've been poisoned and have shooting pains, so won't eat much.

Love,
Frank

P.S. Yes, I get homesick now and then. But generally I want to transplant people over here for the day. I am having an excellent time.

To MRS. SARA PICKERSGILL

Rome, Italy,
December 27, 1938

Dear Mother:

Haven't heard from you for so long: I hope you are enjoying yourself more now. But I still think it was a mistake not to come over to Europe and I can't figure out why you didn't come. It wouldn't have been more expensive.

I came down to Italy on the 22nd of December and have spent the whole time so far in Rome. I'm writing this from the middle of the Roman Forum, sitting on part of an ex-temple. The Forum is very well preserved: I'm having quite a time distinguishing Corinthian and Ionic pillars or Greek and Etruscan styles of building from what I can remember of Skuli Johnson's course in Roman Antiquities III.

This is without a doubt the coldest place I've ever struck. Beats Fort Garry at five o'clock of a winter evening all hollow. There are no means of heating the houses, so that it's just as cold inside as it is outside – and the beds! It's truly appalling. I think they must put all the bedding to soak all day – they couldn't possibly get it so cold and wet any other way. The result is that I've picked up a beauty of a cold – though I've finally broken it so that it doesn't bother me too much now....

Write soon and tell me about your trip. Did you get the book I sent you for Xmas?

Love,
Frank

To J. W. PICKERSGILL

Venice,
Jan. 11, 1939

Dear Jack:

We'll go back to Paris tomorrow night. Just now we are finishing off the rest of the itinerary: i.e., Venice.

Have really had a most interesting trip, but not nearly as fruitful as I had hoped from the point of view of current interest. At any rate I can read Italian now – and hence have perhaps been able to notice things that everyone couldn't notice.

Florence I like tremendously and would love to spend a month living with a family there some time. It strikes me as being the most civilised town I've seen in Italy—much more so than Rome, and Venice caters too much to the tourist trade. Florence preserves its life and individuality in the midst of its "historic sights" in an admirable manner, I think.

However, as a result of this Italian trip, I approve of the Renaissance even less than ever. There certainly are some fine sights in the way of pictures or statues – but in the main what god-awful taste! The way you get beautiful odds and ends in a Church whose ensemble is perfectly hideous and incongruous appals my totalitarian twentieth century mind. (Do I hear rude remarks?)

I'm far from wallowing in mediaevalism (farther than ever in fact) but certainly I'm convinced that from an artistic point of view they knew what the score was back in the middle ages far better than those damned conceited Renaissance Italians. The statues – but in the main what god-awful taste! The way you get beautiful odds and ends in a Church whose ensemble is perfectly hideous and incongrous appals my totalitarian 20th century mind. (Do I hear rude remarks?)

I'm far from wallowing in medievalism (fitter than ever in fact) but certainly I'm convinced that from an artistic point of view they knew what the score was best in the middle ages far better than these damned conceited Renaissance Italians. The sculptors may not have known so much about anatomy but the figures in French Gothic cathedrals at least bear some relationship to the whole structure. Mediæval Gothic gives much more evidence that its authors were civilised than that frightful Italian renaissance stuff does. Don't you think those gilt ceilings the ugliest things you've ever seen outside the Toronto Parliament Bldgs? Even the Sistine Chapel (which I had the luck to see on a free day) is pretty awful I think except for certain things which individually are very exciting. But the worst example is St Mark's here. If they'd only left the original Byzantine

Letter from Venice, January 11, 1939

sculptors may not have known so much about anatomy, but the figures in French Gothic cathedrals at least bear some relation to the whole structure. Mediaeval Gothic gives much more evidence that its authors were civilised than that frightful Italian Renaissance stuff does. Don't you think those gilt ceilings the ugliest things you've ever seen outside the Toronto Parliament Buildings? Even the Sistine Chapel (which I had the luck to see on a free day) is pretty awful I think except for certain things which individually are very exciting. But the worst example is St. Mark's here. If they'd only left the original Byzantine structure alone it would have been a wonderful thing I think. But of course with the new enlightenment they had to improve on it by cluttering it up with a lot of lousy apostles and blowsy madonnas with robes flowing all over the place. If they insisted on committing atrocities, I can't think why they didn't go away in a corner and build something of their own to commit them on instead of ruining a perfectly good building.

As I said, this is a damned interesting country, but from the arty point of view I don't know why people rave so about it. Give me France any time. When I get back, I think I'll have to take my first week-end off and bicycle out to wash my mouth out with Chartres.

Re the article for the Montreal *Standard*, I quite see your point. I already think the article was fairly stupid and the last time I read my copy I regretted having sent it. Oh well – I'm trying to remedy this – and will go on trying. Spending more time with studying European politics than mediaeval philosophy, and at the same time doing enough of the latter not to get left behind with my professors. I think this is a good plan as I don't want to alienate the professors. At the same time, I see more interesting possibilities in newspaper writing.

I don't like perpetually wasting your time asking you for advice. My French friends keep urging me to spend (or, as they are apt to put it, "perdre") less time with fourteenth century scholasticism and more time with twentieth century Europe, and both my inclination and thoughts of jobs point in the same direction. And yet I have another feeling that I should be burning the midnight oil over Gregoire de Rimini. Do you think this is stupid Puritanism or a well-founded instinct? I don't mean to imply that I want to chuck Gregoire de Rimini. Nor do I mean to imply that at the moment I'm an industrious soul working like a beaver over mediaeval manuscripts. But here is the point. If I could get an interesting job – either journalistic, radio, or civil service or something of the sort, I would rather do that than university work. I realise that there probably won't be any choice in the matter since people aren't going to shove jobs under my nose – and that's why I don't want to drop any of my efforts to impress somebody.

At the same time, at the back of my mind I can't get rid of a haunting fear of (a) unemployment or (b) being a bank clerk or something; and also a feeling which is fortunately not permanent that I'm not justifying my existence and ought to be working.

Do write me soon and tell me what you think of this as a way of spending the time over here. This isn't the GRAND TOUR and I don't want to waste it in intellectual gadding but want to make something of it. Do you think I'm going about it in the right way?

Love,
Frank

To REV. W. F. BUTCHER
Maison Canadienne, Paris XIV
Feb. 17, 1939

Dear Wilf:

I've been reading Malraux: have you read anything of his? He is a French Communist, who fought in the insurrections in China around 1926 and in the Spanish War, and has written three novels which make most other modern French literature look like child's play. Two about China – *The Conquerors* and *La Condition Humaine* (translated I think under the title of *Human Fate* or *Human Destiny* or *Man's Fate* or something) and one about Spain last fall which has just been translated under the title of *Man's Hope*. If you can possibly get ahold of them anywhere do, and write an article or something on him for something – I would be very anxious to see your reactions to him. As a novelist, he's the most serious thing I've struck since Dostoevsky – and its real epic stuff. You see the characters and the philo-psychological conflicts out through the glaring light of action, specifically military, just like in Homer. His Communism is not Marxism, far from it.

I must explain what I mean by change of direction. I am still working away with mediaeval philosophy and theology. But with considerably less interest than before. And with an interest entirely different. Because it becomes more and more apparent that the philo-theological structures of the middle ages rested on purely human foundations which in turn were based on purely human presuppositions, which dictated the direction the philosophy was to take even somewhat more consciously and openly than do the presuppositions of modern philosophers. The thing has a historical interest, as being an example of these relations of presuppositions to a body of thought ultimately dependent upon them; comparisons of this with later substitutes, and their effects. But *in se*, as a solution of world problems or even as a valid approach to them, the relevance of mediaeval philosophy seems to me to be virtually null. The logic of it and the demonstrability of it cut no ice, as one can demonstrate anything, given the right first principles viewed from the right slant, particularly if the demonstrator knows beforehand the way he's going to go.

Furthermore, the interest is flagging because my interest in the academic life and in academics is flagging very sadly. I want less and less to be an academic, and more and more to get my teeth into something.

For this reason I'm spending much more time this winter in chewing the rag with people, in reading and in studying

Europe, than in Gregory of Rimini or William of Occam or Aquinas etc.

I don't mean to say that I'm no longer interested in Christianity. Not at all. But I've lost all assurance as far as this is concerned. And am somewhat at sea about it. I still see the Christians as being the people who have got their teeth into the problem, and people like Barth, Thurneysen or Denis de Rougemont as, if you see what I mean, as being "right." Yet I'm not right. This gets more complex. But their seizing hold of the problem touches me personally and I see in the same direction; yet their conclusion remains exterior to me in the sense that I lose all assurance as far, not as they, but as I, am concerned. Do you remember the story in the *Brothers Karamazov* of the Woman of Little Faith? I'm like her. And I think I always have been, in a way.

The thing is I'm convinced of the "rightness" (this isn't the word I mean, but anyway) of their position, but I'm not convinced that I myself am caught ahold of personally by it. Except, again, in the posing of the problem, where I am equally caught by Malraux who poses fundamentally the same problem and yet ends up anti-religious. I'm also shocked and repelled by the superficiality of any other manner of posing or evading the problem. And am hence shocked and repelled, among other things, by Catholicism, mediaeval and (for the most part) modern.

Thanks ever so much for the letter for Bulgaria. I'm not altogether sure that I'll be going down that far south, but it's highly probable. The Italian trip was a great disappointment. ...I did not like Italy....

Well, I must go out and have something to eat, so cheerio. So you're getting married this summer. Good work! I hope everything works out absolutely well.

Yours,
Pick

To ELIZABETH PICKERSGILL
Maison Canadienne, Paris,
March 12, 1939

Dear Ducky:
It is ages since I wrote you . . . My main difficulty is the
typewriter ribbon. I'm such a slave to the typewriter now that
writing letters by hand is an infinitely painful process. But I
hate typing with a red ribbon, and at the present time it's all
I've got, and can't seem to get around to buying another one.
. . .

The reactions of "all the best people" at the defeat of the
Spanish loyalists has been one of the most discreditable things
I've ever seen. What makes me shudder is to think of the
people of my age: as I say, I don't know how representative
my friends are, but I should think, fairly so, for university
people etc. But what on earth sort of lives are they going to
have? This sort of thing goes against their grain completely,
they are more and more out of sympathy with the direction
their country and continent are taking, and in a few years
won't be good for anything except as fuel to feed to a
concentration camp. And I suppose we are next. Oh well, I
intend to make the best of what time we have left anyway.
Next summer I intend to plunge really hotly into free-lance
journalism. I've demonstrated to myself that it is possible to
make some money at it. . . . Well, I must think about going out
and getting some lunch, so toodle. My best to Ken – what are
the possibilities of a European honey-moon next summer?
After all, if I stay on, you never know what may happen. I
might get chucked into somebody's concentration camp for life
and you'd never see me again. I'm vaguely wondering at the
moment whether the German Propaganda Department takes
any notice of things published in one-horse countries like
Canada. And if they do, so what? It would be awkward if I
were refused admission into Germany next summer. I suppose

I'd have to go to Eastern Europe either via Scandinavia or via Algeria.

Love,
Frank

To MRS. SARA PICKERSGILL
Maison Canadienne, Paris,
March 12, 1939

Dear Mother:

I got your letter of Feb. 20 – so my fame is spreading to Southern California? *Saturday Night* paid me about $22 for my German Article, and haven't yet paid me for the Italian one. The *Free Press* paid me about $15 for the one I sent them. All very encouraging. I shall see next summer now, whether it will be possible to eke out a living doing free-lance journalism, and if it is, whoopee. I will have found my calling – for a while, at any rate.

The Spanish business seems to be clearing itself rather favourably for France and England. Sending Maréchal Pétain, the great hero of Verdun etc., and the Grand Old Man of France over there was a stroke of genius. When these people make a gesture its nearly always a pretty effective one. My friends tell me that the Maréchal is a complete dotard now, but he has been surrounded by a staff of exceptionally good diplomats, and what a figure he will cut! Talk about stealing Italian thunder. And then the English lent a ship to France to conquer Minorca with. The Italians have been thoroughly outraged by all this. (So am I, in fact, but there's no denying that for shrewdness it takes the cake.) What makes me feel bitter about the business, is that all this shrewdness and diplomacy, which is all very well, could just as well have been put to a decent and honourable use, the last two years, in winning the war for the Spanish loyalists. Undeniably the security of Europe in general is much more important than the internal condition of Spain. But the Spaniards are people, and Europeans, and a lot finer people than the wops and dagos and Nazis that Chamberlain and his gang have been nosing up to for the past four years. And other things being equal, there's no reason why there shouldn't have been a decent government in Spain instead of a government by a lot of colonels and corrupt parsons. And other things aren't even equal, because there is no certitude that the French and English efforts at the moment are going to be successful in beating Mussolini at his own game.

Well, must go to lunch, so good-bye for now.

Love,
Frank

To GEORGE FORD (New Haven, U.S.A.)

Paris,
April 15, 1939

Dear George:

Feverish activity: I've practically given up the doctorate altogether, what with dynamism, projects etc. I got an interview with Madame Tabouis, you know the only French woman journalist the other day and sent it off to the *Free Press*. And there is a whole series of other interviews on the immediate horizon.

Furthermore, there is a 99 per cent chance that I'll get the job of translating a novel which was one of the two or three howling successes of the year. It is *La Nausée* by Jean-Paul Sartre, his first novel. Pouillon, one of my pals, is an intimate friend of the author and says there won't be any doubt about Sartre giving me the translating job, and after it's finished, he's just brought out a book of short stories which I can start on. It's a sure winner – it's had a terrific sale in France. Of course on the other hand I would henceforth be done for from the point of view of a job with Wesley College or the WCTU and I'm going to have to brush up on English obscenity laws. This book is not cheap stuff like Aldous Huxley, but look what happened to Flaubert and D. H. Lawrence. Pouillon is going to see Sartre about it tomorrow. So, as you can judge, there is every prospect of my imminent rolling in the filthy.

Last week, when I was stony-broke and horribly in debt and trying to figure out ways of earning money quick, my friend Varille, whose fertile mind is always full of projects, suggested a gigolo job for me in the night clubs. This attracted my fancy for some days until I got ahold of more conventional sources of revenue.

I've got everybody caught up in correspondence. Jackson has for two weeks been writing me a letter a day and sending them airmail! Some others have stopped writing to me, I wonder why. I can't go around all my life on tip-toes trying to avoid irritating people. It's never been my policy and I'm not going to start now. If people can't take me neat, so much the worse. I can't and won't make myself over. One changes insensibly all the time I suppose, and if somebody has been away for a period of time, the change in the interval is noticeable, even in letters. Then by the irony of human incomprehension it's put down to snobbery, or affectation. The fact that I've acclimatised myself over here is going, I'm afraid, to have some sad results, when I get back to Canada. It makes me a bit afraid to go back. A problem which is worrying Teakles too. He is here for a time and I've had several long talks with him and feel quite differently about him. He's developed into a pretty good fellow and interesting to talk to. He himself nearly dies of shame when he thinks of his undergraduate days – which is a good sign. Anyone who doesn't ought to be castrated.

The Yurrupean situation looks worse and worse. I guess there's not much doubt now – it's just a question of time. We can thank people like Bonnet and Chamberlain I suppose – but first our own inertia – I mean the inertia of all ordinary people in the civilised world during the last six years, me included.

Why did the Front Populaire government accede to non-intervention? It wasn't for lack of goodwill to the Spanish democracy. It wasn't "political machinations." Its hands were tied by London financial interests—and, in turn, we Americans and Canadians went blithely on a course of goodwill and cheering on the sidelines and not wanting to "entangle" ourselves when a tangible recognition by the American continent that Non-intervention was Intervention would have enabled Blum and Delbos to finish off that affair and thus to damage the prestige of Fascism so effectively as to paralyse German and Italian activity. An effective Franco defeat under the open aegis of France and the U.S.A. – and then there would have been no Austria and no Czechoslovakia, and no war. Now we'll be in it up to our ears anyway – that's certain. And from a spiritual point of view, France and Spain represented something that Americans could ill afford to lose – all that remained and was really dynamic of Europe.

Because Germany and Russia, though dynamic enough, are something else and something alien and (Germany at any rate) fundamentally hostile to the (damn it all, I won't say "democratic") Jacobin orbit—France, Spain, U.S.A. Spain's done for; and France's spiritual condition is desperate which is appalling to think of when only two and a half years ago there was a revivification of the moral forces of the French revolutionary spirit which was absolutely tremendous. It has fundamentally been a Civil War – without bloodshed – which has killed it here too – a Civil War with the same polite and secret English intervention and the same American neglect which permitted its murder in Spain.

By the way, did you know that Irving Babbitt condemned the right of workers to organise on the grounds that it was against the Inner Check? The dirty fat smug old blackmailer. God how I loathe people who are hypocritical in their selfishness and fatness. If he'd come out straight and said: "I and my friends are liable to find our standard of living going down if workmen are permitted to fight for the rights of decent food and clothing – therefore etc" – it would at least be honest.

Or if he even *thought* it. But they persuade themselves into thinking they have all sorts of profound or spiritual motives for these things.

Gooooom,
Pick

To ALBERT FYFE (Galt)
Maison Canadienne, Paris,
June 23, 1939

Dear Albert:

I'm sorry to have been so negligent in my correspondence – but as you so aptly put it, I've been ignoring everyone in the most highhanded fashion – largely because the journalistic work I've been doing has exhausted me from the point of view of writing letters, and recently I've been turning out stuff at a terrific rate. The mental strain is enormous.

I've just been playing with a couple of wire-haired terriers who have interrupted my train of thought.

Well re practical questions, your fees will depend on the work you intend doing. If it's a Doctorate, Inscription fees are $5.25. Living in Paris has gone up a bit – I think you'd have to count on spending 2,000 francs ($52.50) a month for everything – though since you don't smoke and won't be obliged to drink very much, you can probably do it for less.

My thesis has stopped in its tracks – it was on Gregory of Rimini and very dull indeed. I rather imagine I'll be here for another year yet, but am not entirely sure. There's a money question which is of considerable importance. I am writing this in a park which is crammed full of fruits buzzing round each other like mosquitoes and diving in and out of urinals at two minute intervals. As the atmosphere is getting heavy and I'm fed up with being made eyes at, I think I'll clear out, so goom.

Yours,
Pick

To GEORGE FORD

Paris,
June 30, 1939

Dear George:

Why the Hell don't you answer my last letter – I'm not out of favour with you too, am I? I'm pulling out of Paris tonight for a couple of weeks in Germany. I hope I don't get flung out of the place. Dick Herzer managed to get a permit and was shown through the Dachau concentration camp, but I'll probably get put in jail because of my articles in Winnipeg newspapers. An American student at Heidelberg recently made some silly joke about the Nazi régime and got thirty days for it.

At the moment I feel shamelessly cynical about the situation here. I take a malicious pleasure in the slowness of the Anglo-Soviet treaty. I think Chamberlain can be held entirely responsible if it fails: his attitude (until just yesterday) of regarding Russia as something disgusting that he was obliged to dirty his fingers with had every reason to meet with Russian disapproval. And the Nazis have sent a "commercial mission" to Moscow –

Well, I have a bit of a headache and some packing to do, so will close until such time as you see fit to write me!

Yours,
Pick

To MRS. SARA PICKERSGILL

Berlin,
July 5, 1939

Dear Mother:

Well, the trip has started. I'll be here two weeks and then on to Poland. . . . Had a very amusing but tiring train journey. Compartment full of Belgians. And talk about Western Ontarians, Belgians have them beaten forty ways from Sunday for family gossip. These Belgians were all from Liége and within half-an-hour found out that they knew each other's second-cousins-once-removed. One woman announced that she had been an unmarried mother at the age of seventeen but that the man had made an honest woman of her. The man in question sitting opposite blushed modestly and looked vaguely arch, although the whole story was very ancient history, the infant thus produced now being twenty-three years old.

Last evening, in my search for hotels, I ran into the usual German friendliness. Went into one place and asked if they had rooms but it was only a Beer-Hall, not a hotel. As I was turning away, disappointed, an old chappy in a corner with his wife called me over, stood me two glasses of beer, and then took me out and walked me half across Berlin to a Youth Hostel sort of place where he knew I could stay cheap. Unfortunately though his intentions were excellent, I only stayed there one night as instead of a room I had a bed in a dormitory. And not only was it annoying to have German Youth tramping in and out of your room and getting up at 4.30 in the morning to go on hikes and commune with Nature (with a capital "N" of course) but I have too much money and valuables on my person to risk sharing a room with strangers.

I must be getting to bed.

Love,
Frank

To HELEN MAGILL (Winnipeg)

Warsaw, Poland,
July 25, 1939

Dear Helen:

This town at first sight is breath-taking – it's so like
Winnipeg around the C.P.R. station and North Main Street
that you have to prick yourself to make sure you aren't
dreaming. As you come into it, it straggles all over the place,
with vacant lots, tumbledown shacks, little wooden or brick
houses, discarded rolling-stock just like Winnipeg. And then
coming out of the station onto Jerusalem Alley you'd think you
were at the corner of Higgins and Main. The same grime and
oil and Yiddish signs and the same racial types dressed in
exactly the same way.

Other parts are quite Russian and Oriental – the river bank,
for example, looks like something out of a Russian film – no
embankment – long low grassy banks crowded with people just
lying around doing nothing or swimming or something – right
in the middle of the town. Then another quarter is just like any
other mediaeval European town. I've never seen so many
startling contrasts in one place before. It's pretty ugly and
depressing, especially at this time of year with the suffocating
heat, and it's grown much too fast. This country is
industrialising at a fairly rapid rate of speed which gives all the
large towns that ham-strung Chicago look about them. Lodz is
apparently frightful.

The language problem grows more acute all the time; in
western Poland, I now realise, it was very simple – as one could
always find someone who spoke German. Here nobody speaks
anything – they just gurgle Polish and some of them announce
proudly that they gurgle Russian too.

Getting to this place I'm staying from the station was a real
adventure. I knew it was near a certain square, so after going
through my rigmarole of "Do you speak English? Parlez-vous
français? Sprechen sie Deutsch?" several times and just meeting
with blank looks, I started snooping around street-car stops

until I finally found the name of this square – the usual twenty-four letter word with one vowel in it. So I got on the street-car with the corresponding number and looked grimly at the conductor and started in. After I'd got out the first twelve consonants, and was approaching the fainting-point, he caught on and muttered something which I suppose was the price. I tried to look intelligent as though I understood perfectly what he had said, and handed him a 20-zloty bill just to be sure. As he gave me 19.80 in return, I'd know what "20" was in Polish if I could remember the peculiar gurgle he gave. I finally reached the place and got off the car and started looking about furtively to see if I could find the actual Students' Hostel. Not having any luck whatever, I went up to a particularly seedy looking individual sitting on a park bench and without saying a word thrust a grimy hunk of paper with the name of the hostel on it under his nose. He pointed vaguely, I looked, he nodded, and I went off in that direction. I got the place, but the desk clerk couldn't speak anything but Polish either. We looked at each other hopelessly for a while, and then I saw the telephone and remembered a fellow I knew who lived here. So I pointed to the phone book, then to the desk clerk, then gave a sort of strangled noise which I hoped he would interpret as a request to use the phone. No reaction, so I courageously grabbed the phone book and looked up the number and telephoned. No one at the other end could speak anything but Polish, but Indo-European kinships enabled me to make out the fact that the fellow wasn't in Warsaw. I hung up in despair, and at that point the desk clerk started to talk to me in pidgin-German. Silly ass, why he hadn't done that in the first place I don't know. In any case, I got a fine room, with this desk on which I can really write and type – and a comfortable bed and running water – and all, thank God, cheap. Fortunately I go to my family on Friday, and will live free for a month. Otherwise I'd have to rob a bank or something. I've sent off another article, a rather bad one on Danzig, also in quadruplicate, which means seven in all to date, and if some of them don't take, I'll eat my shirt.

I miss France. If I must live in Canada eventually pray God it may be in Montreal, in spite of the French Canadians. Or in Ottawa. (This as you will remember, was the sort of attitude I railed against a couple of years ago. Well, that's how it is.)

Love,
Frank

To MRS. K. SEABORNE (Elizabeth Pickersgill)
Warsaw, Poland,
July 25, 1939

Dear Ducky,

I've run into a Canadian from Winnipeg who has been in Warsaw five years. He is a hustler, a go-getter, an anti-Semite, an ardent Winnipeg old-timer (that is, he wants to get all the latest gossip about Isaac Pitblado, Mayor Webb and other figures about whom nothing exceeds my indifference), judges everything, food, mealtimes, working hours, ways of spending time etc., by Winnipeg standards which he seems to regard as a sort of absolute, has a Y.M.C.A. secretary manner, pokes you in the ribs violently whenever he makes a point – is, in fact, all the things I abhor. Furthermore, he has taken charge of me since Sunday, and arranged my "program" in Warsaw in a most dictatorial fashion. He means well, I suppose, and I don't want to hurt his feelings . . . but it is just about all I can do to be civil to him . . .

I've sent off seven newspaper articles already which isn't bad for three and a half weeks. Typed them in quadruplicate and sent them to four different papers. Five of them on Germany, of which I think four were quite good, one on first Polish impressions, and one on Danzig. Danzig was disappointing all the same. I didn't see much, beyond, of course, an amazing movement of troops, "tourists" being carried in army-trucks out toward the East Prussian frontier, SS men who disguised themselves as Danziger Heimwehr men by the ultra-simple procedure of sewing a tab with "Danziger Heimwehr" on it to the sleeve of the SS Uniform. They barely even try to pretend that they are Danzigers and not recently imported from Germany, they wander about in a lost fashion in the streets, and patently don't know the town. They don't make any bones about it any more. I guess things are really going to pop in about a month. The end of August is, at any rate, the date people in Berlin give for Hell to pop. Obviously, if there is a war, my wretched plans don't matter any more, and I'll probably stay here – I don't know what doing.

The Poles certainly know how to eat. The food here is almost as good as it is in France. It's certainly a welcome change after Germany. I'm trying to learn a bit of Polish. I'm hopelessly bogged in a complicated network of case-endings and verb-forms and when I try to plough my way out I just sink deeper in the morass. I can't figure out how little kids can learn to talk at all.

Well, gooom, and give my best to Ken. I hear indirectly that you are being moved to Calgary. Permanently? Tell me all.

Love,
Frank

To GEORGE FORD

Warsaw, Poland,
July 27, 1939

Dear George:

Well today's scheduled for the end of the world according to some Mexican astronomer or other so I don't suppose this document will ever reach you. I hope that makes you feel somehow proud and humble.

I hear you have the summer job again. Congratulations. You had better earn some money at it and come to Yurrup again this winter. Probably you will be here anyway in the trenches so such suggestions are superfluous. Have you read Dos Passos's *Three Soldiers*? It's rather good on that.

The crisis is scheduled for about early September, very slightly before the one of last year. I suspect it will be war this time. It has ceased to have any connection with democracy or any other ideological considerations and it's just a naked question of interest. If I were English or French I'd want to cut Chamberlain's throat, but as a Canadian I feel more like sneering cynically this season. There aren't any more issues that matter a damn involved in it, except accidently. Not that we won't be all dragged in too.

These Poles are half hoping for a war as they figure on getting Danzig and East Prussia out of it. They are unpleasant people from a political point of view. They have profited by every war that's been fought in Europe since the Partition (including the "guerre blanche" of last September when they got a rake-off in the Czechoslovak deal) and the result is that they're aggressive and ambitious.

I got a letter from a friend of mine in Paris with the addresses of two Warsavians and the following dubious recommendations. For the one: un jeune homme, très gentil, quoiqu'un peu bête. For the other: la fille d'un journaliste, légèrement communiste, je crois, aime bien discuter, très laide. I'm going to take a fling at the man – the woman I don't quite dare to tackle. Unhappily the man is doing his military service and is in Warsaw only five hours today.

Well, Georgiiiiii, I think I'd better go out and look up this bird. Goooooooooooooom,

Pick

To MRS. SARA PICKERSGILL
c/o Klobska, Dabie u/Nerem, Poland,
August 12, 1939

Dear Mother:

I do hope you're feeling better. I am so worried about the whole thing as I have no idea what you are to be operated on for. Is Elinor Black going to do the operation? I hope that it won't ruin a possible trip to Europe.

I'm leaving this place tomorrow to spend two weeks at the Fuldes' at Kalisz (they are the people I should have gone to in the first place if it hadn't been for the skulduggery). I planned this move twice ... but feared this family would destroy my mail if I went over.

The change in their attitude is, I think due to a political discussion at the dinner-table last night. The night after night examples of chauvinism, anti-Semitism, Red-baiting etc., were getting to the limit of my endurance. Last night (I never introduce a political subject and always avoid talking – and when I do, generally either tone down my views or lie outright) Mrs. Klobska who, as I think I told you, spent four years in U.S.A. told me that an American friend of hers wrote her that the vast majority of Americans had sympathised with the "Reds" during the Spanish War, was this true? I said, oh yes, it was largely true. Oh, she said in a horrified voice: "you'll *admit* it – like that – right out?" This got me fighting mad, and gripping the table to keep my hands from shaking too much I said in as frigid a tone as I could conjure up: "Oh certainly. I've been 100 per cent for the Spanish Government from the beginning of the war." Trying to keep the rage out of my voice and maintaining all the amenities of polite conversation I went on – I got wound up and it wasn't any good trying to control myself. She proceeded to pour abuse on my head – shocked horror and amazement rather than abuse, I should say – about her not having realised she had a red beneath her roof. Finally my lid blew right off. I've told you what German haters they are. Well, I finally said: "You know I find it difficult to see

120

how you, as loyal Poles, can be pleased to see Franco's victory which means turning Spain into a German garrison. You no doubt have a very good opinion of your army – but you surely count on needing a bit of help from France and England in the coming war – and now France and England are going to have to waste men and munitions guarding the Pyrenees – which they wouldn't have had to do if his most Christian excellency General Franco and his German and Italian legions hadn't conquered in Spain. That means all the fewer men and munitions to help you."

I didn't add – though it nearly slipped out: "Of course, last September and October, when you were pro-German and our enemies, your hatred of the Spanish Government was understandable as the proper politics of an Axis-partner. Your alliances of this season ought to result in a change of attitude on this subject."

I don't know why I got so worked up about this fairly trite question – I suppose it was the cumulative effect of repression and tongue-holding for two weeks.

In any case the atmosphere got chilly and I think they went to bed afraid that they might be murdered in their beds by this "Red" they were harbouring. (As far as I can make out, I'm the nearest thing to a Communist they have ever met!)

This morning, when another message came to me from Madame Fulde, it was suggested that perhaps it would be only fair that I divide my time up. I'm so glad and relieved to get away from here ... I can't say the prospect of living out the war in the midst of these frightful chauvinists is an altogether charming prospect, but then neither is the war.

Well good-bye for now Mother, and do let me know at once about the operation and your general health. I'm very worried about you.

Love,
Frank

To HELEN MAGILL
c/o Fulde, Kalisz, Poland,
August 18, 1939

Dearest Helen:

I shouldn't be writing letters as it's three weeks since I've turned out an article and should be reserving my forces – but it is well-nigh impossible to write one here ... Anyway, I'm having a month of "Polish family life" and should work up something out of it.

Poles are a curious race: as far as I can see utterly untouched by the ideas which floated about Western Europe in the nineteenth century and which conditioned me, at any rate, to such an extent that I can't help having Liberal reflexes whatever my reflection may be afterwards. Poles professed Liberalism in the nineteenth century, but only to get their country back. Liberalism in the sense other than strictly political, i.e., a certain measure of tolerance, of humanitarianism and egalitarianism never has seemed to mean anything to them. And the result is – among the people I've met – feudal aristocracy untouched to the smallest extent by inquietudes about the immutability of the Natural Law which gives them such and such rights over such and such of their fellow-men. I don't know about England, but certainly in France the pitiful remains of the aristocratic tradition yells of course loud enough, but their yelling is in a tone of self-defence. They are obviously unsure of themselves in the face of Free-Masons, "that Jew Blum," CGT, meridional peasants, rising business men et al et al – and methinks the gentleman doth protest too much.

So it's a curious and really utterly new world to me. The intolerance and inequality and racial hatred and so on that Fascism is developing at such a fine rate in Italy and Germany and – indirectly – in France and England, here needs no development. It has a long and perfectly established tradition – nothing else has ever existed: and considering the way the country is going and growing, I'm inclined to see in it a prefiguration of the New Europe. All the more reason for wondering if the game is worth the candle. The twelve children I've always wanted to have will either be shot at dawn or be hateful to me. It would be so much simpler to be an out and out Communist because then one could feel it a virtue to be motivated by hatred and intolerance. Psychologically they're in the swing as much as the others though from the point of view of power I think they are doomed to lose out.

The presumption of the nineteenth century to imagine that Liberalism was "here to stay," as though it was anything more than a nice dream egged on into existence by the peculiar economic circumstances of nineteenth century expansion ...

Pardon this diatribe. My mental reactions are doing their best to spoil a physically agreeable stay here playing tennis, swimming etc. – but after all I came on this trip not for the tennis but for the mental reactions, so I suppose it's all to the good. German intellectual and moral atrocities never depressed me as much as Polish ones do, because, I suppose, I persisted in kidding myself that the Germans were our psychological "enemies," and as such we represented a higher level of something-or-other. But the Poles are our "allies" and it becomes increasingly plain that there isn't the slightest moral or ideal issue involved in the coming struggle whatsoever. The Poles are at least barefaced about this – whereas the French and the English –! well, the best of them kid themselves and the worst of them are, I suppose, in their way as barefaced as the Poles, only sournoisement.

Thanks for going to see Mother. Go as often as you have time for, please. I'm very worried about her.

Love,
Frank

P.S. This is a dismal and doleful letter. Sorry. Try to do better next time. Central Europe must have a bad effect on my liver. Yet Polish food is excellent.

To KAY SINCLAIR (Toronto)

c/o Fulde, Kalisz, Poland,
August 20, 1939

Dear Kay:

Yesterday I read your letter on my back. Today I reply on
my stomach – the reason for the change being that yesterday I
got my front sunburned and don't dare expose it. It makes me
feel like Napoleon's army.

I'm having a pleasant time earning my living here for a
month by talking French to the family. The month will be up
next Sunday when I go to Bucarest. Provided, of course, the
war doesn't break out before next Sunday . . .

Speaking of French-Canadian Journalism, would you do me
a favour? If possible get hold of some numbers of *La Relève*
published, I think, in Valleyfield, Quebec, and then tell me
what you think of them. *La Relève* is the French-Canadian
offspring of a French parent called *Esprit* which I find the
outstanding French monthly mag, and the only journalism I've
seen in any language to which I could apply the word
"inspiring" (if you like I'll send you some numbers). It's
editorial board is made up of Catholics, Protestants and "Free-
thinkers-recognising-certain-spiritual-values." I admit it
sounds a little SCMish and would be in any other country but
France where people have the guts to talk about their "souls"
without getting sentimental. It is political, entirely – and Left in
the following sense: without being commie or, on the other
hand, programmish, it adopts the principle that the working
class and working class movements are the only spiritual force
of any value – or at all disinterested – in modern politics. Hence
it is more syndicalist than definitely socialist. This is typically
French and I might say Latin, where all Left-wing thought
worth the paper it's written on has tended away from
doctrinairism towards anarcho-syndicalism. *Esprit* is
anarcho-syndicalist with a Christian (in its *very* best sense) bias.
Thus it was Front Populaire while most Catholics felt obliged
to abjure the Front Populaire and "that Jew Blum" as the

works of Satan, and it was perhaps the most sincere and devoted supporter of Republican Spain in Europe.

The French Socialist party is petering out intellectually. The Communists are distinguishing themselves by a degree of stupidity, bigotry, hypocrisy and "mauvaise foi" which is unusually high even for them. I speak, of course, in terms of parties, not of men. I don't know about Canadian commies – except that the *New Frontier* used to irritate me furiously once a month – but (outside Russia) I find the European Communist Party insufferable. The Russians make use of these half-baked bigots and doctrinaires as an unofficial diplomatic corps – in which they are quite justified if they can take the fools in – but it is a shocking commentary on the intelligence of these people who go on believing or pretending to believe that Russia is serving a disinterested cause and not simply playing her political game like the others. The bare fact is that the days of disinterested causes are over in Europe, and the Front de la Paix no more resembles the late League of Nations than Al Capone's gangland rivals resembled an hypothetically honest police force. I think Russia comes out of the business with the cleanest bill of the lot, but that's not saying much.

I agree with you (and with *Esprit*) on the need of supporting working class movements – and even at times the CP – but take more and more a syndicalist view and regard the Communist Party as being just as potentially dangerous to the working class as any *other* Fascist party. The Communist Party differs from other Fascist parties in its foreign policy, and this is approximately all. As I see the problem, is the economic, social and personal life of the workers going to be subjected to political state control – whether those of the Fascists or those of the Commies – or are they going to defend themselves on their own ground?

This is the corrupting influence Latin culture has had on me. It has turned me too into an anarcho-syndicalist.

I'm terribly fond of France and would really like to live there now. And not because of the Opera, or wine or "French Culture" or any of the other nonsense prigs talk about, but because it is the only place I've struck which seemed to me really democratic. The muling and puking about democracy in Anglo-Saxon, particularly Canadian newspapers, almost sickens one of the thing as well as the word. But in France, where they don't yap sentimentally about it, but *have* it, one realises at first hand (or at least I do) that democracy is the only air in which one (at least I) can breathe. I mean by democracy principally the social situation in which everybody including the bootblack has sufficient self-respect and personality that you are not only permitted but obliged to treat him as an equal – a thing which exists all too little in Canada and is impossible in England. This may not seem much – but I'm convinced that it and France's radicalism and social justice depend on one another for their existence.

The most painful thing to me about this coming war is that it will be the end, I'm afraid, of this democratic France. It will bring all the "salauds" to the fore in the name of "défense de la patrie" – a process which has started already – and the marvellous country that I've known for a year is likely to be swept into the mill pond of stupidity, hate, reaction, bigotry and oppression into which most of the rest of Europe has already jumped.

Poland is god-awful. These people are very enthusiastic about the coming war because they count on grabbing hold of East Prussia and Silesia at the next Versailles. With Germany destroyed, and France and England exhausted after the struggle, I predict that Poland will rapidly assume Germany's place as the greatest "potential menace to world peace." ... Talk politics to any Pole and you quickly discover that his much lauded "patriotism" resolves itself into hatred of the Jews, hatred of the Germans, hatred of Russians, and hatred of the Czechs. And when I say hatred I don't mean something abstract like, for example, Masons' hatred of Catholics or Catholics' hatred of Masons. It is a concrete affair so that they consider it a patriotic duty to play mean scabrous and filthy tricks on individuals of their acquaintance because they are of Jewish, German, Russian, and sometimes Lithuanian origin. I have seen examples of this and it's pretty sickening I can tell you.

Country isn't Fascist but parliamentary. Very very aristocratic: remember they had serfs until the 1860s. But they don't need to be whipped on by a half-mad dictator.

On the other hand, in their defense, one is obliged to admit that they were roughly handled in the nineteenth century and have had only twenty years to forget it. To me, as an "ally," they are charming, but I can't say I like them much taking everything into consideration. Except this family where I am who are somewhat exceptional ... (I hope there is no censorship of mail in this country but am rather afraid there is!)

As you may gather, I'm not altogether enthusiastic about our "allies" for this season. I'm very glad, though, to have made their acquaintance as it will prevent any possible hasty idealisation of the "little Poles" when the Time Comes. I hope Canada stays out of the dog fight but suppose it is an utterly forlorn hope. We *are* a people of benighted idiots. The ideological question petered out in three stages: Ethiopia, Spain and Czechoslovakia. It won't matter, from the human point of view, who wins the bloody war as any countries with decency left in them will be so exhausted as not to count any more. And Poles and Germans are just Tweedledum and Tweedledee. And if I hear any more talk about "honour" I'll drive a knife into somebody.

The Left is doomed in Europe. By the Left I don't mean the Soviets which I consider Fascist, though from an international point of view the only decent form of Fascism, largely because of their geographical advantages. Fascism I consider not the last stand of Capitalism but the control of society by state control. The capitalists thought that Fascism was their last stand in Germany and Italy, but Fascism fooled them badly and after people like Hugenberg put the Nazis into power the Nazis turned on them in no uncertain terms. One of the irritating things about the Communists is their refusal to recognise certain elementary and obvious historical facts such as the handling by the Nazis of German Big Business. Of course, in recognising such facts, they would cut the ground from beneath their feet because they would remove the sole difference between Fascism and Communism.

And that is why I'm a syndicalist: because I see the political game of Fascism (or Communism) versus Liberalism or what you will as one which is working itself out in the inevitable direction of state control. In the face of that, all the factors making for defence of personal and human liberties should be mobilised into the most efficient organisation possible for the defence of those liberties. The unions *must* learn to work together.

Have you ever discussed integral syndicalism with any of your left friends? Not the Communists, of course, whose answers could all be predicted beforehand.

I concur with your sentiment re C.C.F. and mistrust thoroughly all Parliamentary Socialism. That is to say, Parliamentary Socialism is hopeless by itself and can only be of use when aided by the non-political, revolutionary forces of the syndicates. The C.I.O. in the U.S. seems to a certain extent to have understood this essentially non-political character of syndicalism, and its attitude to Roosevelt in this respect resembled the attitude of the C.G.T. to the Front Populaire, support and aid but from the outside and in a more or less parallel line....

Somebody sent me an announcement of Brock King's wedding. I haven't written him yet but will. I like Brock very much.

I was truly delighted to get your letter and to find that you hadn't begun viewing me with alarm too. Having replied so promptly to yours of the 5th, you can't have the face to leave me hanging fire another ten months.

Yours,
Frank

P.S. Whatever parts of this letter may suggest, I'm *not* a Trotskyist!!

To J. W. PICKERSGILL

c/o Fulde, Kalisz, Poland,
August 20, 1939

Dear Jack:

This family is awfully nice. So much pleasanter than the other place.... In the heat of the thing I wrote a passionate and probably equally unpleasant diatribe on the subject to Mother who, poor soul, will have to put up with it in the middle of her illness.

I find that my French is getting rusty: I can still fool Poles but not Frenchmen, which I could do the last month or so in Paris. It appears that I have "le don des langues" but also, the "don" for forgetting them. It would be nice to land up with a job in Montreal – a French-speaking one – but if my alarming adaptability in respect to language continued, I might develop a French-Canadian accent – horrid thought. It certainly has an unpleasant and stupid sound to me. No, I think it *has*. Because the great and distinctive virtue of French (in the sound of it) is its lack of long and short or accentuated syllables—whereas French-Canadian is more heavily accentuated even than Italian or German. The lack of accentuation in French accounts for the nervous, intelligent sound of the language, I think. I don't think there exists a language that sounds stupider, more spineless and uninteresting than Italian – where the accentuation is perfectly regular, everything ends in a vowel, and they can't pronounce two consonants together.

Polish is *impossible* – it's too complicated to get anywhere with in less than two years and the pronunciation is fierce. Try *Chcquasc* or *brvmy* – and don't put any mute "e's" in between the consonants! I can say the days of the week, the months; count to 1,000, "hello," "good-bye," "please," "thank you," "isn't it?" and "the Greek bandit is cruel" – but that's the extent of my repertory.

Life here is very smooth despite the trenches, machine-gun nests and barbed-wire entanglements which cover the Fuldes' property. We are 40 kilometres from the frontier and between Kalisz (a town of about 50,000) and Germany, and all preparations are getting in order. I have my doubts about war this season though, in spite of my being *here* which, as G. Ford said quoting you, ought to result in a major crisis. My reputation in this respect is spreading over two continents; several of my French friends wanted to kidnap me to prevent my getting to Danzig and Poland. But I made the grade in Danzig and will perhaps get through to Roumania! Have doubts about the interest of Hungary and wonder if I shouldn't do Bulgaria instead. I'm disappointed about cutting my trip short – but can't eat my cake etc.

Must rush to picnic so cheerio and give my love to Margaret –

Love,
Frank

P.S. The translation job (the Sartre novel) has fallen through owing to inability to find an English-speaking publisher. I have Sartre's and NRF's permission – but the English-speaking public is apparently uninterested. One of my friends suggests making the translation in my spare time and sending it to Hemingway or Dos Passos to act as foster-father. I don't know though. It's an awful job to tackle on spec – and pretty flimsy spec at that.

To MRS. SARA PICKERSGILL
c/o Fulde, Kalisz, Poland,
Aug. 21, 1939

Dear Mother:
Just a note to let you know I'm still alive as I'm once more

in the throes of composition. Your Ashern-history project strikes me as excellent . . . if you come to Europe this winter we can work on it together.

I do hope you can come: if a bit short of money couldn't you borrow a bit from Tom – or have I already bled him white? If my Journalism were a howling success I could – but you can't count on that as I may even have to go on living off my relations to some extent for a bit yet in case of emergency. I can't tell you how grateful I am to all my own family for the encouragement I've got this year. Jack has been really marvellous; I've never really told him how much I appreciate it because I find it so difficult telling people things like that – but not only the money he has lent me but letters he has written at psychological moments to help me over rough spots when I was discouraged or had totally lost what little self-confidence I possess, or had qualms of conscience about the way I was spending my time – have been an aid just as great or greater than the money.

He just sent me an air-mail letter telling me about the *Free Press* publication of my articles. I'm so pleased about that – and hope they print them all and rally round quickly with the pay!

Dinner gong must rush. Must tell you though how nice this family is. If only I'd been able to spend the whole time here! (But the other was probably good experience.)

Love,
Frank

To J. W. PICKERSGILL

Cernauti, Roumania,
August 26, 1939

Dear Jack:

My first experiences in Roumania are stirring if nothing else. The British Consul in Warsaw, an awfully nice bird, got the telegram from Ottawa yesterday morning, just as I got in to Warsaw from Kalisz. He advised me to beat a hasty retreat from Poland to Bucarest. . . . He agreed to change my zlotys into lei which he had left over from a former trip at the Black Bourse rates which would give me nearly enough to live on until I could get in touch with Paris again to send money.

Here I am: a wait in the station of two hours and twelve more hours of train ahead of me, and I go into the station to have a bite to eat. When it's time to pay for the meal I produce a coin. "No good – we changed our money a couple of years ago and these coins are no longer of any value." I had enough zlotys left to pay nearly all the bill – except for 10 lei (roughly 10 sous). After considerable melodrama, and calling into conclave of various female relations, waitresses and officials, the restaurant-manager decided to be magnanimous about the 10 lei.

The worst of it is that I get into Bucarest tomorrow (Sunday) with nothing but worthless coin in my pocket . . . all of which has assumed a more important place, temporarily, in my mind than the Kriegsgefahrmstand.

I naturally can't post this until tomorrow as I have no money for stamps.

Out of the two howling children, three whining restless women and one stinking man with whom I shared the compartment last night, I got a fine dose of fleas who have been making merry over me all day. If I have another night without sleep I'll have greater difficulty coping with a day without food tomorrow. Well why worry: in six months I'll be eating bully-beef in the trenches probably – if there is any bully-beef. I'm not going to describe in detail the last three days (a) because I'm too tired to concentrate on it and (b) because I want to exploit it, and so don't want to get it out of my system beforehand. I feel vaguely as though I'd been wrung through a wringer – the emotional strain of the last days at the Fulde's was heavy. If Europe has many more crises the continent as a whole ought to be a good candidate for a looney bin. The wringer feeling is getting chronic with me.

Love,
Frank

Bucarest three days later –
Got in touch with Consul and got money. Now they say there is nothing doing and unless I'm definitely attached to a newspaper I'll be a nuisance here too if war breaks out. So they're sending me back to Paris by the Simplon Express tomorrow morning. If I wait around till the war starts it'll be via Cape of Good Hope! It looks as though it really were here this time – and only last week I was congratulating myself on scaring away crises!

This is a round-about way home. However I've got three more articles out of it – still in my head and not yet written – no time till I get on the train. With war here I suppose I'll have to go back to Canada eventually – I haven't thought the thing out much lately as I've been too busy but will have to start. I haven't joined anybody's army yet though.

Love,
Frank

To MRS. SARA PICKERSGILL

British Consulate, Bucarest, Roumania,
August 28, 1939

Dear Mother:
I'm here in what for a while, at any rate, will be the safety zone ... I doubt if this country will go to war (unless Hungary attacks them) until Poland looks done for. Then they'll probably be forced in. The atmosphere is very much that of a neutral onlooker – sympathetic, though, to France, England and Poland.

The last days in Poland were pretty harrowing: I came to have a much more sympathetic view of Poland before I left as a result of leaving the Klobskis and seeing the other people. I particularly liked Mr. Fulde. His estate, as I've told you, is only twenty-five miles from the German frontier and of course will be all smashed to hell in the first week. He has built it up and is very attached to it – the morning we all left, Thursday, he was mobilised into the civil government of Kalisz, and when he left he nearly broke down. Poor man. He's a quiet, very kind, peaceable sort of person – and you know what happens to civil governors of towns in occupied territory. He'll be shot as soon as the Germans go in. I wish from a personal point of view that this damned awful thing had started last September before I made a lot of personal friends all over Europe who are going to be shot to pieces. The inconsequential Robillot, who writes marvellous poetry and can't pass an exam to save his skin – and his luck is very bad, he lost a finger mountain-climbing at the age of thirteen, broke a knee-cap skiing last winter – and is so impractical that, if he isn't bayoneted, he'll go in the wrong direction one day because he misunderstood the command and will be shot as a deserter.

I can't really believe yet that it's possible – it's sort of like trying to imagine yourself dead. Up until this minute I suppose I really thought of bombs, machine guns, etc., as properties of an opera or something and not really for serious use. We can even talk calmly about the bombing of Madrid, because we didn't *know* any of the people who were bombed. I imagine that's why I haven't yet been at all frightened: I couldn't really bring home to myself the reality of these things.

Those people were pretty wonderful really, the last hours before the household broke up. I think the Germans are going to have a hard time conquering that country. When all the men are killed the women will start in on the invaders with their bare teeth!

The point I think is the Poles know what they're fighting for, and most of the poor Germans don't really. They're just bewildered – and how long they'll go on blindly trusting the omniscience of the Führer once they start getting their heads blown off it's hard to say. Czechs and Austrians will almost certainly revolt in large numbers. . . .

Concentrating on strategy, tactics and politics, one can forget the personal implications for a bit. In the last few days I've worked out a whole plan of action for the British fleet in the Mediterranean!

I really think it's here this time: no more bluff like last September.

You should have seen the Jews in the Roumanian legation at Warsaw! They all had brand new Palestine passports and were getting transit visas through Roumania en route to Zion! This crisis has caused an amazing conversion of Polish Jews to Zionism. Polish anti-Semitism is fairly understandable. The Jews have been pretty well-treated and (especially in the face of Nazi invaders) you would expect a certain degree of loyalty. But not only are they clearing out of the country, dashing to and fro and doing their best by their panic to demoralize the country, but they have in their own little way done their best to create a crisis in the Polish monetary situation by hoarding coins because of their fear of the devaluation of paper money (bad economics incidentally which is curious in Jews). There is, of course, an incredible number of them in the country.

Well, Mother . . . there's not the slightest need to worry. I'm perfectly safe, and I have a mother, father, brother and sister in the British Government. This trip is almost turning me into an Imperialist! You can't imagine how nice they've been . . . I've already borrowed money from them and will continue to do so until I leave Roumania.

Remember that here I'm quite secure and don't worry.

Love,
Frank

Part V

THE PHONEY WAR: 1939-1940
(age 24-25)

*"The trouble with this 'war' is that so little is
happening that people have too much time to
think."*

(F.H.D.P., February, 1940)

*"In the future, the place of the artillery barrage
as preparation for an infantry attack will be
taken by revolutionary propaganda, designed to
break down the enemy psychologically before the
armies begin to function at all."*

(Adolf Hitler, *Mein Kampf*, 1927)

During the first ten months of the war, before the Nazi armies
and air forces crashed through the Lowlands and overran
France, Frank Pickersgill remained in Paris. After his return
from Poland and Roumania he gave up all plans for writing an
academic thesis and tried to support himself as a free-lance
journalist in order to stay afloat in France. Although he managed to have a number of articles published in Canada, his
venture into full-time journalism could not be styled a success
– at least financially. One great difficulty was his growing concern about his personal relationship to the war which made the
role of a mere observer difficult for him. He was frequently in
search of other means of making enough money on which to
live. His letters refer to various possible jobs such as driving a
morning milk truck or writing articles about Canada for jour-

nals in France. For a time he was elated about the possibility of what he could earn by translating Jean-Paul Sartre's novel, *La Nausée*, into English, but the two sample chapters sent to Allen and Unwin of London did not attract that publisher's interest, in view of the international situation, and the project had to be terminated. It should be remarked here, nevertheless, how once again Pickersgill seemed to be ahead of the market. As a friend, Alison Grant, remarked later: "It seems typical that Frank would be translating Sartre five years before Cyril Connolly discovered him in England, and at least ten before the ordinary reader knew the word *Existentialism*." Finally, as a possible way of regularizing his precarious situation, Pickersgill contemplated entering the Canadian Department of External Affairs, and early in 1940 passed the written examinations for that Department with a brilliant performance. To complete the requirements he was to take an oral examination in London in May, but in the chaotic state of affairs that month, he never made it to London. In short, existence during these ten months was precarious in more ways than one.

Most of his French friends of the Maison Canadienne group of the previous year were mobilised during this period and were away from Paris. Pickersgill himself elected to move out and to settle into a small room in a Left Bank hotel, the Hotel Lenox, where James Joyce had stayed. For Pickersgill the attraction of the hotel was not its associations with Joyce; he settled there to have the company of another group of friends, three young women who were working at the British Embassy. One of these, Kay Moore, was an old friend who had been a student at Manitoba with him. They had renewed acquaintance when she came to Paris before his Polish expedition, and on his return he sought her out at the Lenox, where she was living with Madeline Probert from England, and Mary Mundle, a stunning-looking Scot. All of them were to be closely associated with his life later during the few months he spent in London in 1942-1943. In Paris they saw each other almost every day at the hotel, and also, in the spring of 1940, at an apartment on rue de l'Université which the women had rented.

When his hostesses were ordered back to England by the government, they left Pickersgill with the key to their apartment (the rent had been paid until October). Kay Moore describes their association:

> We were a screwy sort of gang that autumn [1939]. Frank began to spend much time with us. Even if he came in very late, he used to pop in and say goodnight to us all when we were in bed. The hotel was small, very gloomy with horrid blue lights in the hallways as the blackout was not complete. We had no social life at all. During the first raids or alarms we all descended out of our rooms dutifully to the cellars and sat, talking in English about love, life and the pursuit of happiness.

After reading Pickersgill's letters from this ten month period, Madeline Probert commented:

> I could hear Frank saying every word, and as far as I was concerned it really did bring him to life again. I could still see him sitting in my room at the hotel, haranguing Kay and me about Poland. I could hear him saying: 'God, I feel dismal!' – as he so often said when he came in in the evening after a dispiriting day; and he would look dismal, even to the lobes of his ears.

A different response to this group of letters was expressed, shortly after the war, by a platitudinarian who remarked: "Well it's easy to see why France fell to the Germans in 1940." Perhaps it was easy to see, five or six years later. But the isolationist point of view expressed here was not exclusively French; it was widespread in North America, where, in most cases, it lacked the sequence of reasoning indicated in this correspondence. The reader may be referred back to the letters written during the Munich crisis (September 26, 1938) in which the necessity of working out the "moral problem" is described.

One seeming solution to this "moral problem" was to plump for some form of pacifism, a point of view often linked with isolationism, and popular in the 1930s in many countries. When war broke out, anyone with such beliefs could strenuously seek to be classified as a Conscientious Objector. It is of interest that Francis Cammaerts, a schoolmaster who became one of the most effective and dedicated agents in the same organization in which Pickersgill was later to serve, began the war in England as a declared C.O. Cammaerts had acquired his convictions as an undergraduate at Cambridge and stuck by them for more than two years until finally deciding that there were devils abroad that he must fight, as he was to do most impressively from 1942 to the end of the war. To Pickersgill this Conscientious Objector solution, however prevalent in the 1930s, seems never to have appealed; isolationist and non-interventionist yes, if need be, but pacifist, no. Although at this time certainly no militarist, Pickersgill viewed the pacifist solution as essentially pointless. Yet ruling out that solution did not solve the real dilemma in which he found himself during the opening phases of the war. He wanted passionately to participate somehow. But participation required a cause, and to his mind, as to the minds of thousands on both sides of the Atlantic, there was no cause left by September, 1939.

Robert Lapassade, one of the Maison Canadienne group, who was himself to become a resistance leader, reports that "in 1939 Pick certainly never imagined that he would one day be a hero and that his heroism would cost him his life." Nevertheless, especially during the first week of war, he was afflicted with what he called "enlist-itis," an ailment well-known to Canadians (in two wars, Canada has relied almost exclusively upon voluntary enlistment rather than upon conscription).

It was also during this period that Pickersgill started to write a book called *France – the First Year of War*. As he said in a letter to his brother, Tom, the book was to deal with "the evolution of French mentality and public opinion since the beginning of the war (especially the opinions of younger Frenchmen)." Sam Dashiel, a United Press correspondent, strongly urged him to write such a book and assured him it would sell well in America. Inasmuch as none of his letters describes what conditions were like during the opening days of war, a chapter from his book is introduced in the following section in order to fill the gap. It also serves as a sample of his formal writing.

The story of how this manuscript survived may be of interest. A few days before his first arrest by the Germans in 1940, Pickersgill informed his French host, M. Paul Philippar, that he wished to hide some manuscripts he had written, earlier in the war, which were outspoken in their comments against Hitlerism. His host advised him to hide them elsewhere inasmuch as the Germans would be sure to search the house when they came for him. Nothing more was said on the subject, and when the arrest took place, the incident was forgotten. Over a year later, M. Philippar happened to look in the pocket of an old raincoat, which was hanging in the front hall, and was astonished to find it stuffed with typed manuscripts! They were thereafter hidden in a less prominent place and, after the war, sent to Canada. *The Cloudburst*, which follows, was the second of four completed chapters.

THE CLOUDBURST

Paris, September 1, 1939: it was 3.00 o'clock in the afternoon when I got into the Gare de Lyon in the Simplon Express. I was a sort of Polish refugee; having left Warsaw six days before, I had borrowed and begged a weary journey through Roumania back to France. Three days on the train from Bucarest, three days without news of the war that was being prepared in Europe. The train was a buzzing hive of wild rumours of every sort, ending up, toward the French-Swiss frontier, with stories of Polish capitulation and a general settlement, stories which no one quite believed but which were nevertheless listened to with that mixture of relief and alarm, hope and shame about one's own hope, which should by now be familiar to all followers of European crises.

It was a relief to be coming back to Paris, after the past turbulent months in Central Europe, and I was looking forward to seeing my friends, revisiting my favourite cafés and so on, in fact it was like coming home. I jumped out of the train into a subway. There the shock met me. Still I hadn't seen any newspapers. But the subway crowded worse than a sardine tin was as dismal as a funeral home on a wet January Sunday. I was unnerved from several sleepless nights on the train and had expected more from Paris than this inexpressible gloom oozing up out of the subway's heat. I finally managed to look over a man's shoulder and read the newspaper headlines. Germany had invaded Poland, the Franco-British declaration of war would be a matter of days, or of hours.

The subway got too much for me. I struggled out of it with my luggage and piled myself into a bus. There were crowds everywhere, terrific crowds. Never before had I seen crowds completely silent. Some people were already carrying gasmasks. They knotted up round the posters proclaiming the general mobilisation, "provisions for three days including knife, fork, spoon, tin cups, tin plate," etc., etc. They were reading the proclamations over and over as though expecting them to change. Two people got off the bus to be sick. I was afraid I was going to be the third. People were unusually kindly and careful about not getting in each other's way or bumping into each other. I was sore all over, mentally, and felt afraid to touch anything or anybody for fear that I would yell; the cautious, considerate way in which people avoided each other and kept their voices down suggested that I was by no means alone in this feeling.

I went out to my old home; as I walked up the boulevard in the direction of the Maison Canadienne, I saw Eugène's wife coming down the street. Eugène was the concierge, the good-natured, humorous bird who had served us our breakfasts in the House the year before. "Madame Eugène"!, "Monsieur Pickersgill!" we shouted simultaneously and practically fell into each other's arms. The house was closing down: some day it would be a military hospital, and poor Eugène was in the throes of evacuation. He was called up, one year off the age-limit; he was leaving that night. He had been through the last one and had won the Médaille Militaire for an extraordinarily skilful and courageous bit of bluffing with a machine-gun. There were four of them with three machine-guns, and they had fooled the enemy into thinking they were half a regiment.

It was my first chance to talk about the war, down in the kitchen with Eugène and his wife over a cup of cold coffee. The war and the heat were stifling. "Maybe it won't come to anything; maybe Hitler'll back out of Poland when he sees that the French and the British are firm."

Nobody wanted the French and the British to back out; as for Hitler doing it, it was too wild a pipe-dream to be taken seriously except at a moment like that, when you were ready to take anything seriously that sounded like bringing back the fresh air and the heart-beats that wouldn't drown every other sound out of your head.

"He has forty-eight hours to make up his mind in," said Eugène. ' 'If he hasn't withdrawn his troops from Poland by that time the heavy artillery gets into action and everything gets blasted to hell."

We had all seen newsreels of the wars in China and Spain. And pictures showing the atrocities of the last world war were crowding in on my memory. I looked at Eugène's wife: she had a blank look of horror in her eyes; she was from Toulouse, but her southern volubility was dried right up. "What a filthy business; what a filthy business," was all she could get out; the blank eyes and the sharp, bitter tremble of her voice spoke of the scenes which were flitting across my mind's eyes like a *March of Time* film; the poison gas, the incendiary bombs, the pillboxes full of their deadly stenographers tapping out blood, brains, guts, broken bones on their machine-guns.

"You are leaving tonight?" I asked Eugène.

"Yes, to look after a bridge, or be a station-agent or something of the sort. I'm too old to be sent to the trenches right away. Oh well, I haven't much to be afraid of; I'll be safer where I am than here in Paris once the bombing starts."

Eugène was taking it in his stride very much like an overturned coffee-cup. In his laconic way however he had managed to conjure up a sudden and pretty vivid picture of the totalitarian war which everyone knew this was going to be.

I had spent the rest of the afternoon helping him evacuate the House. The hard physical work had made me forget my nausea and I was very tired, but I wished my heart wouldn't make such an impossible din, like the dull thuds of bodies falling in detective stories, and what wouldn't a person try to believe at that point? So when the rumour started spreading late that evening that Hitler had submitted and was backing his troops out of Poland I was as ready to believe it as everyone else was. The excitement over that story was terrific, and all the more so as no one really believed it, yet we were all wishing so hard that it was true that we had ourselves half convinced, and were arguing with ourselves and each other to try to persuade ourselves outright.

The week-end passed like ten years in the blazing heat. The first night, before going to bed, I was given two long strips of blue paper and some thumbtacks. I was to pin the paper over the windows, for the blackout. Then I was to shut the shutters, the windows and the curtains and keep them shut, all three all night. I was given my gas-mask and told to have it ready beside my bed in case anything happened. And I was to leave my light on for the bare minimum of time necessary to undress and get into bed. Official nerves were being tried by this waiting about; since the war, the blackout regulations have never been so severe as they were that week-end before the war began.

Sunday morning in the midst of the rumours, the news came through at 11.00 o'clock that Great Britain had declared war on Germany. That was a sharp bit of news at least, slicing into the sultry week-end of uncertainty and wild stories. The jangling nerves produced a laugh.

"What's so funny?"

"I was just thinking; France hasn't declared war yet. I suppose it's the first time in history that the English ever got in there first."

France hadn't declared war, but the trap was closed up and

practically speaking the suspense was over. It had been a radio bulletin. The report was of course not yet in the newspapers. After lunch, sitting having coffee on a terrace in the Place Saint-Michel, the three of us, an English girl, a Canadian volunteer in the Royal Air Force, and myself, hadn't much to say. There was a noisy group of alleged students, of that dubious, pasty-faced, greasy-haired, Central European and vague South American variety which haunts the cafés of the Boul' Mich' and which is usually pretty non-committal about what it is studying: they were singing bawdy songs and making a frightful row in the interior of the café.

The waiter and several of the customers on the terrace kept giving furious, nervously-irritated glances in the direction of the interior. "What the blazes are they howling about?" exploded a harassed-looking little man.

"They didn't hear the radio this morning," the waiter explained. "They don't know anything about it."

The nerve-wracking irony of this exuberant yelling made it sound like deliberate mockery. A bitter indignation surged up against these noise-makers: the full venom of the phrase "sale métèque," dirty foreigner, seemed suddenly to be poured into the sticky-hot atmosphere of the café.

At five in the afternoon the sound of the "Marseillaise" penetrating to the street from a radio, was the sign of the French entry into the general massacre. We were out of the café, and heard no more singing; the "Marseillaise" was not being repeated in the streets, nor were they singing Tipperary or anything else. There was more than tragedy about the Parisians' faces that day; it was vaguer than tragedy. They all looked as though they had been hit by a blunt instrument.

The younger generation in Western Europe has been fed on the horrors of war; the older generation has seen them and been taught to believe that each new war will be automatically, inevitably bigger and more horrible than the last. In Ethiopia, Spain and China, modern warfare had demonstrated itself. It was now doing so in Poland, where the civilian population was already being bombarded. As I had come into Paris from the south-west I had been able to see the roads lined with automobiles, bedding, bags, personal effects piled all over them, leaving Paris: the fortunate evacuees who had places in the country and automobiles to move about in. And the Gare de Lyon had presented another and more unpleasant spectacle. Crowded to the doors, as were all the other stations in Paris, with tired women and children waiting about, waiting for trains to be made up, waiting to take their places in order – not that they would be able to sit down once they boarded the train. The trains leaving Paris that week-end were jammed with people, lining not only the corridors but even the spaces between the seats in the compartments. Leaving Paris to evacuation centres, to live in barns, granaries, school-houses, any place where there would be room, fleeing from the toppling buildings, the incendiary bombs and the poison gas.

There were not many people who went to bed that night expecting an undisturbed sleep. This thing was going to make the war of 1914 look like a Sunday-school picnic, and the thought of war was the thought of air-raids. Paris would certainly be bombed, and probably at once.

We had not yet got used to the blackout, and when night fell there was stumbling and bumping in the streets. Half the street-lights were entirely extinguished; the others had blue blinkers over them and let a little stream of light trickle down to form a puddle around their bases, and nothing more. Most people were carrying their gas-masks now. The automobiles had their headlights blinkered, and the streets were full of the screeching of brakes, the crash of bumpers and the cursing of people trying to avoid being hit by something they could barely see coming at them. The corridors of the House were equally badly lit, and I had a job finding the right door.

At a quarter to five in the morning I was awakened by the siren. The sinister, dizzy shriek was rising and falling rhythmically; it climbed in the windows, it rushed down the corridor and through the cracks in the door and seized you by the throat and started strangling you. It was a noise with a personality, some sort of vampire-personality. You weren't scared of the bombs that were coming, you were scared of that evil noise. I could hear the galloping of feet in the corridor outside my door; some people were already out and charging away propelled like robots by the rhythm of the alarm-siren. No one really took the time to get dressed; you slung an overcoat over your pyjamas, and without lacing up your shoes you stuffed your bare feet into them, and you made for the stairs, the front door, the street, the air-raid shelter. It was dark, and some people tripped and fell. Everyone was running, running away from that noise, but you couldn't get away; it was the perfect nightmare. It stopped just as I was plunging down the steps into the shelter. An hour of dead silence, waiting about in the shelters freezing in the September dawn. We were two limp round-shouldered rows of depressed humanity, sitting staring at each other on the benches against the concrete walls of the shelter. Several refugees took out their masks and tried them on; we were supposed to have them out of their cans, anyway, and hanging round our necks ready for use. No one said a word for fear of drowning out the sounds we were all listening for.

The sounds did not come; the shelter was so bitterly cold that we had to get out and circulate a bit to warm up. The air was clear outside and still no sounds of an alarming nature. Finally we had enough. A drift back to bed started, and I do not believe that anyone waited up for the all-clear signal.

The following morning we found out that there had been no bombing whatsoever. But there was something very wearing about these nocturnal disturbances that followed each other on successive nights; everyone was suffering from lack of sleep and the effect on the morale of a long series of such nights was a problem which was worrying many people. The following day, after one tranquil night, the noon paper *Paris-Midi* appeared with the cheering headline: "One undisturbed night in three: an excellent average."

But during those days no one really questioned anything that was going on. The darkness and the stumbling, the harshness of the various and sundry rulings, and their uncertainty, the censorship, the conduct of the war, the reasons for going into the war, all were accepted as right, good and inevitable, the effort to think otherwise under the nervous strain of what had happened and was (we thought) going to happen was too great, it would have made us yell. Just like touching something or talking too loud that first day in the bus.

And the French premier made the best radio speeches of his political career those days; speeches whose tone was calculated to harmonize perfectly with the general feeling of devastation: "this war imposed on us," "this utterly futile, horrible and stupid war" – phrases which warmed people to Monsieur Daladier and to the government and to national solidarity more than any amount of band-playing enthusiasm, chauvinism or ideals could have done in a hundred years.

Imagine the Communist leader, Maurice Thorez, a deserter three weeks later, writing a passionately patriotic, sincere and tragic letter to the editor of one of the leading Paris morning papers about the middle of September! It happened: even the group which has since broken the "sacred union" of the nation was caught up during the first weeks of war by the feeling that swept the country, the instinctive response to a situation bared of all its implications in the minds of individuals.

You cannot keep a critical sense when your main immediate interest in life is finding others of your kind and crowding up miserably against them. The war had started, and with it a solidarity which could not be called chauvinism, war psychosis or any other of the pet names dished out to cover these mass sentiments. Nobody was being psychopathic, nobody hated the Germans, because nobody was even thinking about the Germans.

This "dirty business" was not being blamed by the French on any particular group of people; it was the thing that had cracked down on them on the nape of the neck, pulverizing the whole scheme of their various existences, which was occupying their minds, and that thing was impersonal, was War, and had nothing in particular to do with Germans or with any other group of people.

They were being shoved together instinctively and the same instinct was working on me: automatically I sent out post-cards to all my friends to find out their whereabouts, when they would be mobilised, and what they were doing. Huddling together, really: I wanted to find the people I knew, who were suffering or going to suffer, and huddle with them.

When I found Maurette he was in the process of pinning blue paper over the windows of the family apartment. He dropped his paper and thumbtacks, and started to laugh. "Pick! what the devil are you doing here? You ought to be in Poland being fêted by Smygly-Rydz or Beck or Rydz-Smygly."

He was not to be mobilised until September 16: still a few days of grace for those who had put off their military service to finish up their studies. I had got a letter from another of the old group of last year; he was waiting round at home, at Le Havre, to be mobilised, also on the sixteenth.

"I've got the Austin out again. We'll drive down to Le Havre in the morning and camp on the Pouillons for a day or two."

I was enjoying myself for the first time since my return to Paris. I was back with the people I knew, and had at last found a connecting link pulling me back into some sort of continuity with the pre-war world in which I had lived before leaving France for Eastern Europe.

To J. W. PICKERSGILL
Hôtel Lenox, 9, rue de l'Université, Paris,
Sept. 9, 1939

Dear Jack:

I suppose you got my telegram through the Legation. It is true that I can't go back to Canada even if I wanted to for ages. I'm doing my best to write an article – or rather a series – on the trip back to Paris in wartime. I shall struggle through it as quickly as possible but it's hard at the moment as I am in such an unsettled and uncertain state of mind.

I wish I could talk things over with you personally... Never have I – or anybody else I've seen in France for that matter – been so far from the famous "psychose de guerre" as at this minute... but I feel I have to stay here and do something.

I am fortunately under no need to hurry into decisions. I can't go back to Canada even if I wanted to until November. But if they don't convoke me for defence work in Paris – which from every point of view would be the way I would most want to act in this affair – I'll have to do something else.

My first reaction would be to join the French army. Except to see my family, going back to Canada seems so futile. If I went back it would be to enlist in the Canadian army, and considering everything it would be almost a betrayal of my principles to do that.

Don't get the idea that I want to fight or feel in the least heroic. It's not the case. Oh God it's hard to explain – even to you. No one has put the slightest moral pressure on me – in fact I've discussed my case with no one. The point is that unless and until I can feel myself of no importance, either to myself or to anybody else, I'll have no peace of mind. War profiteering, whether morally or financially, is the last activity I want to engage in.

(An advantage of the French army if it came to that would be that I'd have decent cigarettes to smoke.)

Well, there you are. I hope and am sure that you will see my point – obscure as it may be! I might add that had I been in Canada at the outbreak of war I might have thought very differently.

Things are going very smoothly and we have had three nights in a row without an alarm.... Give my love to Margaret –

Frank

To HELEN MAGILL

Hôtel Lenox, Paris,
Sept. 22, 1939

Dear Helen:

I've practically given up writing letters as I've been exerting all my concentration, which has recently been none too efficient, to get off some articles to earn a bit of money ... I have applied to the Defense Passive here for ambulance work or something but nothing has come of it yet, and when the British Red Cross gets organised will try them too. I shall do all I can not to have to leave France and return to Canada.

It is very discouraging getting pre-war mail. It doesn't seem to make any sense whatsoever. Here it is amazing how rapidly one adjusts oneself to a new routine of living; of course we're barely aware yet that there is a war but we will be one of these days I expect. I don't think Paris has ever been so beautiful – the Place de la Concorde is a veritable seventh heaven. Leaving it at any time would be a difficult process; now, well-nigh impossible. It's going to get its claws into me more and more – what a town!

Living here becomes very much a day to day matter. I've seen quite a lot of Madeline Probert and Kay Moore recently who are living in the same hotel but working feverishly seven days a week. I have the cheapest room in this hotel and get a bit off my rent by moving people's luggage for them, but it's still too expensive.

With the Russians messing up the works, this thing may go on for years, which is a nasty thought. I wonder what people will be like after it's over. I hate to think of that.

I met one of my friends (Maurette) last week and we went out to Le Havre in his car to see Pouillon and spent the night in the mouldiest hotel I've ever imagined possible. We had eaten and drunk too much, and the place was alive with mosquitoes and I've never passed such an agitated night. . . .

Both he and Pouillon are now in training in artillery – he as sub-lieut and Pouillon as a private. I've heard from another

150

friend (Robillot) who is a private in the infantry but since he
lacks the index finger of his right hand I don't imagine he'll be
kept there. I hope not, poor devil.

Love,
Frank

To HELEN MAGILL

Hôtel Lenox, Paris,
Oct. 6, 1939

Dear Helen:

All sorts of hot news (a) I'm passing the permis de conduire
poids lourds to qualify to drive a milk-truck for the Laiteries
Maggi – who are apparently very Canadiophile and will take
me likely with permis. I had put in an application for passive
defence work but nothing came of it (b) I got a telegram from
Jack yesterday saying that I have a job with the *Vancouver Sun*
– writing articles from here – a *regular* job! . . . I take it all back
– the *Vancouver Sun* must be the best paper in Canada: they
know a good man when they see him. But isn't it an extraordinary stroke of luck? I don't know which way to turn after
all this.

Last night – no – this morning at 6.30, the siren of our
quarter went off by accident and everyone got themselves
routed out of bed and ready for the air-raid. It was damned
annoying and I'm still feeling vaguely in bad humour about
the whole thing.

Lord I'm glad to be able to stay over here now. I'll have to
be around at least for the Peace Treaty too. That ought to be a
terrific show.

Madeline Probert is going to Madrid to work in the Embassy
there. It should be terrifically interesting. Lucky Spaniards:
their war is over!

I got a very sad letter from Mother the other day. I guess the
war is getting her down badly. Everything has settled down

very quietly here. We were all pretty upset until we made the adjustment. I was reading Canadian papers in the Legation the other day. God what exaggeration.

I haven't heard from Bessie since last spring . . . We have the Polish government living on our street now which makes us all feel somehow proud and humble both at the same time. Kay Moore is in excellent spirits. She's a very amusing person . . . and it's nice to see one other Canadian who is unconditionally enthusiastic about this country.

Well cheerio for now and write when you have time and energy.

Love,
Frank

To HELEN MAGILL

Hôtel Lenox, Paris,
Oct. 30, 1939

Dear Helen:

I was certainly glad to hear some news from you . . . Was out to Fontainebleau Wednesday to see my two friends Maurette and Pouillon in training there. Maurette has his uniform now and is one of the wildest sights I've ever seen. There are only three sizes for the privates; he being taller than I am and skinny as a rail took the largest size and the tunic hangs about his body in long and grotesque folds, the sleeves come up to the elbows, and the kepi is several sizes too big and rests quietly on his ears.

However he is in the army getting ready to be a lieutenant in the artillery – and trying to learn to ride horse-back.

Cinemas and things are reopening and the Ursulines is right back in form next week with, Monday night, three René Clair: *Chapeau de Paille d'Italie, Entre'acte* (his surrealist thing) and 14 *Juillet.* The following night is *Opéra de Quet 'Sous* – which I'll probably go to see for the sixth time. And I'm reading again – Proust at the moment – I'm a hound for culture you know.

The worst lack is theatres. The Opera is running, but I hate opera and won't go and be bored at it. The Odéon has opened but I hate it too. I wish Jouvet would get back into action. Oh yes, Sacha Guitry is at it again but I hate him too. But the Concert Mayol (Allo, femmes nues!) has opened again.

I got a letter from Mother this morning which indicates that she is in much better spirits. I was into Shakespeare and Company today and read the latest *New Masses* to arrive. Of all the god-awful tripe I've ever seen, I think that hits about an all-time low. Nobody, whether to the Left or to the Right, seems capable of saying anything about Russia these days without talking arrant nonsense – except Leon Blum in the *Populaire* who has written some moderately sensible things on the subject.

Well, I have a belly-ache as a result of something I've just eaten so will stop. It appears that Margaret (Tom's Margaret) is going to produce ... next spring. I must take steps measures and proceedings.

Love,
Frank

To MRS. SARA PICKERSGILL

Hôtel Lenox, Paris,
(posted early December), 1939

Dear Mother:

Just a note as I'm in a rush for today's air-mail. I'm so glad you're at Ottawa and hope the war isn't getting you down too much. Don't spend the winter freezing solid at Pt. Rowan. I'm glad you were able to see Bessie and Ken before leaving Winnipeg. Bessie is putting on weight eh. Don't tell me that means another nephew.

The war is getting me down a bit. My friend Lapassade (with whom I stayed when I was at Biarritz last spring) is coming to Paris at the end of the week on a ten day leave. He's a sub-lieutenant in the artillery and has been at the Front for the past month. His letters suggest more danger of death from boredom than from any other cause just at present. His life is a dull round of digging trenches and playing bridge.

Well, I must type an article and pack all this off on the air-mail.

Love,
Frank

To J. W. PICKERSGILL

Paris,
Jan. 12, 1940

Dear Jack:

I see your point about free-lancing. I was much too optimistic at first on the basis of the exceedingly high prices paid last year. But as rates seem to be now, I'd have to publish about six articles a week to make a living from it ... The worst thing is that every so often I get thoroughly discouraged and at such moments writing is difficult. The *Standard* wrote me asking for articles. I'm going to send them two or three at the beginning of the week and hope they'll take them.

I may have a publisher for the translation of Sartre's novel. It's not at all sure, but I'm translating the first fifty pages to send them to see if they are interested – have them nearly all done.

Ah yes, the External Affairs exam. In the morning I wrote

the essay – on American literature as an interpretation of American life – came out thinking I had defended myself respectably. Then in the afternoon the general knowledge paper, where I met my Waterloo on South American geography and some of the terms in Question 2. I felt quite depressed about the afternoon paper. However, Scott Macdonald read them both over, and said the essay would almost certainly be head and shoulders above anything else that was submitted, and that I had, in spite of my pessimism about it, defended myself well enough in the afternoon to assure myself of being one of the first ten on the ensemble. He thinks I stand an excellent chance.* And he wanted to take time to copy out my essay and to keep it, claiming it was the best thing he had ever seen on American literature!

I hesitated on the three subjects: "Christianity and Paganism in the twentieth century"; "French Literature" – and American, and don't particularly know why I chose the last.

I see from this morning's papers that Germany is letting Italian arms pass through the country with destination for Finland. Can it be that Germany is going to try to work round into the anti-Communist crusade at this late date? I wonder what the attitude of the Western powers would be then.

Since the real issue in the war seems to be the anti-revolutionary one, I should think such an expression of piety on the part of the Nazis would cause a certain embarrassment to the saviours of civilisation. After all, on the principles of international morality and other rot there is no more reason for indignating against Russia and Germany than against Italy and Japan – this ingenuous soul wonders if perhaps there isn't something else in the backs of the minds of our war lords.

– Like the French Canadian last night who was accusing Maurette and Pouillon of being unpatriotic, and getting quite hot and excited about it, and Pouillon, pointing to his uniform

*It was later learned that he had gained one of the three top places. There were 360 candidates writing the examination, and most of them had been preparing for it for some years. Pickersgill had made no formal preparation whatever.[G.H.F.]

155

remarked: "Mon vieux, when you are wearing one of these you will then have the right to give us patriotic lectures, but not before."

Well, being a civilian in wartime hasn't yet turned me into a rabid militarist, spy-hunter and treason-expert, though that seems to be its effect on most people. Every single "patriot" I know is beautifully placed for the duration of the war, either unmobilisable, or "in the administrative end."

Europe is a queer place already – after four and a half months of war – and will be a hell of a lot queerer after it's over. I don't really want to leave but I think I should this spring anyway and get myself established at home.

The idea of joining an army has disappeared completely. I'm not anxious to do anything in this bloody war unless I have to, so shall wait for conscription in Canada.

It's painful this perpetual cold – I wish I could get rid of it once for all. Never in my life have I been so bothered by colds as this winter – it is sapping my vitality.

I have been reading Suarez's life of Briand. He is a stupid writer but full of information, and it is a very instructive book though hopelessly badly written. Also Lenin's *Imperialism: the Last Stage of Capitalism*. I wonder.

Scott Macdonald said it was Veblen who wrote the *Acquisitive Society*, but I'm convinced he is wrong. I think I know all the titles of Veblen's books ... In any case, that was one of the questions I didn't get. Also Blackstone's *Commentaries on the Laws of England* but that was because I was ill and my mind wasn't functioning properly, as I'm not *that* ignorant – but I'd always heard it referred to in abbreviated form as the *Commentaries* and simply didn't rally round. When Macdonald said it was Blackstone I could have kicked myself to the ceiling. Well, I think I'll stop and get to work on an article to send with this.

My love to Margaret.

Love,
Frank

To HELEN MAGILL

Paris,
Jan. 19, 1940

Dear Helen:

I'm writing this in a café and the person at the next table has
a face I want to smack. I can't get my mind off it and I shall
either have to leave the café and write elsewhere or take steps,
measures and proceedings. I'll probably meet him in a month
or two and discover a kindred spirit but at the moment the
temptation to push his face in is getting irresistible so I'd better
leave and start afresh somewhere else. Good God! another
even more unpleasant-looking person has just come in and sat
down on the other side of me: it's the last straw, I'll have to
leave.

I should like, on returning to Canada, to do newspaper or
radio work rather than anything else.

Nothing is doing here and it gets harder and harder to think
up subjects to invent newspaper articles about. I'll have to try
to crash the American market – which pays so much better.
Everybody is getting fed up to the teeth with this bloody war –
particularly as a dreary future seems promised for all – except
perhaps the Russians . . .

I have been reading the odd Canadian newspaper and am
agreeably surprised to see that, except for McCullough's rag
the *Globe and Mail*, there is virtually no hate-mongering in the
Canadian press at all – the war, in fact, seems to be exciting
considerably less interest than, say, the Royal visit of last
spring.

Since the Royal visit was not just Art for Art's Sake, I
presume that its success was not as signal as the cheering at the
time might have led one to think.

I cannot figure out what Chamberlain thinks he's
accomplishing in ditching Hore-Belisha. Especially as he was
clumsy enough to do it without blackening his character first.
Chamberlain is of course succeeding in the short run in getting
rid of all the energetic and intelligent people in the Party

(except Churchill who is too well-entrenched) who might be a danger to him. But he must know that in the long run the Edens, the Duff-Coopers, the Hore-Belishas will come back, and when they do it will be with an awful bang and Good-bye Mr. Chamberlain. The extraordinary political intriguing and ambition of a man of his age astounds me. Chamberlain and Daladier: what a pair! It is to be hoped that in this famous struggle to save civilisation those two are not representative of the civilisation that is being saved. . . .

In this café it's cold as Greenland and I must get to work so will come to a.

Love,
Frank

To J. W. PICKERSGILL

Paris,
Feb. 9, 1940

Dear Jack:

Enclosed is a very long article,* subject suggested by Scott Macdonald. He seems to think it very good, but it may have difficulty in finding a Canadian publisher, owing to the subject-matter.

I'm in a mood of terrific depression, due to a number of small causes, which was so bad at the beginning of the week that I didn't eat for two days – it is pretty bad when it comes to the point of cutting *my* appetite. I had another bad attack of enlist-itis among other things. Things would be so much simpler if I hadn't got so into the life of this country; then I could go off home and think no more about it. But I cannot get rid of the feeling that I am getting out of something that all my friends have to put up with, and it is horribly unpleasant.

*"The French Communists and the War." This article was not published. Scott Macdonald was the counsellor in the Canadian Embassy. [G.H.F.]

And I know I'd rather be in the French army than in the Canadian expeditionary force, if I were obliged to make a choice! Not that either of them really appeal to me in the slightest – but here there would be more leaves, and the company would be more congenial.

This is silly nonsense – I wish I could get it out of my head. It has been preying on me all week. I haven't been able to work eat or sleep properly.

God I feel dismal.

Well cheerio, and try to write soon. I've heard no sort of news from Canada for so long it might almost as well not exist any longer. My love to Margaret.

Love,
Frank

(The following letter is translated from French)

To JEAN VARILLE (Lyons)

Paris,
February 12, 1940

Cher vieux:

Yesterday evening, as I was having an aperitif at the Café de Flore before dinner, I saw the girl of my dreams. A Spanish girl, Celtic type, somewhat blonde, who bowled me over like a bolt of lightning. She was in the café for twenty minutes, and during those twenty minutes I didn't take my eyes off of her. I returned home and couldn't get to sleep until 3.00 a.m. and then dreamt of her for three hours. I woke up in a fever at 6.00 a.m., and at 8.00 o'clock got out of bed, trembling all over, and since then I've searched for her at that café every hour of the day, and I haven't found her. If I can find her and can insinuate myself into her attentions, I'll ask her to marry me. I'm out of my mind. It's terrifying; I never believed that a girl could be so incredibly beautiful.

How goes your factory job? Pouillon, who is about to be married in eight days or so, told me about your letters to him.

I've been trying to recuperate this past week. If I only knew the reasons for my state of depression, I might be able to get rid of it more easily; as it is, I've only vague insubstantial suspicions about what's wrong, and I fear that the treatment would be worse than the malady.

I'm at the point, I believe, where initiative has got to be taken – to act – in some sense of the word. I shall have to decide what I'm going to do. Perhaps that will turn out to be returning to Canada, although probably not that. This thought of returning home makes me even more depressed. Desert islands are perhaps a good thing – but desert continents – there isn't any thing to be said in favour of those! And to top all this off, I'm now engaged in translating Sartre's *Nausea*, and in my present state of mind, that's a disastrous occupation. If it would bring in some money, that would be great. But how depressing this novel is! To work on translating it even for two hours is so desolating that I get the urge to throw myself into the Seine.

What lethargy I feel. What apathy of spirits. More and more I seem deadened. And perhaps there's a more respectable job to fill waiting for me in Canada about May first. But I'm fed up with that prospect for it would not last long. The general elections in Canada will end up by saying only one thing – for me, personally – that about the beginning of 1941 I'll be returning to Europe in a beautiful uniform with a maple leaf on my cap.

What baloney! What imbeciles!

In 1937, when I was a student in Toronto, I attended a sort of recruitment meeting for volunteers to participate in the Spanish Civil War. I'd had enough of Canada, and I wanted to see Europe. The Spanish Republican cause filled me with enthusiasm, but I failed to commit myself. If I had done so,

perhaps at least I'd have got killed for a cause worth the pain –
at least I'd have believed it – which would have perhaps been a
consolation.

I'm disgusted with everything, myself included.

Au revoir mon vieux – je t'embrasse.

Pick

To MRS. SARA PICKERSGILL
Hôtel Lenox, Paris,
Feb. 23, 1940

Dear Mother:

I won't make this a long letter as I'm feeling pretty rotten. I
am catching another cold, and have two wisdom teeth that are
nearly driving me insane. I'm having them out this afternoon
at 3.00 o'clock. I'm having them pulled by a Spanish Jew who
is the family dentist of the girl who married one of my best
friends yesterday. I hope he gives me gas but I'm afraid he
won't. Well, I'll soon know.

I'm leaving Paris to spend a month in Brittany. I'll get
material from there, and a month in the country will perhaps
rid me of the cold-flu germ which has been persecuting me all
winter.

I got a letter from Helen yesterday – she says that the
Canadians are singularly unexcited by the war. You say you
get little or no war news; but I envy you the chance of listening
to the American radio and getting some news that isn't a pack
of lies.

The lies and dissimulation that are handed out from all
European radio stations, Allied, German and neutral alike are
pretty annoying I can tell you.

According to the Gallup Poll, the Allies are losing sympathy
at a rapid rate of speed in the U.S. They certainly are in all
neutral countries in Europe – and at the beginning of the war

the neutrals were almost solidly behind them, except for Spain, Italy and Russia.

Well I'm really feeling too rotten to write a real letter so will send this off as it is.

Love,
Frank

To GEORGE FORD

Landereau, Brittany,
March 7, 1940

Dear George:

If this letter appears totally incoherent the reason is elation. Along with your letter of this morning I got a letter from the Press Association "Opera Mundi" offering me a job. No details. I hope it will earn me a living and am so excited at the moment I can hardly walk. I shan't get tight to celebrate until tomorrow night at Tours where I'm heading, where I can celebrate with a pal who is mobilised there. I'm leaving here tonight at 7.30. This is a crazy sort of trip I'm taking to get the Paris winter out of my bones. I'm going from one mobilisation centre to another, visiting friends.

What an army! The discipline is about as casual as anything you could imagine. I was down at Quimper, on the south Breton coast, last week, where I have a friend mobilised [Jean Jezéquellou]. He is a "fascicule bleu," that is, he had served in the last war and wasn't called up until February. For three nights after his mobilisation he slept in a requisitioned movie house which served as a camp – but the company got on his nerves. So on the fourth day, my friend took a room in a hotel in town, eats all his meals in town restaurants, and shows up for about half-an-hour a day for roll-call unless he feels like doing something else – in which case he doesn't show up and nobody minds. Of course his group are all war veterans and nobody has quite the nerve to discipline them. One day he was told to take the men out and exercise them – 120 of them. They went out to the country and had a drink in a pub and then started back. He got back with forty men – the others had buzzed off to see their wives or something. He said he didn't care – he had no responsibility anyway being only a private soldier, but nobody asked any questions about the missing eighty – nobody seemed to care in the least what had happened to them.

Here at Landereau I have a friend [Henri Robillot] who is a pupil officer, the discipline is allegedly more strict, but he seems to have inordinate freedom of movement, never shows up at exercises any more, and has forty-eight hour leaves to go to Paris with monotonous regularity. The magnificent indifference shown by the average Frenchman to all rules and regulations definitely strikes an answering chord in my heart.

Brittany is astonishing, because the people really do talk Breton, and most of them talk French very badly with a sing-song accent which has the same sound as an Irish accent in English.

And dumb! The average Breton reaches the rock-bottom of anything I've ever encountered for slow-wittedness. They are very friendly but in the main so stupid that you can hardly believe they're human (don't tell Mlle Ballu that I said that!) They pickle their brains in alcohol, of course, which may account for it.

However, it's wearing, all this good-natured dumbness, and I'll be glad to get to Tours, back to more human intelligence. It's nice country around Tours, but I suppose I'll be obliged to "do" one of the Loire chateaux – a prospect which appals me to the uttermost.

I've had wonderful luck in all the people I've met in France. I seem to get along with them like a house on fire and to make friends extremely easily. Without boasting, really, I've yet to see the Anglo-Saxon who is *tutoied* by as many people as I am after less than two years here. Oh Hell, it's too fine a country to leave – even if it is swamped in a stupid war and on the verge of a dictatorship.

I'm beginning to have doubts about the future horribleness of this war, at least on the western front. The magnificent strength of both the Maginot and Siegfried lines seems to assure a certain protection, for both sides, from inordinate bloodshed. Neither side is going to attack the other's line I think, and have half its men massacred in the fray. And, if the Allies can hurry up their aerial preparations, the same holds true of aerial bombardment.

Unless someone goes nuts and tries a new Verdun, the fear of reprisals ought to keep land and air warfare within reasonable bounds of inhumanity this time. Besides, the morale in the Allied countries is so low (about on a par with mine!) that they couldn't hope to make war without a full-scale campaign of propaganda for six months or so, in order to whip up the people's fury, hatred etc. Well, we'll see, I suppose. I must go for a walk, so gooom.

Pick

P.S. Gide is not to be put on a par with Aldous Huxley, in spite of his flimsiness. He is too sure a writer, and he does think concretely and sincerely and writes accordingly, which is more than Huxley could ever do.

I'm astonished at you even mentioning Thomas Wolfe in the same breath as Dos Passos. And to accuse Dos Passos of "journalism" is not worthy of you. Dos Passos's "journalism" is as artistically relevant today as Shakespeare's dramatic technique was then, or Fielding's novel technique when he wrote. Dos Passos, Hemingway and Caldwell have had the courage to write in the form which corresponded to their twentieth century American experience. Wolfe just "wrote a novel" or several – which puts him on a par with *Gone With the Wind* and *Anthony Adverse* – better stuff of course, and more real, but hell – nothing to write home about.

The universal interest aroused by Dos Passos, Hemingway and Caldwell ought to make English professors in American universities sit up and take notice. They are read over here, and the important younger novelists such as Malraux and

Jean-Paul Sartre and even Celine read them and are definitely influenced by them. Sartre rates American literature as the only living literature of today, and his interest turns especially and above all to those three authors and to William Faulkner. About Faulkner I disagree with Sartre, though he told me that I'd read all Faulkner's lousy books and none of his decent ones.

A writer to watch will be Arlen Campbell. He'll be publishing a book of short stories in New York this summer, and they will be worth reading. He's one of the few sincere Americans in Paris, and, with a woman named Miriam Beck who writes for the *Chicago Tribune*, *New York Times* and *New Yorker* and will publish a very good book on Germany this spring (out of which I made her cut certain purple patches) the only two Americans I have anything to do with here. Beck's thing is first rate human interest reportage, and if people object that she hasn't explained the political situation or solved world problems in it, so much the worse for them.

FHDP

To MRS. K. SEABORNE

Paris,
(Posted March 26, 1940)

Dear Ducky:

Your letter has given me a bout of homesickness. As Jack may have told you, there is a fair possibility of my being installed here indefinitely as I've just got a decent job writing articles on Canada for the French public. . . . It'll enable me to get rid of the last shreds of stiffness and stuffiness, heritage of too much university education. I have lost all my prejudices against writing for the great reading public, which is a damned good thing, and this will teach me how to write for it.

I had a world-problem-solving session with a friend who was in town last night (result, something of a hangover) and he has a theory that there never will be a war, but just a new division of the world into hemispheres. . . . It isn't as impossible as all that: Neither side can hope to win a victory by just sitting and sulking behind a fortified line. The blockade is rendered even more inefficacious by the economic co-ordination of Germany, Russia and Italy – and when they take the Balkans (and how can anyone stop them?) the blockade will just fall to the ground. And as for trying to crash either the Maginot or the Siegfried line to win a *military* victory, it seems quite impossible. So –

Besides, the morale in Germany, France and England just won't stand a really bloody war right now. People are still too tired from the last one – all anybody seems to want is peace. One of my best friends is a fellow who fought in the last war and who has just been mobilised again – he knows what it's like – and after the failure of the last twenty years he goes back into uniform in the firm conviction that the last war, and this one too, are just put-up jobs arranged by high-finance and the armament manufacturers to sell their products and reduce unemployment by killing off a few million soldiers. You couldn't persuade him otherwise – and it's a pretty common opinion of re-mobilised war-veterans.

I do all my writing (letters and articles) in cafés – most of them in this café – which is a sinister locality, in fact, except in the morning and early afternoon. Full of idle Americans, central European refugees, spies and international gangsters of one sort or another (three people were arrested here the other day and one of them has already been shot!) In the morning it's fine though, and I come here for breakfast because the coffee is good and it's the only place with good coffee in the Quarter. But last week I made the mistake of dropping in for an aperitive at 7.00 o'clock, just before dinner. – The elongated Central European fairy making eyes at me from the table opposite; the Czech ex-professor wandering about vaguely and blinking, full of magnificent projects for writing articles containing sensational revelations on something or other and for getting to America where he'll be APPRECIATED – and, of course, not ever doing anything but wander about blinking vaguely and getting fatter and more livid every day; the crowd of movie-Jews who have managed to get themselves exempted from military service or put on some special soft job keeping them at Paris in civilian clothes – making smart conversation in another corner – etc., etc., etc. – well, I gulped down a mouthful, paid as quick as I could, and rushed out into the fresh air thinking "My God, if I were a German I'd certainly be a Nazi."

Central Europe is certainly an extraordinary phenomenon, and if the Germans can clean it up a bit, more power to them!

The Nazis committed a lot of atrocious crimes against the German industrial workers individually and as a class – which is the basis of my hatred of Naziism.

One of the sinister things about this war is that the Allies waited to make war on Germany until Naziism began evolving – and started kicking out Rauschning, Fritz Thyssen and Hugenberg – the same big German industrial magnates who had financed National-Socialism in the beginning, and who were in particular responsible for Nazi attacks on the working class.

The war is one between rival systems of oppression – The only thing in favour of the Allies is that the Anglo-Franco-American system of oppression is less odious in its results than the Italo-Russo-German one.

Well I must start work on an article on Saskatchewan wheat-farming. So will stop. My best to Ken.

Love,
Frank

To THOMAS PICKERSGILL
9 rue de l'Université, Paris,
April 8, 1940

Dear Tom:

I just got your letter announcing the arrival of lil' F.D. – and am very excited about the news. I just took time to wash one

167

pair of socks, darn another and hop into bed, where I'm writing this. Being an uncle is a new role, and having my first nephew sprung on me as a namesake into the bargain is quite overwhelming all at once. But you'd better be careful about his political career or he may end up in a concentration camp with his father and all his uncles.

I'm very glad he and Margaret are doing well. I presume the father is improving steadily and giving out daily communiquées with a little more in them than 'Calm Night – Nothing to Report.' The new uncle is in any case doing fairly well – in fact so well that he may not be obliged to recross the Atlantic this summer. I have a sort of job with a Press Association here called Opera Mundi, not badly paid. . . .

According to the (reliable) people to whom I've shown my stuff I really am a good writer now. I've learned a lot since starting this racket and my style is a lot more supple than it was. So you can understand why I'd hate to leave right now. I want to give myself this chance, and then if it falls through I'll go back to Canada content (well – at least resigned). If I have got some talent in that direction, it's what I'd most like to do, and I'm getting the journalist's habit in so many ways now that I don't know how well I'd ever get along in anything else.

Also, I like this country so much, in spite of the war and the disgusting aspects of Allied politics, that I really don't want to leave it!

The war seems to get crazier every day. The dissatisfaction and boredom here surpass all bounds of imagination, and the disillusionment following the crash of Finland was directly and solely responsible for the fall of Daladier's government. I'm very pleased about that of course. Daladier, Bonnet and Chamberlain are more responsible for the war than Hitler, Stalin, Mussolini and all the dictators between here and the Pacific Ocean. . . .

Unless the Americans are willing to pay for the war it can't go on very long, anyway, which is one comfort. However it looks as though they are going to pay for it – in spite of Cash and Carry. Of course, the Siegfried Line is damn good, but then so is the Maginot Line. And I doubt if either side will dare attack. Britain thus stands to lose everything (Iraq, Iran, India etc.) and France virtually nothing – except by exhaustion. Which explains a lot of things. I think that unless the war starts in the north there will be a gradual demobilisation here. In fact it has already started, with the demobilisation of all farmers down to the Class '19 and the long agricultural leaves for others. Otherwise after ten or twenty years of this sort of war people will just starve to death! Besides it's too damn soon after the last war really to fight another bloody one. I know this consideration has an important effect on the morale in this country. I hope the same holds true for the Germans!

Give my best regards to Margaret and to the little goof.

Sincerely –
Frank

To J. W. PICKERSGILL

Hôtel Lenox, Paris,
April 13, 1940

Dear Jack:

Well, I got your air-mail letter of April 1 and was pleased to hear from you after your protracted silence. I wonder what you are thinking of the new developments of the war; I'm feeling optimistic for the first time since the beginning of the Finnish affair. It looks as if the Germans have really bitten off more than they can chew in Scandinavia, and Swedish iron is very important to them!

Personally I've got into a rather nasty scrape. At the end of the crisis in Finland I was feeling very blue and wrote an extremely pessimistic and bitter letter to Stan Jackson. It was opened by the censors and sent to the Department of the

Interior as defeatist. I was sent for the day before yesterday, and the man who came for me gathered up all the papers I had lying about and we went down to the Security Police. The papers – carbon copies of articles – all spoke well in my favour, but the wretched letter was the object of their concentrated attention. Inasmuch as it read almost like a Communist tract, no wonder. Anyway the man who was hauling me over the coals told me that I'd better get ready to go home as they were going to expel me from the country. I went down to the legation afterwards and talked it over with Scott Macdonald who said that the threat of expulsion was almost certainly to throw a scare into me, but that if they carried the thing any further they would be certain to come to the legation for information, and there it would be explained to them that they shouldn't, because of a momentary aberration, expel one of the best propagandists for France in Canadian journalism! He told me not to worry and not to let it interfere with my work – that there was no great danger of it coming to anything, but I cannot help feeling pretty sick about it. I've said nothing about it to Mother as I don't want to worry her unduly.

Dashiel wants me to send my stuff to the U.S. Inasmuch as you know better than I what has been published and what hasn't, and have all the manuscripts in your possession, would you send them to Miss E. Kane, c/o Wm. Lengel, Literary Agent, 654 Madison Ave., New York City. Give Margaret my love.

Love,
Frank

P.S. It's midnight and I've been working on my book! Have the first chapter (there should be twelve) almost finished and it reads not badly at all. But am sleepy so I'll go to bed now.

To MRS. SARA PICKERSGILL
Hôtel Lenox, Paris,
April 13, 1940

Dear Mother:

I got your letter dated March 22 last night: the postal service seems improving. Apparently I've had some good luck with publications recently and have "made" the *University of Toronto Quarterly** among other things. I hope soon to try the U.S. which pays so much better and gives one all kinds of prestige.

The situation seems to be looking up considerably and I'm getting optimistic again. If they can really push the Germans out of Norway maybe they won't have to play around at conciliating Mr. Stalin who would seem to be a dubious ally at the best estimate.

I'm sure that the new government here is in part responsible for the renewal of energy. Reynaud has lots of guts whatever people may think of him personally, and appears really to be taking the war seriously as a *war* – and when he went to London it is significant that the Interallied Council underwent a serious revision and Chamberlain was put out of it and Churchill put at its head.

I often wonder how all this strikes you who have already followed the events of another war and no doubt had moments of pretty extreme depression. Judging from Canadian newspapers the population of Canada is still so absorbed by its elections that it has little energy left to think about the war, but maybe now with the Greenland scare they'll start getting excited about it again.

Well, I haven't much more to tell you today so will close. Give my best regards to Aunt Bessie.

Love,
Frank

*"The French Press and War Aims" published in April, 1940, in the *University of Toronto Quarterly.* [G.H.F.]

To MRS. SARA PICKERSGILL

Paris,
April 16, 1940

Dear Mother:

Just a note hurriedly to send with Scott Macdonald. He's leaving tomorrow. I've got to rush out and help Kay Moore who is being shipped off to England. She's feeling very cut up about it but there's nothing to be done about it. I think London is more dangerous than Paris but she, of course, can go to her family in Ireland which is a neutral country and hence safe for a day or two.

What a madhouse. There is no doubt about the war being on now and the awful thing about it is the sort of disorder it brings into life because you don't know how long you're going to stay in one place.

The buses have all been requisitioned and I suppose cars will go next. There'll be an awful run on bicycle shops. I wish I had one.

Love,
Frank

To J. W. PICKERSGILL

Hotel Lenox, Paris,
April 19, 1940

Dear Jack:

I enclose an article which *Maclean's* might like. I've finished the first chapter of my book and half finished the second and am working on an article on French Syndicalism and the War.

I haven't anything much new and am writing and thinking so much about my book that I have little mental energy left.

Am reading Hemingway's *Men Without Women*, a book of short stories. I figure I should read several pages of Hemingway a day – for style! He does write marvellously. Give Margaret my love.

Love,
Frank

To J. W. PICKERSGILL

88 rue de l'Université, Paris,
May 29, 1940

Dear Jack:

I have done little or no work for a considerable time but must try pulling myself together and doing some. The waiting round for news about my External Affairs oral and job, the shattering effect of the real war, and the lost feeling of having nothing definite to do in the middle of all this have rather got me down, and though I've been reading terrific quantities of stuff I've done no writing for ages. Regarding the job in External Affairs I feel pretty sick about it. Dupuy told me that after my oral in London I'd probably be taken on here in Paris ... and now I cannot go to London as I can't get an exit permit. Whether they don't consider the reason sufficient, or whether it is that bloody business of the letter cropping up again I don't know ... but if I lose out on this fine job through not being able to be present at the oral I'll really feel that the fates are agin me.

Everything seems of relative unimportance as does my exam, the future and everything else pertaining to my person at the moment in face of this god-awful slaughter in the north ... When I think of these people I know and these towns I know it almost makes me scream. I've got to make every conceivable effort to stay in France until this war is over. I could earn board and lodging in an ambulance corps if nothing else came through. Do you think I'd just be indulging a personal desire in staying? I really don't think so. But after eight months of this war, I can't be sure of my own sincerity any more – I'd be prepared to do anything to stay in France now as long as this thing lasts. And not out of morbid curiosity – I'm sure of that.

You like this country; you must know what I feel about it. The two years I've been here I've changed so much that what I owe this country would fill the Encyclopaedia Britannica ... God knows I'm further from feeling any thrill about participating in the guerre courte fraîche et joyeuse than ever. I'm pretty self-indulgent and have no urge to be a hee-row. Damn this filthy world anyway. We are beginning to hear stories about the battle of the Meuse – and by heaven I can understand now why the "post-war generation" was that way. Please God let me stay in France at least until this war is over.

Well, I put this in the box and hope it'll reach you before too long. I enclose a letter for Mother.

Love,
Frank

To MRS. SARA PICKERSGILL
88 rue de l'Université, Paris,
Thursday, June 6, 1940

Dear Mother:

Just a note before going to the Legation to find out my future fate to let you know I wasn't hit by a bomb the other day and didn't even know they had dropped any bombs until I read it in the paper the next morning. There was a lot more noise than usual during the raids – but I thought it was just the anti-aircraft shooting more than usual.

I hope this afternoon to find out what is to be done about my oral exam. I'm having a three-power conference with

Dupuy and the Minister (General Vanier) at 4.00 o'clock and will know then – but unfortunately must send this off first.

Got your birthday card the day before yesterday, I feel a lot older than last year but not because of the birthday!

This uncertainty about what I'm going to do is getting me down more than anything else. I hope to know something definite this afternoon. Almost all my friends have left Paris either to the Front or elsewhere and I feel more than ever the futility of wandering around waiting for something to decide my fate. Thank heavens I only have another fifteen minutes to wait which means I must stop and get this off. Good-bye and love.

Frank

Don't worry. There's a splendid cellar to this building and no bomb'll ever be able to find its way down there.

Part VI

INTERNMENT AT ST. DENIS: 1940-1942
(age 25-26)

The protracted inquiries which Frank Pickersgill had been making at the Canadian Legation came to an abrupt end. On June 11, leading elements of the German Panzer divisions (which entered Paris the following day) were only a few miles away. He found that the legation had moved to Tours and that he was in a bad fix, without either money or transportation. Arlen Campbell, the American writer, gave him a bicycle and they headed south together for Tours along the roads already jammed with refugees. At Tours, he found that the legation had moved again, and so he decided to head west for Brittany in search of friends who might be able to assist him to escape to England. Campbell, who was unable to dissuade him, proceeded south to safety.

After a series of adventures which he described in a letter two years later, Pickersgill arrived in Brittany near Quimper, on June 19, and was given lodging in the summer home of a stranger, M. Paul Philippar. The Germans had also arrived in Quimper on June 19, and Pickersgill was naturally unable to conceal his presence from them. For six weeks he remained at liberty, helping his host with the vegetable garden, teaching English to some of the children, and cycling round the country to determine whether or not he could make a break for the unoccupied zone of France. This fantastic situation terminated on August 3 when he was arrested by a small party of German soldiers who surrounded the house. He was taken off to prison, together with eighteen other British civilians, in a POW camp for French soldiers near Quimper. In the next two years he was to serve time in no less than nine German prisons and concentration camps. In this, the first of them, the Caserne de la Tour d'Auvergne, he remained only eight days before being transferred to Montreuil-Bellay, near Saumur in the Loire Valley, where he spent two grim months of autumn with a mixed group of prisoners: British civilians, German Jews, and Canadian priests and seminarists, Spanish Republican civilians, and soldiers from Indo-China and Morocco. The German camp commander was a tyrant, and as Pickersgill later reported in a memorandum: "Except for those who were actually bedridden, every man in that prison had to work from 8.00 A.M. until 6.00 P.M. at exhausting manual labour." The food, too, was execrable, although some relief in his case was provided by extra rations smuggled into the prison by a French construction engineer, Jean Boucher, with whom Pickersgill had long talks after working hours. Boucher commented, after the war, on Pickersgill's extraordinary command of French. He lamented that the Canadian had chosen to become a secret agent when instead he could have served more safely as an interpreter for the Allied armies.*

From this camp Pickersgill made plans to escape, for he was within easy striking distance of the demarcation line between the German occupied zone of France and that pocket of the country under the jurisdiction of Petain's government at Vichy which was called, for the next two years, Unoccupied France. As a letter written later reveals, the escape plan had to be abandoned, and on October 15, 1940, he was transferred, together with 180 other British subjects, to the prison at St. Denis, a former French army barracks five miles north of Paris. Here he was to spend the next year and a half.

Life at St. Denis seemed idyllic after what had gone on at Montreuil-Bellay. On his arrival "in rags" he was enthusiastically greeted by another internee, a journalist from Delhi, whom he had known in Paris, Girija Mookerjee, who told him about the relatively decent conditions in the camp. Quarters for the 1,700 internees were indeed crowded. They were also

*"Votre frère, avec sa connaissance parfaite du Français et même de l'argot, aurait rendu de grands services comme interprète aux armées."

inadequately heated as was to become painfully evident in the icy winter of 1941, and the food was sparse, but these liabilities were offset by the fact that no one was ill-treated. As Pickersgill himself stated: "We were neither man-handled nor insulted." And best of all there were privileges. In October, 1940, internees could send and receive mail. And by spring, 1941, Red Cross parcels began to arrive, which were a godsend. For Pickersgill the most enjoyable privilege was being able to see his Paris friends for a half-hour of talk every two weeks. A hundred visitors would line up on one side of a long table extending from one end of a large hut to the other, and a hundred internees would line up on the other side of the table to talk and sometimes to receive pre-inspected parcels of food and clothing from friends. Although there were chores to do such as chopping wood or shovelling coal, most of the time was free for recreation. Pickersgill read extensively and played endless games of bridge with his friend and hut-mate, Whitmore Hicks. Hicks, who served on a Recreation Committee which organized concerts featuring a full-size jazz band, describes their activities: "In the summer we had sports every day. There was tennis played on the court we made, and there were other games as well. There was soft ball with the Canadians and cricket with the others. In winter we had football, and for a month in winter we had ice-skating and ice hockey on the tennis court."

There were, of course, some drawbacks, aside from loss of liberty, in what otherwise sounds like an idyllic life behind barbed-wire. The internees were a mixed lot in more ways than one. Although all of them were classified as British subjects, about half of them could not speak a word of English and had never seen England in their lives, which created complications. And some of them, as might be expected, were racketeers whether inside or outside the prison walls. According to Hicks, one of these loathsome types ran the canteen. Characteristically he would charge 5 francs for a toothbrush costing a franc.

Pickersgill too was to complain about such scummy characters, but to all appearances, he himself seemed to have found the whole experience of internment a kind of lark. In January, 1941, Ake Malmaeus,* from the Swedish Legation in Paris (married to a Winnipeg girl) reported after visiting him that he was amazingly well and cheerful:

> He is treating it just like a football match and thoroughly enjoying every contact he makes with peculiar and interesting people.... He shovels coal four hours a day and thinks it's great sport because he can steal a little extra for his own room.

This account coincides with the tone of the few letters written from St. Denis included below. These letters are simply typical prison-camp communications, short, non-committal, and primarily designed to sustain the morale of one's family by picturing the happier aspects of a life of confinement. Inevitably he was unable to write about his real state of mind and his profound change of attitudes, let alone to hint at his absorbing preoccupation with plans to escape. Recently it has come to light that one plan of escape, not mentioned in his later letters, was to try to pass himself off as a French priest. One of his acquaintances in the camp, Dr. William Moran, who had church connections, had been taking lessons in Latin from him for some time. Pickersgill solicited Moran's help to have priestly garments smuggled into the camp, which was done, and when he donned this garb – the deception being aided by his balding forehead – the young Canadian (according to Dr. Moran in an interview in 1977), could readily have passed as a typical French priest, even though an unusually tall one.

Evidently this engaging strategem had to be abandoned and another escape plan substituted for it. The reader will acquire the full story of these developments later, in a long letter written from London, October 30, 1942. Meanwhile, because the Pickersgill story, even more than most stories, is full of might-have-beens, one question may well be asked. In the light

---

* He was to become the Swedish Ambassador in Ottawa in the 1970s.

of this account of his secure and seemingly carefree existence at St. Denis, what would have happened if he had simply elected to stay in interment camp? As a civilian, rather than a POW, he was under no code that encourages attempts to escape. To have stayed would have been perfectly honourable, and in all likelihood, after the Allies liberated Paris some two or three years later, he would have been released, little the worse for wear, and probably with a lot of writing of his own to his credit (the manuscripts of what he had written at St. Denis had to be left behind at the time of his escape and have never been recovered). But the safe choice was not to be his choice.

Interne Britannique No. 1135,
Grande Caserne,
ST. DENIS (Seine), France,
29 Oct., 1940

Dear Jack, Mother, and family,

I'm sending this to you Jack, to send on to Mother and the rest of the family. I think you will be able to reply, also via the Red Cross. So I hope to get some news from home some time soon.

It's great to be in Paris. My friends come to see me on my visiting days. From August until the beginning of October I was in a camp near Saumur, between Tours and Angers, and was too far away from anyone to be seen. They are loyally rallying round with parcels, clothing and what I need. There were no casualties among my friends, but two of them are prisoners, apparently.

Life here is as good as it could possibly be without liberty. I'm keeping in excellent health, am now able to do some reading, thinking and so on, and hope that the war won't go on too long! And what a lot of things I'll have to tell my grandchildren.

Well, this was just to let you know that I'm still quite alive so good-bye for now. I'll write as often as I can.

Love to all,
Frank

St. Denis, France,
Dec. 14, 1940

Dear Jack:
Hope to hear from you soon. Am in excellent health, reading, shovelling coal, seeing friends on visiting days.

Love,
Frank

May 12, 1941

Dear Mother:
Letters from you, family, Helen Magill. Delighted. Health and spirits splendid. Send canned goods, tea, coffee. Read, write and teach school.

Love,
Frank

July 7, 1941

Dear Mother:
Got your letter of May 14 the other day, and we all got parcels from the Canadian Red Cross a couple of weeks ago. Your letters all come and are a joy. Could you send me another pair of running shoes same size (9) for a friend and a size 9½ for me. If the war goes on toward winter could you

send me a pair of ski-boots (9½ or 10 I suppose) and a pair of ski-slacks. I spend my spare time sun-bathing. See my friends regularly three times a month. The place looks nice now with roses and other flowers blooming all about and the caserne itself is a fine piece of architecture. I miss Paris and Winnipeg! It seems funny living five miles from Paris for nearly a year and not having been there. I'm reading a great deal and am just going to start in on *The Brothers Karamazov* (for the third time).

Love to all,
Frank

July 20, 1941

Dear Mother:

I am pleased to hear that you are established in Winnipeg comfortably. It's curious; your regular letters and my visits give me two islands of reality in the outside world: Paris and Winnipeg! I've just moved: am no longer in the big building but in a log cabin for sixty. Eight of us have a corner which we have fixed up splendidly and we have a kitten. I have more things to ask for: bath towels (big), a quantity of chintz cloth, olive oil (or other), T. S. Eliot's poems, Dos Passos's *U.S.A.* (Jack has my copy I think), American cigarettes or else Buckinghams or Winchesters. As my internment goes on I'm getting to be a better and better carpenter: I can probably make a fortune in that line after the war. I hope everyone is still well. Do you count on spending the winter in Winnipeg?

Love,
Frank

Dear Mother:

I just got two of your letters and one from Mademoiselle Ballu. Tell her how much pleasure I had in hearing from her, and to write me as often as she thinks of it. I'm still feeling fine. The morale is excellent. I'm going to collaborate in a Christmas musical comedy with David Askell, a pal of mine here, the son of the man who wrote the stage version of "1066 and All That." I don't know Baby Bjornson's husband but heard about her marriage in a letter from Ford. If you see her tell her to write me. Heard also from Frank Jones. Mademoiselle made some characteristically obscure remarks about rabbits at the Clearwater Bay cottage. What's all this?

Love,
Frank

St. Denis, January 6, 1942

Dear Jack:

I got Mother's first letter from Florida last week and was pleased to hear that she is well installed. I don't think I congratulated you in my last on your fatherhood. All these nieces and nephews in *absentia* are beginning to bewilder me. I got a letter from Paul* last week. He had tried to get news to you without success. He's been in Arry since October, 1940. Everyone in the family is well, he tells me, and he is going to try to come down to see me.

We passed a very agreeable Christmas and New Year's, the Christmas menu including oysters, moules mariniere (my bed-

---

*Vicomte Paul de France, friend of Jack Pickersgill's, with whom Frank had stayed in 1938.

mate's cuisine), chile con carne (my fabrication) four bottles of good wine and two of gros rouge; the New Year's one much similar with coques replacing the moules and beefsteak frites replacing the chile con carne. If I see Paul I can doubtless give you more news of him. Try to send cigarettes.

Love to all,
Frank

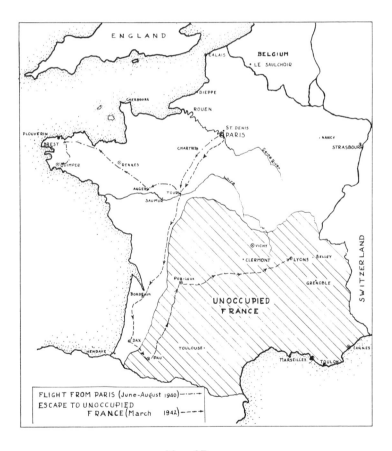

Map of France

PART VII

UNOCCUPIED FRANCE: 1942
(Age 26)

Frank Pickersgill's escape from St. Denis to Unoccupied
France in March, 1942, is vividly described in a letter from
England many months later. His escape was contrived with the
assistance of his French friends from the Maison Canadienne
group, Pouillon, Maurette, and, in particular, Lapassade. It was
Lapassade's brother-in-law, Louis Saint-Calbre, an architect,
who arranged to get Pickersgill across the demarcation line into
the unoccupied zone and who accompanied him on his journey. Another Paris friend who helped was Jean Jezéquellou
who, before the war, had been a waiter at the Café de Flore.
This was the café from which Pickersgill wrote most of his
letters, and he and Jezéquellou had become close friends.
Whitmore Hicks, a British subject but French-speaking, his
hutmate at St. Denis, was Pickersgill's accomplice in the escape
and was with him for two months afterwards. A hefty six
footer like Pickersgill, Hicks himself was later to become a
secret agent, in 1943, in the same service in which Pickersgill
was to enlist. His organizing of resistance groups in the south
of France led eventually to his arrest by the Gestapo and
deportation to a concentration camp. Because his captors fortunately lost his papers, he survived his imprisonment although

he contracted TB as a result of maltreatment in Germany.

As soon as they reached Unoccupied France, Pickersgill and Hicks went to stay with an older brother of his friend Maurette, who was living in a village near Perigueux. Two happy months were spent with this family. His host said later that for him it had been a moving experience to watch Pickersgill's eager enjoyment of his newfound life of freedom. From May to September, while waiting for exit visas that would enable him to get to Portugal, Pickersgill lived in or around Lyons, part of the time at the home of his old friend from Paris days, Jean Varille, and at other times in quarters provided by Americans from the United States' consulate.

Through Varille he made a number of new friends among a group of Frenchmen, only one of whom survived the war. This was General Pierre Jacobsen de Rosen, an officer of the Legion of Honour. At the time of attaining his rank, Jacobsen was thirty years of age, which made him the youngest general in the French army.

The first news his family received of the escape was a cable to Jack Pickersgill which reached Ottawa on March 18. Translated, it read as follows: "Your brother arrived here in good health. Try to send underwear shoes money advice. Paul Maurette." For fear the message might be intercepted by the Germans, no reply was sent, but the United States' authorities were at once asked to use their good offices to assist him inasmuch as direct correspondence seemed too dangerous, and in this way, he was able to receive funds and other help. As a result of these precautions there is only one letter written to Canada during the whole period of six months, and a couple of notes to friends in France, and hence we do not know much of what he was doing at the time, except that he drove a milk-truck for the Red Cross for a period and did other odd jobs. Even when he got to England he wrote to his brother: "I think I'd better skip my activities in Lyons – even to you – until after the war!"

This reticence suggests the likelihood that in Lyons, months before he was to become a full-fledged agent, he had already established some contacts with the secret service in which he would later serve. There is a hint of this in an October letter in which he mentions "spending four months in Lyons doing illegal propaganda" and of his daily fear of arrest at the time by the Vichy police. Kay Moore, because of her work at the War Office, was able to be more specific on this point: "He was mildly involved in helping a group who were doing some sort of resistance. He had been with some people at Lyons who were well-known at London Headquarters to be active resistance people and who were being used by the British." *Duel of Wits* (1955) by Peter Churchill (himself a British agent but no relation to Winston) describes the activities of these groups in Lyons at the time Pickersgill was there. One of the most colourful of the agents working for London in Lyons was Virginia Hall. When the Germans took over the city in November, 1942, the commander of the Gestapo affirmed that he would give anything "to put his hands on that Canadian bitch." Miss Hall, as it happened, was not Canadian. She was an American from Baltimore, and she had good friends in the American consulate where Pickersgill also had established friendships. If my surmise is correct about his activities that spring and summer, one can appreciate why he did not want to compromise any of his contacts by talking about them afterwards.

Aside from such conjectures we do have one clear account of his life during this period in a letter to his family from Miss Constance Harvey of the United States' consulate at Lyons. One incident, not covered in her letter, should first be mentioned. Late in the summer Miss Harvey arranged a visit for Pickersgill with Gertrude Stein and Alice B. Toklas, who were living out the war in Unoccupied France in a country house east of Lyons. This visit is mentioned in passing in one of Pickersgill's letters, but when he was in London he expanded on his impressions. The two Americans struck him as "like two little old New England ladies rocking on the front stoop, but very loveable and impressive." He liked to tell of Alice B. Toklas taking him aside and complaining that when visitors came it was she who was sent outdoors to hoe the potatoes while Gertrude remained behind to enjoy the interesting conversation.

Miss Harvey's report follows:

It must have been July, 1942, when Pick came to us. He had recently escaped from St. Denis and was waiting round pending his departure with a regular visa for Lisbon. (We were able to get him out as a non-combatant because of his deaf ear, but it took a long time.)

Pick had expressed a desire to do something to help while waiting for the visa, so I got him to work on some translations of news bulletins for private circulation among French friends. Pick's French was perfectly amazing. He not only spoke – but what is much rarer – wrote beautiful, accurate French. A number of the young lads at the 'Science PO,' sons of friends of mine, were eager for more information than was contained in the broadcasts – foreign editorial comment, and that sort of thing. I discovered that Pick knew many of the same type of boy, and so we wrote for them.

One of the things that most struck me about Pick was his remarkably wide acquaintance among French lads of his own age. He had friends all over France who already were 'the new élite.' Some of them, such as the youngest Michelin boy, used to come to see me after Pick was gone.

I had rented a lovely old country place in the Ain half way between Lyon and Geneva for the summer. Although I was hardly ever there, it seemed a good place for Pick to live. Lodging in town was awfully uncomfortable. Moreover, Pick had next to no clothes! It was always a problem to try to clothe the lads who kept turning up. We did the best we could for Frank but it wasn't very good. We had to give the most solid clothes to people who were going to need them for a long time and Pick was "going out" soon to the great world where he could get anything he wanted. Somehow the contrast between Pick's grave courtesy and the particularly shabby suit found for him by one of my colleagues made him even more charming.

So I took Pick down to Le Chanut with a party for the week-end, and he stayed on, with occasional trips to town. He used to tour the countryside by bicycle and talk to the country people, or go to see friends of mine who had a place seven kilometers away. Once he went off visiting some of his own friends for a week but came back afterward. I think the country did him good and it was possible really to feed him up. He was so tall and hungry after months of St. Denis! He said to me once in his funny dry way: 'I don't know what your cook thinks of me! I'm really ashamed of eating so much!' Of course my cook and my housekeeper and I were all perfectly delighted. Any woman would be! My chief, Mr. Vance, spent ten days down in the country with Pick and was very happy. I had ten days there with him myself. He was such a nice guest! In spite of his youth Pick was such a mature, even a rather comforting person! One felt so clearly that one could depend on him completely. His judgement about political matters was extraordinary. We talked a lot. He told me about your whole family and about your mother and the way she brought you all up. I thought then – and even more now – that Frank was one of the best things our new continent has produced, from the old stock.

I didn't want to involve Pick in any particular work at that time. He himself felt instinctively that he must go back to his own people for orders. Although he did not know exactly what he was going to do, one felt that he had solid ground under his feet, and would only take the next step when he knew where the next bit of solid ground lay.

When the visa finally came, I hated to see Pick go. Yet I was glad that he was going out to the free outside world. I felt sure, however, that he would come back – under orders. He seemed so prepared for the work, and so serene. As I look back on it now

I believe that your brother had a good life, although it was so short. If the job he did later – and the end – was lonely, yet one feels sure that, unlike many others, he had the strength to bear a hard fate, and to do a difficult job, for which he was superbly fitted. You must be very proud of him. His friends in France feel that it was a gift to have known him.

(The following letter is translated from French)

To J. W. PICKERSGILL (Ottawa)
c/o M. Paul Maurette, Les Jalots,
Trélissac, (Unoccupied France)
March 23, 1942

Dear Jack:

You will already have received my telegram (I hope) before this letter reaches you. I'm impatiently waiting for word from you either directly or through the U.S. consul. You've doubtless figured out from the telegram that I escaped from the camp where the Germans had us interned. I managed to get away with a pal of mine, and we had a regular comic-opera escape.

Everything has gone beautifully up to this point, and I'm getting my position straightened out with the French authorities. I'm with some friends here who have been magnificent, and in fact everyone has been marvellous to me, especially my friends in Paris. But what am I going to do from now on? That is, what am I entitled to do, and can you help me straighten out my position further?

If you can send parcels here, I'm desperately in need of underwear and shoes. Madame Maurette would be also very grateful if you could send certain things such as cotton material for making children's clothes. I don't know what food you can buy. If you could send her dried apples, chocolate, Klim milk or condensed milk, she would be delighted. She has three children, and the whole Maurette family have sacrificed so much for me that I'd do anything under the sun to be able to reciprocate a little.

Will it be possible for you to send any money? In any case you will probably realise that the Germans retained my passport and identity card, so that I'm here without any sort of identification. Then there will perhaps be difficulties about obtaining any funds, especially if I'm going to be repatriated. On every account, therefore, I'm waiting for news and advice from you.

You've doubtless spread the glad tidings. Write to me by air-mail here, and have the others write too. I'm thirsty for news. Send my greetings to everybody collectively and individually.

Frank

To PAUL DE FRANCE* (Chateau d'Arry)

Lyons
June 9, 1942

My dear Paul:

I hope that you received my last post-card safely. My plans here are in good shape. I've already obtained two of the three visas that I was waiting for, and expect to leave next week, or at least by the end of the month. There's no news yet from my family, but that will be taken care of soon now.

I never stop relishing the joys of liberty these days. I have many excellent friends here, and the time passes very agreeably.

Bien amicalement
Frank [tr]

* Vicomte Paul de France, friend of Jack Pickersgill, with whom Frank had visited in 1938. [G.M.F.]

To HENRI ROBILLOT (Morocco)

Lyons
Thursday, July 3, 1942

Cher vieux:

I have just returned to Lyons after a week in the Puy-de-Dôme and found your telegram.* I was delighted by the news and hope that child has found a suitable name.

I know she will be brought up with the GREATEST RESPECT AND VENERATION for her godfather!

Send me word when she is named.

Still no news from Portugal. The delay is becoming really exasperating. Patience is a virtue I don't possess.

Je vous embrasse tous les trois.

Pick [tr]

*News of the birth of Robillot's child, Frank's god-daughter, in Morocco. [G.H.F.]

Part VIII

LISBON AND LONDON: 1942
(age 27)

With his long-awaited papers in order, Pickersgill arrived in neutral Portugal, via Madrid, in late September and reported at the British Embassy in Lisbon. Discreet enquiries there led to his obtaining the addresses of army agencies in London where he could apply for special work in France. First, however, there was the problem of getting a plane flight to London. What complicated matters was that his family in Canada, who had not seen him for four years, were understandably keen to have him return home, even for a brief visit. An animated exchange of cablegrams flowed between Ottawa and Lisbon throughout October. He was assured, by cable, that there were useful services for him to perform in Canada, and the National Film Board even offered to pay his plane fare home. Despite the attractive prospects of a reunion with his mother and brothers and sister, he told the British Ambassador that he had urgent work to do and could not consider returning to Canada; what he really feared was that if he went home he would never get back to France to fight. A flight to London was therefore arranged for October 24, and upon arrival he reported to the War Office. His family, however, were still hoping to see him and greeted him with a cable: "Family delighted. Want you home." Within three days of his arrival in

London he was able to counter this proposal by a cable reporting of his having been offered "a job of extreme importance ... as a British officer." His family was therefore reluctantly persuaded to accept his urgent sense of priorities and to give him their blessings. Through the efforts of Jack Pickersgill, it was arranged by the Minister of National Defence, Colonel Ralston, in late November, 1942, that his commission as Lieutenant would be in the Canadian army (General List) rather than the British, and he was "loaned," as the expression has it, to the War Office, which, when translated, in his case, meant that he was to be trained as a secret agent.

This month of October in Lisbon also involved Pickersgill in a personal relationship as well as in military commitments, a relationship occasionally alluded to mysteriously in his letters but which must have been important to him at the time. A young English girl, Jacqueline Grant, who had been living in Unoccupied France at La-Tour-du-Pin, had escaped to Lisbon with her mother en route to England to take on a war job. She and Pickersgill fell in love, and for the first time in his correspondence there are references to the possibility of his getting married. It is known that there had been a girl friend in Paris, to whom he had smuggled out a letter from St. Denis in 1941, but the word *marriage* crops up here, for the first time, in December, 1942. For some time after their arrival in London the young couple saw each other frequently for long walks and for spaghetti suppers at a little Italian restaurant in the Brompton Road. He also introduced her to a group of his Canadian friends with whom he stayed when on leave, and there were parties. After a few months, however, the engagement was broken off, without bad feelings. In an interview twenty-two years later, Jacqueline Grant (herself married in the interim) explained: "We didn't have much in common to talk about you see and this is really why it folded up. I was aware of the fact that he was much too intellectual for me to, you know, keep up with." Pickersgill himself commented on the relationship in the spring of 1943: "I guess I'm not just the marrying type."

Other personal relationships, perhaps more important, were to develop in London with his Canadian friends, but these can be related in a subsequent chapter.

To J. W. PICKERSGILL
Hotel Rosa, Caldasda Rainha, Portugal,
Oct. 1, 1942

Dear Everybody:

This isn't going to be much of a letter, as I have a touch of flu, and anyway am going down to Lisbon on Saturday whence I'll send a cable, and write a longer and more interesting letter from there. I've been champing at the bit in Vichy-France for six months waiting for my visas – although I really did have a very interesting time there. Here, it's just heaven. The food just knocks me cold. The idea of going to breakfast and having rolls made with white flour – *and* as many as I want without the horrid feeling that I won't have any tickets left at the end of the month – *and* of being able to smoke – oil and butter à volonté, and potatoes, real *frites* at every meal – is overwhelming and I still think I'm dreaming. Of course I was better off for food in Unoccupied France than in the camp – but that's not saying much.

I'm not going to recount my escape from St. Denis here – although it's really a very exciting and amusing story. But I hope you'll make very public the fact that if it hadn't been for the loyalty of my French friends, who risked their lives to help me get out, I should still be there. Everywhere in France, Unoccupied as well as Occupied – any amount of sympathy and helpfulness. There is nothing wrong with the French people and nobody will make me believe otherwise.

I'm going to England. The Consul here wants me to go by air and as quickly as possible – hence the cable that you'll probably have received before getting this letter. I'll try, once in England to regularise my situation (if it's not too late) as

195

regards the Civil Service exams written in 1940. Then I expect if they have me I'll go into the army.

I feel bitterly sorry for all the worry I must have caused you all since June 1940. The circumstances were really beyond my control. – I was left flat without any money. I tried as best I could to *faire l'évacuation* without funds, but as a result of lack of money got pushed around in the tide of refugees and ended up in Brittany too late to get a boat for England. I tried to escape from Montreuil-Bellay in September 1940 but was given away by the treachery of one of my charming fellow-prisoners. Well, I hope that you haven't worried too much – I tried to give as rosy a picture of things as possible – anyway now that it's all over I consider it has been an invaluable experience.

Also the six months in Unoccupied France. I did some work at the American Consulate at Lyon and became very good friends with Miss Harvey, one of the vice-consuls there, who is the real backbone of the Consulate and is doing a splendid job in France. I learned a lot and am dying to tell you about it all in some detail. It's from her account in Lisbon that I'm going to pay my air passage, and I hope you'll be able to deposit the sum to her bank in Buffalo.

I'm very keen to get to England – although this place makes a wonderfully agreeable rest-cure – as I'm sick to death of doing nothing.

Well, that's all for now and you'll hear much more from Lisbon.

Love to all,
Frank

P.S. The Consulate here is very good to these repatriated people and in particular to me. I came rather apologetically – it seemed rather cluttering the place up – didn't expect to be treated as a hee-row and find it rather uncomfortable!

(The following is in reply to a cable advising immediate return to Canada)

To J. W. PICKERSGILL

Lisbon, Portugal,
October 12, 1942

Dear Jack:

We've had the cable from Ottawa for a few days now and I'm trying to get used to the idea. I'm terribly anxious to see Mother and will be relieved to have her see no pieces are missing – and of course would give anything to settle down to a long world problem-solving session with you – but nevertheless feel perfectly god-awful about not going to England. You see in that hole where I was kept one gets so dulled and nerveless that it requires a terrific effort of will to get up the energy and guts necessary to escape. I only got away thanks to an *idée fixe*: that I'd make my way to England to fight, or at any rate to suitable work in the danger zone. As I was waiting for my visa I became more and more fanatical about my *idée fixe* – and here in Lisbon I'd already seen the people who were going to put me in touch with the right people in London. (As I found out that the medical exam for the army would certainly disclose my burst eardrum, I've been very careful about making my plans to get seen and heard by the right people to get me into what I wanted to do.)

As I say, I realize what a joy it would be to see you all, and would like nothing better than to come back to Canada, report as it were, and spend about a month with the family, then buzz off to England and the war. But I'm afraid such a prospect is a pipe-dream and that once in Canada I'd have the devil's own time getting back to Europe.

I do hope you'll understand what I mean. I've seen and done some things which have rather radically changed my outlook. After seeing a French soldier clubbed to death by German cops at Quimper, after starving in a gravel-pit at Montreuil-Bellay and getting blood-poisoning through being made to put up barbed-wire entanglements without any gloves on, and after sawing my way out of St. Denis through a barred window, and spending four months in Lyon doing illegal propaganda and not quite sure from one day to the next when I might be "*repéré*" and arrested – well I'm afraid I'd find it pretty difficult to settle down to pushing a pen in an Ottawa office for the duration of the war and trying to convince myself that it was "useful work."

However if I must go back I must, but for heaven's sake get me out of this fool's paradise just as soon as possible – with God knows what priority on a Clipper. I was all set to get off to England this week-end and have a furious desire to get at whatever I'm going to do. Waiting here will be even worse than waiting in St. Denis or in Lyon, because here there's far too much to eat and people are far too comfortable. Also do keep your eyes peeled for a chance, if there ever is one, to get me at something that will satisfy my passions! I'm convinced that as far as this war is concerned there are certain jobs I could do better than anybody, but about a handful of people – and surely that would be the most suitable thing for me to do. That such jobs would be dangerous is just one more thing in their favour. If any preparing the way can be done, do prepare the way so that I can see and talk to the right people. I'm sure I can convince them there as I've been able to do here – or seem to have. Remember, I kept my eyes wide open wherever I was.

I'll go back to Canada *la mort dans l'ame* rather – but I'm sure you'll see my point and if there's anything to be done to help me get back into the war you'll give me a hand.

Love to everybody,
Frank

[CABLEGRAM TO J. W. PICKERSGILL]
London, England,
October 27, 1942

In view of your cable about my return, War Office has offered job of extreme importance and direct value in war

effort as British Officer. Propose to accept, subject your
blessing. Cannot overemphasize certainty this is the right
course. Love to everybody.

Frank

To J. W. PICKERSGILL

Canada House, London, England,
October 30, 1942

Dear Jack:

I've just got your cable and at last feel as though I can write
a decent letter – after the rather hectic trip and one week
rushing around this town like a whirlwind – I got here last
Thursday evening and got my job, after one and a half hours'
interview, on Friday afternoon, and have been rushing ever
since! I'm getting worse than Tom for being busy.

But I'd better start at the beginning and sort of give a brief
history of the past two and a half years. I left Paris (like a
damn fool: had I stayed there I would have been in the non-
occupied zone in July 1940) on June 11, with 50 francs and a
bicycle. I rushed off to Tours – held up of course by the floods
of people on the roads – and got there a few hours after the
Legation had left. I had two francs left and didn't dare go
south without money so dashed over to Angers where I had
friends who might lend me money. They had left Angers. By
this time I was out of the southern direction and rather
desperate about starving to death, so went off to try to find
friends who lived in Rennes. Could not get into Rennes: had
another friend (Jezéquellou) mobilised in a village called
Plouverin in the Côtes du Nord in Brittany – thought he could
lend me money to get to a port so I could get a boat over to
England.

Well, on the way to Plouverin I was picked up as a German
parachutist, taken into a café and just escaped being lynched
by the narrowest margin, then was taken out of the howling

mob by two or three more responsible people who took me to the gendarmerie. The gendarmes were as excited as everyone else. They wanted to shoot me, but I finally persuaded them to telephone my friend where he was mobilised. He vouched for me, but warned them to tell me not to come to Plouverin as he had just had orders to smash his telephone and leave, which he would do in a quarter of an hour. So that, if these gendarmes had waited another fifteen minutes, they would have phoned to a bogus number and I don't like to think of the possible results.

I then made for the first large town, Quimper, feeling badly shaken up and just wanting to get somewhere safe from people who were lynching parachutists – I finally ended up registered as a refugee in the commune of La Forest-Fouesnant (Finistère). I was there at the armistice, was still feeling pretty weak, had no money but was earning some by giving English lessons. However, I decided to pull out in the night and try to get across the demarcation line on my bike. But the day of the night I intended leaving a German soldier came to the place where I was staying to see my papers, and he seemed to take my presence and my desire to go to Lyons (which I knew to be in the proposed non-occupied zone) so casually that I thought they couldn't be intending to arrest me at once. I decided to stay until I'd earned enough cash to do the trip without running the risk of starving to death.

My date for leaving was to be about August 15th, but on August 3 they came and got me. Took me to the Caserne de la Tour d'Auvergne at Quimper where there were 3,000 French prisoners and about eighteen British civilians arrested in the neighbourhood.* This was awful. We were put in the cells – ten in one cell and six in another. No light all day and eating in the dark. The food was good because the French were so kind to us that they sent us everything decent that there was to eat. The cell doors were left open and there was one vacant cell.

* Among the French prisoners was Frank's friend Jezéquellou who escaped shortly afterwards and returned to Paris. [G.H.F.]

The night before we left two German cops obviously drunk dragged a French soldier into the empty cell and clubbed him to death. It took over half an hour and was the most frightful experience I've ever had.

The next morning they took the nineteen of us off to Montreuil-Bellay in the Loire Valley. There we almost died of starvation for two months – my weight went down to under 130 lbs., and I was one of the three people in the camp who didn't have dysentery. They made us do road work and pick and shovel work all day, and in the morning heated water so we'd have something warm in our stomachs to work on, at noon a plate of soupwater with a couple of slices of carrot and a bit of rotten potato floating around in it, at night 250 grams of bread and 20 grams of either fat or beetroot jam.

I once saw a piece of bread in a ditch as I was working on the road. It had been there for years and was black with dust and had a bit of cow dung on it, but I pocketed it all right and ate it when I was in bed that night.

Then the Commander of the Camp was changed and things got a little better – the baker and pork butcher were allowed to sell stuff – but it was even worse in my case as I had no money, and it is terrible to watch other people eating when you're hungry. Of course every man for himself – as another thing proved in this Camp.

I laid plans for escape which would have been easy as we went out on work parties and were only about 65 kilometres from the demarcation line. But I wasn't very discreet and asked a couple of fellows who knew the region what roads to take. It got around to the self-appointed camp leaders – one of whom, a filthy swine, took me into the Courtyard with three men to serve as moral support, said he knew I was leaving and that, if I didn't give my word of honour that I would not escape he'd put a bodyguard around me everytime I went out on work parties to give me away to the Germans if they saw me make a false move. They were all so frightened as to what would happen to them if someone escaped that I began to get infected, decided it would be a dirty trick to escape and settled down more or less for the duration – passing up any number of perfectly easy chances at Montreuil and during the following eight months at St. Denis.

Life the first year was pretty awful. At St. Denis we were much better off materially, the Germans stopped kicking us around, and from June 1941 on, we began getting Red Cross parcels from England and Canada and eating better.

But many people in the camp were such lousy swine (remittance men, jockeys and racing touts, people with small private incomes who were living in France because they could put on more side than if they tried living in England, and so on). And I saw no hope of getting out, no chance of escape, with possibilities of reprisals on the others hanging over my head, and no hope at all about the war, shocked at the Fall of France – a pretty ghastly winter.

Then the first leg-up was when Russia came in. My morale went up 200 per cent. Then in August 1941 two men escaped and no reprisal measures were taken on the Camp, so I knew at once that my job was cut out for me and started preparing. I made one attempt in November which failed. Fortunately I got away without having it detected by the Germans. Then I started looking around a bit more. The lay-out of the Camp was as follows:

It was a barracks with a high stone wall (ten feet) with barbed-wire on the wall around it. Inside the wall was the barbed-wire fence with the barbed-wire entanglement inside that. Work parties generally went outside the barbed-wire to work but never outside the wall. Roll call was inside barbed-wire at 5.00 every night and no one allowed outside on any pretext afterwards. On Saturdays, last roll call of the week was at 11.00 a.m. (until Monday morning) and no one was allowed outside the barbed-wire afterwards except one man, Hicks, who had a special permit as he did the sweeping and dusting in the German censorship office and used to scrub the floor there on Saturday afternoons. The Censorship Office was in one of the old out-buildings of the barracks, built into the wall in one corner, with windows which were barred giving out on

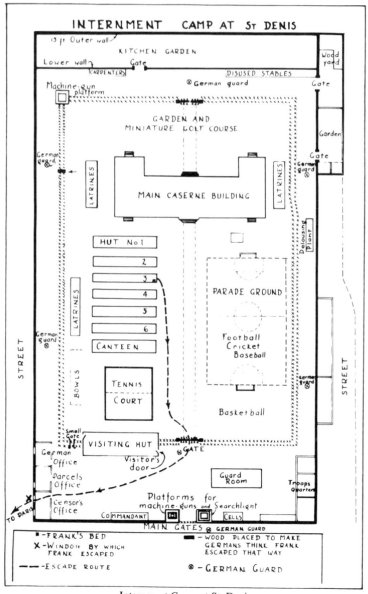

Internment Camp at St. Denis

to the street. In the upper storey of the building one of the Officers Commanding the camp had his flat. Hicks swept and dusted his flat too.

This building seemed like a good dodge to me. The first thing to do was to work on Hicks. His father and two brothers were in the camp, his mother and sister in Paris. Although only twenty-two, he had never thought of escaping, for fear of what might happen to his family. However, in December 1941, a man whose mother was in Paris, escaped and his mother was not even questioned by the Gestapo. I managed to find this out and passed the word on to Hicks who let it simmer for about two hours and came back to say he'd decided to try it and had I ever thought of it. I said I thought of nothing else and was sure his censorship office thing was the way out, somehow. So he told the sergeant in the censorship that he needed help and knew someone that would help him, and I began going out to sweep and scrub, too.

Thus we were getting out on Saturday afternoons after roll call – the only two in the camp – and of course had very black names as 5th columnists as a result! The German officer above had a mistress in Paris and left every Saturday at noon and didn't show up again until Monday morning, so he was no problem. In theory, a sentinel was put on our tails while we were working, but as they all got to know us and were lazy, they didn't bother coming after a while, except on rare occasions. Thus the stage was set and we lacked only the raw materials. We needed the key to the officer's flat, so as to have a sure hide-out until nightfall, and a hack-saw to saw one of the bars on the window giving on to the street, during the night.

I think I've told you in some of the camp-letters that we had visitors. Anyway my friends were arranging a hide-out in Paris for us and a way to cross the line. For the key the thing was easy. Hicks put some plasticine in a cheese box and slipped it in his pocket. The officer had the negligent habit of leaving the key in the door when he made the rounds, and Hicks' presence was normal upstairs as he swept and dusted there. So one day he just laid the key in the plasticine at every angle. On my next visit, I slipped the cheese box across to my friend Robert Lapassade who works in the Mint and a fortnight later, while shaking my hand across the barrier, he left a nice new key (furnished by the Mint!) in my hand.

I then told him we needed a hack-saw – damn difficult to find in Paris nowadays – and to send it concealed somehow to Hicks who was known in the parcels office and about whom the Parcels Control was careless. I added that when the hack-saw was got to us he was to come past the window at 3.00 o'clock every Saturday, and on the first propitious Saturday we could indicate by some sort of sign whether they were to expect us in Paris that night or not.

On Friday, March 6, Hicks got a parcel containing a four pound loaf of bread. When we took the end off it we found a hack-saw inside with three blades. The next day, Saturday, the cigarette ration for March came along at 2.20 p.m. and at 2.30 we went through the barbed-wire to scrub the floor. We had no sentinel – the coast was clear. At five past three I began looking out of the window. Suddenly across the street I noticed a girl staring in at me, and she grinned when she saw I was looking at her. I said to Hicks (who doesn't speak English: a help on the journey as there was no temptation): "Tiens, on a fait une touche."* He came to the window and we began grinning at the girl. Then she flicked her eyes in the direction of a shop beside her and through the shop window we saw Lapassade buying razor blades. In a minute he came out, walked up the street, put his arm round the girl, crossed over to our side and down past our window, apparently engrossed in courtship, head turned and bent towards hers and, incidentally, toward the window, apparently whispering sweet nothings in her ear, among which was "We'll meet you at the Gare du Nord at 11.00 o'clock." They disappeared and we put

*To say that Hicks didn't speak English was an exaggeration. Son of an English father and a French mother, Hicks had been brought up in France, and French was his preferred language, but he also knew a fair amount of English as well. [G.H.F.]

away our brushes and sneaked upstairs and locked ourselves into the officer's flat until nightfall.

We made tea on his electric plate, then began looking through his drawers and cupboards but all we could find was a pound of coffee (worth its weight in gold twice over in France now) so we took that.

Then Nature began calling violently and the only Johnny was in the court yard (the factor one always forgets about in these affairs) and, after looking about desperately, we found two empty wine bottles which we duly filled. But that by no means satisfied Nature's every desire – there was more solid work to do. The Officer had left a pair of boots in a corner and I wanted to use the boots, but Hicks rightly pointed out that if we left traces like that behind us it might go hard with us if we were caught. We finally found an enormous piece of wrapping paper which we spread out on the floor – and took turns leaving a souvenir on it. Then we made it into a neat package and when night fell sneaked downstairs with the two wine bottles and the neat package which we had, of course, to take away with us. Couldn't leave traces like that around.

We found the hack-saw made so much noise that there was nothing doing until after the curfew at midnight. So we tried to keep warm till then and at 12.30 started sawing the bars. It took us four hours to saw the bar – the anguish of those four hours is indescribable. The damn thing made enough noise to waken the dead – there were cops on the square fifty yards away and the sentries just inside going the rounds. And of course we had to stop at the slightest noise. It's amazing what human nerves will stand when they have to, though. Anyway at 4.30 the bar was sawn and we subsided into a corner of the room and relaxed till 7.30. Then we climbed out the window with the wine bottles and the package which we deposited at the foot of the lamp post and walked about two miles – in the same direction – God what a joy! – toward Paris.*

*Hicks's account of this incident, on which he prepared a report, adds a few details. After the crowds in the streets diminished at midnight, the two men

In general I can say that I have been going from one thrill to another since that morning, and I've never really known what it is to be in love with life until, well, the last seven months. But that was the first thrill and it was pretty intense.

Then we got on a bus and rode into Paris listening to the workmen enthusiastically discussing the bombing of the Renault factory which had taken place four nights before. Then we took the Métro – what a heavenly smell it seemed to have! – and found my friend who had found a hide-out for us in an empty flat. That evening several of my friends came round and we all went out and had a meal in a restaurant nearby, and it seemed as if two years had simply telescoped into nothing – in spite of two German S.A. men dining at the next table.

My friends had found a French soldier (named Saint-Calbre) on temporary release, subject to removal to Germany if he tried any funny work, who was crossing the line clandestinely the next day near Dax, and who had the necessary indications and would go with us. So the next morning we took the train at the Gare d'Austerlitz. We reached Dax at 8.00 p.m. – there was a bus leaving at 10.00 the next morning for the line – so we went out and lay down in a field for the night, but didn't sleep as it poured rain all night. The next morning we got on the bus.

began sawing. "Pick was watching at one of the windows while I was sawing one of the bars of the other one. For four solid hours I sawed this bar, which was about one and one-half inches thick. We could hear the sentries walking outside and French policemen talking about fifty yards from the window. Twice during the night we thought the sentries were coming into the office. Once we heard a sentry scraping his feet outside the door, but he didn't come in. At 8.00 in the morning we got out the window, closed it behind us after putting the iron bar back into place. I learned later that the Germans only found out about the bar two months later." That the two men were missing was, of course, discovered early. According to a letter to me from Hicks (July, 1977) the unfortunate commandant of the camp, Colonel Von Arnim, was sent to the Russian front as punishment for having allowed the successful escape to happen. Other escapes occurred later (Hicks' brother escaped twice), but the men were almost invariably caught soon afterwards. [G.H.F.]

When we were about fifteen kilometres from the line, we saw a French gendarme at a bus stop. He let all those get off who were getting off at that stop, then got on the bus and started asking people for their papers. We assumed that the game was up – there were so many witnesses that he would have to arrest us. He must have seen the bleak look on our faces, for when he got down to our level on the bus, instead of asking for ours, he turned his back directly on us and bent over to ask the people in the seat across the bus. We took the hint and got up and walked out – trying not to walk too fast. Then we went down the road feeling pretty sick, as, without the French soldier, we would probably get lost or picked up. We'd gone about two hundred yards when there was a honking behind us, the bus drove up, stopped, the driver opened the door, and, in the most casual, matter-of-fact tone, said "It's all right now, he's gone, you can get back in." Everybody in the bus had grins a mile wide.

About a mile from the line the driver stopped and said to us that this was about where we should get off and indicated the direction through the bush. Off we went and got lost in the bush. But we came to a farmer, making hay who kindly took us to the line which was a highway, went over first to make sure there was no patrol and then beckoned us to come over. We went through a gate with DEMARKATIONSLINIE: Uberschritt strengst verboten! on it.

We went about thirty yards and then the relief of safety set in. My legs suddenly collapsed and I just faded out into the road and sat there trying to keep the tears back. The French soldier decided we needed food, took out a piece of bread and pâté from his haversack and divided it up and gave us some. The effort of swallowing was too much for me, and I started to cry like a baby. When I had pulled myself together we went into a farmhouse where we were given a couple of bottles of wine to drink and rested a few minutes. Then on. We walked about ten kilometres and I found myself whistling a rather nice tune (sung by the French Bing Crosby Jean Sablon who now sings in some New York night club. If you're ever there go to hear him, he's sure to sing the song) "Je tire ma reverance – par les routes de France – de France et de Navarre" – anyway that pleasantly silly song now moves me more deeply than any other music I can think of, which suggests interesting thoughts on impurity and suggestion in artistic appreciation!

Then at the first telephone we phoned for a taxi which took us to Pau where we spent the night in an hotel, having made out phoney hotel slips. The next morning we took the train for Perigueux. We found Paul and Arlette Maurette who were wonderful. They put us up, and kept us for two months until we got settled and fixed as it were, and the first week without food cards – and I don't know whether you can appreciate what that means. We reported to the police who were very friendly and helpful, straightened out our identities and got us new papers (of course, the Germans had our passports and identity cards), got our food cards, and even the special clothes tickets which are given to escaped French prisoners.

By May 7 I had my residence permit for Lyons, thanks to poor old Firmin Roz who is slowly dying at Vichy, and whom I saw there later in the summer. I was shocked when I saw him. He was appallingly ill. I also had my passport from the Americans and my medical certificate enabling me to get out of France, and had applied for all my visas.

I stayed in Lyons, except for trips to visit friends to Marseilles, Grenoble, Clermont, Vichy, St. Nectaire and Bellay (where I met Gertrude Stein, a very impressive old woman indeed), until September 19, by which date all my visas had arrived and I started off.

I think I'd better skip my activities in Lyons – even to you – until after the war! They were, at any rate, terribly interesting, and I made many wonderful French friends and one wonderful American one, Miss Harvey, vice-consul there (who lent me passage money by air from Lisbon to England).

All this time I had no real intentions whatever of going back to Canada. This rather curious complex of experiences had left a fairly profound imprint and I saw only two possible or conceivable alternatives (a) go to England with vague intentions of "joining up" or (b) staying in France, under certain conditions, which should be obvious, at least to you. I was in the war up to the neck and I think I should have died of spiritual starvation had I been wrenched away from it. In other words I suppose in a sense I had become a fanatic.

I got to Lisbon, and more definite plans as to what sort of work I should do began maturing in my mind. I got on the trail of some people and was about to set off to England when the cable came from Canada saying I was to go straight back. I was so cut up about it that I didn't sleep for two nights – hence the two rather hysterical letters I wrote you from Lisbon. I was relieved by the reprieve which came a few days later and which would give me a few days in England to try my luck. The rest you know from the cables.

I shall be enlisted next week I think, so am very much afraid there won't be leave to go back home on.

I think this country's simply marvellous, I can't get over the exhilaration of being able to think out in the open. I'm sending new photos to show no pieces are missing. I'm actually in glowing health, could fight my weight in wildcats, and have every intention of doing so, have never had so much energy and ambition, and have got back nearly all the pounds I lost. My whole experience I consider to have been invaluable and really wouldn't have missed it for anything. Life is simply *formidable, mon vieux*.

I don't remember any addresses and would be grateful for information as to how to write to people. Also, how many nieces and nephews have I got and belonging to which parents (with names, dates etc.)

Love to you all,
Frank

Part IX

TRAINING IN ENGLAND: 1942-1943
(Age 27-28)

"The need was for unconventional men and women who understood that the Second World War was ideological and fought against terrorists. The guerilla and the agent had to forgo the certainty and tradition of regimental life."

(Lester B. Pearson, *Mike*)

Before the Pickersgill story is resumed something needs first to be said about the history and objectives of the organization into which he had volunteered to enlist. This organization was not concerned with spying or gathering military intelligence (except peripherally), nor with counter-intelligence (the locating and neutralizing of enemy agents), nor with propaganda. Special Operations Executive, or SOE, was organized in London in July, 1940, after the fall of Norway, Denmark, Belgium, Holland, and France. Its special assignment was to build up resistance forces among the shattered populations of Europe, forces that would be equipped by the British for sabotage of important installations, and for harassment of the Nazi armies of occupation. In the desperate situation in Britain in 1940, Winston Churchill was eager to discover some way of fighting back (bombing raids would come later), and hence organized subversive warfare had his enthusiastic endorsement. He called the ministry under which SOE was established, in a memorable phrase, "the Ministry of Ungentlemanly Warfare."

SOE's operations involved sending trained agents, usually by parachute, into countries of occupied Europe which were bristling with hostile police forces and armies – "dropping into the arsenals of Hell" as it was called.[1] These men and women agents would need to know the country and its language and be able to assume false identities as inhabitants. The agent's role, after landing, was to establish contact with trustworthy persons who were willing to take the risks of resistance activities. Such persons would be organized by the agent and trained by him how to receive the weapons, explosives, and funds dropped by parachute from RAF (and later, American) planes, and then how and when to put these weapons and explosives to work against the enemy. Radio contact with headquarters in London was an essential feature of such operations. It was to be especially important about the time of D Day, June 6, 1944, in co-ordinating how the secret armies would emerge to launch a full-scale harassment of German supply lines and troop movements – as was done with telling effect by tying up some eight German divisions, which had to be disengaged from combat against the regular Allied forces, for the duration of the war.

As might be expected, SOE got off to a slow start in 1940-1941, but by the time Pickersgill joined the organization it was expanding rapidly, and by the end of the war it was impressively vast. According to E. H. Cookridge's *Set Europe Ablaze*:

> From the SOE training schools 7,500 men and women were graduated and sent from Britain to Western Europe; 4,000 more were sent from the Mediterranean bases to Italy, Yugoslavia, Greece, Albania, Poland, Czechoslovakia, Hungary, Rumania, and so on.[2]

Like all organizations, especially military organizations, SOE made its quota of mistakes (as some phases of Pickersgill's

[1]See H. Montgomery Hyde, *The Quiet Canadian* (London, 1962), p. 470.

[2](New York, 1967), p. 26. Published by Thomas Y. Crowell.

mission will illustrate), but its overall success is incontestable, as affirmed by Allied generals like Eisenhower, and by the German commander in France, General von Rundstedt, who credited SOE's resistance forces as having shortened the war by six months.[3]

SOE headquarters, after being established in Baker Street, London, was divided into sections each concerned with different countries. Two sections operated in France. One, the "RF" section, consisted of agents from De Gaulle's Free French organization. The other and larger section consisted of agents who were predominantly British subjects by birth, including, of course, Canadians, although there were also some Frenchmen in this section as well. "F" section as it was called, under the command of Colonel Maurice Buckmaster, was the unit in which Pickersgill was to serve. The first "F" section agents began operating in France in the spring of 1941 at the time Pickersgill was still holed up in St. Denis.

Prospective agents for "F" section had a number of special requirements to meet before being selected for training. Ordinarily they were already in the army or air force. Pickersgill, a civilian until November, 1943, was an exception. John Macalister, who was to be his radio operator in France, was more typical. When war broke out, Macalister who had been at Oxford as a Rhodes Scholar from Guelph, Ontario, had joined the British army as a private in 1940. He thus had some years of military life behind him at the time of his volunteering for special service. Obviously a candidate had also to know French and France (Macalister, for example, had a French wife whom he had married in Normandy). Many "F" section persons had lived in France as businessmen (Buckmaster was one). Others had been teachers of French, or former students like Pickersgill. In any event, the connotations of *secret agent* that may be evoked by the world of the James Bond movies are inappro-

[3]See M.R.D. Foot, *S O E in France* (London, Her Majesty's Stationery Office, 1966), p. ix. In general, see also Foot's later study, *Resistance: European Resistance to Nazism: 1939-45* (London, 1977).

priate to characterize most SOE officers. As the historian, M.R.D. Foot states: "All SOE's agents were enemies of one enemy, Hitler. . . . Their motives were as diverse as their origins, but with few exceptions they were patriots – British, French, Polish, Canadian, or American – rather than adventurers or knaves."

Finally, what should go without saying, all candidates had to be volunteers, and even after having been accepted they were assured plenty of free choice to withdraw from the program without loss of face. The emphasis on an agent's attitude towards his role as being the crucial requirement is brought out in an observation by Colonel Buckmaster:

> It is a commonly held idea that the type of subversive warfare in which we were engaged in France demanded the employment of thugs to carry it out. . . . We quickly found out the error of such a theory. . . . We found that the intellectual, the professional man, or the straightforward commercial representative, did much better work in a good cause. He put his heart and soul into outwitting the German forces.[4]

Readers of Frank Pickersgill's letters will recognise how appropriately his state of mind corresponded to Buckmaster's profile of a model agent. Another officer in "F" section, Vera Atkins, head of the training section, has spoken of Pickersgill's "moral strength" as his chief asset for the role. Knowing occupied Europe at first hand, he was fully aware of the hazards likely to be encountered, but his vehement determination to participate is everywhere evident.

The making of a secret agent took some five or six months of intensive training conducted at a series of camps which had been first set up in Britain late in 1940. It is worth noting, in passing, that similar training camps, staffed by SOE instructors, were established at Oshawa, Ontario, as early as December, 1941, with cordial co-operation between the Canadian govern-

---

[4]*Specially Employed* (London, 1952), p. 17.

ment and the special British headquarters in New York headed by William Stephenson.

Before Pickersgill began this course of training he was given three weeks of leave to enjoy himself in London and to get used to wearing an army uniform. It must be said that his sudden initiation into a military career had its lighter sides. All his life he had hated any form of regimentation. One of his newspaper articles from Germany in 1939 reflects his contempt for the parade-square antics of a German Youth Camp. During the Phoney War he once saw a straggling procession of French troops, marching all out of step, with sunflowers stuck in their lapels, and the spectacle had delighted him. Pickersgill was a practising individualist.

His early days in the army showed some of the results of his individualism. His first appearance on the streets of London as an officer in the Canadian Infantry Corps was an epoch-making one. He had not managed to purchase his entire outfit at once, and consequently was attired in his khaki serge but with a civilian's blue shirt and a bright tie. The Military Police, of course, soon picked him up and took him to headquarters for questioning. On another occasion, while drawing his equipment from stores, he horrified the quartermaster sergeant by ingenuously asking to be shown which was the front and which was the back of his helmet. And, as was to be expected, for the first week or so he did everything possible to avoid salutes.

He was nevertheless resolved to adapt his individualism to army life, and as his training program progressed, he was soon at home in his battle-dress uniform and even able to return a salute without wincing. Before he left for France he was promoted to the rank of Captain.

In addition to relaxing during the interval before training Pickersgill visited some Canadian regiments and gave talks about conditions in France. He was shepherded, on this tour, by another officer from Winnipeg, Mervyn Sprung.

In December he began his first three weeks training program at Wanborough Manor near Guildford in Surrey, a strenuous session of physical training, basic weapon training, map reading, and Morse code. Peter Churchill, in his *Duel of Wits*, provides a vivid account of the exhausting pace demanded of the trainees. In Churchill's group of fourteen, four dropped from the program at this point, and, of the remaining ten, only three completed the whole sequence of courses.

After leave in London for Christmas Pickersgill was sent to the highlands of Scotland for the month of January, 1943. This training camp was located in the rugged wilderness of west Inverness at Loch Ailort. In a letter Pickersgill patriotically described the area as "the nearest equivalent to the Lake of the Woods that could be imagined in Europe." Other trainees were less complimentary about this bleak location. They found the foggy dampness, on twenty-five mile cross-country exercises, to be execrable. The inculcation of toughness in Scotland included instruction in techniques of unarmed combat, which Pickersgill would himself put to good use a year or more later in a Paris prison. Also included were extensive practice in the use of explosives for sabotaging railways and machinery. And by the end of this course, as Foot remarks, most agents "would have got to know their companions thoroughly well, have begun to call them *tu* – an almost universal practice among sub-agents in the field – and have started to get the hang of what they might be called on to do when they got to France."[5] After the war a statue commemorating those who had undergone this rigorous highlands training, both commandos and SOE agents, was erected on a hilltop in the area.

Because secret agents on missions abroad generally operated in pairs, each trainee in Scotland was encouraged to seek a team-mate with whom he would feel especially congenial, and the two would thereafter practise working together. Pickersgill had happily already discovered his team-mate before their course of training began. This was a young Canadian lawyer, John Macalister, who (as was previously mentioned) was to serve as his radio-operator in France. In the course of their training together the two men became extremely close friends,

5 Foot, p. 55.

and they were to be constant companions until their deaths. Macalister and Pickersgill were virtually the same age (Macalister was a few months older), and their feeling of congeniality of temperament was reinforced by interests they shared in all manner of subjects. Like Pickersgill, Macalister had behind him an outstandingly brilliant academic record. In 1937 he had graduated in law from University College, Toronto (where he had also played football), and enrolled at New College, Oxford, as a Rhodes Scholar. During his final year at Toronto he could have encountered Pickersgill, who was also a student there at that time, but so far as we know, the two men did not meet before late 1942. At Oxford, in the spring of 1939, Macalister graduated first in his class of 142 law students, a class reported to have been made up of prospective lawyers from many parts of the world. He continued further studies at the Institute of Comparative Law in Paris in 1939, and in 1940 took his Oxford degree (First Class) and passed his Bar Final Examination in England with the Certificate of Honour.

At the outbreak of war, Macalister was in France, where he had married a French girl. He at once sought to enlist in the French army but was not accepted because his eyesight did not meet the requirements at the time. Despite this minor disability he was accepted by the British army, in July, 1940, and served for two years as a private and non-commissioned officer in the Field Security Service before volunteering for training as a secret agent at the same time as Pickersgill entered the service.

This review of Macalister's career and interests would suggest that the two men might have readily become good friends even under peacetime conditions, but in wartime the warmth of such a friendship was to be intensified by their daily sharing together the experiences of their strenuous program of training.

After successfully completing the course in Scotland, the two men entered the third stage of the program, in February, 1943. This third stage involved practice in parachute jumping from low altitudes. Their school was located at Ringway, near Manchester. Four or five jumps were required, one by night. Agents were taught to jump in pairs, ten men to a plane, and were coached from the ground by a jump-instructor calling out to them over a loudspeaker. Pickersgill's letter describing his first jump is certainly a classic record of the experience.

The final stage, extending into May, took place on an estate at Beaulieu on the south coast of England near the New Forest. Emphasis here was on how to carry on in France in order to evade detection by the Gestapo or by French collaborators, the use of identity papers and ration books, and the kind of security to be expected from an agent if captured and interrogated and tortured. One amusing sideline of the Beaulieu training, reported by Peter Churchill, was the employment of some seductive pickup girls, planted in pubs in the area, who could test out an agent's capacities not to talk indiscriminately. Overall, agents were coached at Beaulieu to blot out their British identities and to live out a new French identity, symbolised by the French clothing they would wear (which had been meticulously put together for them), and a reliable demonstration of French eating habits such as enthusiastically soaking up the gravy on a plate with pieces of bread – no problem for Pickersgill.

Pickersgill's new *alter ego* was to be called *Bertrand*. His radio-operator, Macalister, was called *Valentin*. These new identities were even tried out in London. One of their friends records having gone to a London Buttery expecting to meet Macalister in his Canadian Lieutenant's uniform. Instead she was confronted with "this funny little Frenchman with a tartan tie." Pickersgill, even though not little, was similarly disguised. Although he did not care at all (as he told Alison Grant) for the incongruously drab personality he was required to assume by his cover-story as Bertrand, there is no doubt that by June 13, as he wrote in his last letter, Bertrand was "raring to go."

Of course the making of a secret agent did not consist exclusively of strenuous training sessions. A fair amount of time was free for leave, and agents were encouraged to locate themselves in London in congenial and secure quarters. During his eight months in England Pickersgill had the good fortune to be the welcome guest in one such establishment. Almost immediately after his arrival in London in October, 1942, he had looked up Kay Moore and Mary Mundle, whom he had known at the Hotel Lenox in Paris. They had rented a house at 54A Walton Street, in the Knightsbridge-Chelsea area, which they were sharing with Alison Grant, a former art student from Toronto whom he met here for the first time. Because all three women were working hard in War Office roles (two of them had important jobs in SOE and the other, Alison Grant, was in MI5) the household was certainly a secure one. The house itself was a comfortable place, three storeys high, featuring a large living room with a fireplace, and extra bedrooms for SOE guests, one of these in the attic being used by Pickersgill. Here he was encouraged to "fatten up" after his arrival, and it was here, in subsequent months, that his leaves were spent, often accompanied by his team-mate Macalister. Rather than going out to eat in crowded Soho restaurants, the two visitors preferred long talk sessions around the Walton Street fireplace – "Russian evenings" as they were described. At this "Canada House Annex," as the house came to be called, there were also occasional parties, informal gatherings of an interesting and assorted crowd of people, of mixed military rank, where there was good talk to be enjoyed. The talk was varied and often hilarious; moreover reference to secret agent missions was rigidly excluded. Pickersgill's good spirits and restless energy made him the centre of an extraordinarily lively group, as the following account, supplied by Kay Moore, will illustrate:

> Frank brought a breath of new life into our home. Everything to him was of interest, intense interest and delight – even a bus ride down Piccadilly fascinated him. He was most anxious to hear everything about everybody. He said, I remember, that he had two years of cinemas to make up and he was always disappearing into the distant suburbs to see some old film. We had in the house the back numbers of *New Yorker* for about a year and he devoured them from cover to cover.
>
> His talk ranged over a most incredible variety of

subjects; and never was there so much talking in our house. He seemed impatient of any time we spent away from the fire in the evening. Again and again we would state that there were household tasks which had to be done in our all too meagre spare time. I remember one evening when we were drinking tea – he had learned to brew innumerable cups of tea in the camp – and did so at our house at all hours of the day and night – he treated us to an exposition on the globular content of Mother's milk and why it was hence more digestible than cow's milk; immediately afterwards he discussed certain Tibetan practices in some religious orders, followed up with a discussion of the black masses practised in some sects in Lyon and Paris. We teased him frequently about his incredible knowledge – and cried out sometimes 'useless fact Number 2389'; this because he one day admitted that when he read or learned a thing he never forgot it.

He enlisted in the Canadian army, coming back one day to the house very cross and disgruntled. He said he had had a series of intelligence tests – a thing he hated. The tests had apparently consisted of a long paper with pictures of various tools and gadgets and the examinee had to name each. He said with some rage that opposite one he had written: 'I do not know the name of this gadget in French or in English, but I used one to escape from prison with.' We soothed him with murmurs of modern mechanisation being necessary evils in all armies and so on.

At one of his courses at P.T. he slipped and cut his knee on a stone and he was obliged for a few weeks to go about with a walking stick. He told us one day that elderly ladies frequently offered him a seat in buses, obviously under the impression that he was a wounded hero recovering from Dieppe. According to him, he always assumed a fatuous and modestly demure expression that was supposed to be read 'Anything for my country ma'am.' He often wanted to say at the end of the ride that he had cut his knee on a stone during P.T., but couldn't bring himself to un-

mask his 'wound' and discomfit the would-be bene-
factor.

One Sunday when we were off duty, we were all
trying to spring clean the house. It was a sunny day
and Frank was out on our balcony shaking a rug into
the street (contrary to London by-laws). He was in
civies that day. An irate woman passing shouted up
at him: 'Young man, you'd do better to go into
uniform.' This again delighted him.

He commented on the fact that he did not feel like
reading at all. I do not think that any of us ever had
the energy to be profound or intellectual about anything.... Speaking of the future – which he rarely
did – he seemed increasingly against the idea of going
into External Affairs. He seemed to have undergone
a metamorphosis (according to him at the time of his
escape) from a thinker into a man of action....
Once, when speaking of St. Augustine, Frank said he
and Mademoiselle Ballu were two of the greatest
influences in his life. He also spoke much of his
family, particularly of his mother and Jack. We always felt we knew his mother well; he had the ten-
derest love and devotion for her.

In the spring, the week before he was parachuted,
he was with us.... A few nights before he left, Alison and I took him to dinner at Prunier's where we
had a slap-up meal and we paid much to the shocked
surprise of the waiter. Frank sat unconcerned,
brawny, tough, and huge, and in wonderful spirits.
He asked us when the man went off with the bill:
'Do you suppose he thinks I am a kept man?' It was
the sort of situation Frank loved.

This account of the farewell dinner at Prunier's takes on an
added dimension when it transpires that for the previous six
months Frank Pickersgill had been deeply in love with one of
his two hostesses that evening, Alison Grant. By Christmas,
1942, his short-lived engagement to Jacqueline Grant had been
broken off, amicably, and a much more serious and intense
relationship had developed with Alison Grant (no relation of
Jacqueline's). In view of the precarious future, of which they

were both keenly aware, there was no talk, this time, of marriage or even of plans of what might happen after the war. Instead there was the here and now of shared interests coupled with a radiant happiness stemming from mutual attraction.

When they first met on a London street in October, Alison Grant noted that he was then "terribly thin and hollow-eyed, but with such a sparkle in his eye." By Christmas-time, this acquaintance had blossomed into a relationship that could itself be described as a sparkling one. The happiness of their encounters during the short six month period of the remainder of his stay in England was of course heightened (as has been suggested) by an awareness of his impending mission. One of Alison Grant's recollections will illustrate:

> His toughness I should mention as unlike John Macalister's. Frank knew exactly what he was doing and getting into. We went to see a film called 'Assignment in Brittany' with Jean Pierre Aumont, all about a double agent. It got pretty grim, and I began to feel uncomfortable, and suggested we leave. Frank said quite coldly: 'If I can stand it surely you can.' That was that.

Alison Grant was the last of his London friends to see him before his departure. After a taxi-ride, they said good-bye on a streetcorner, and she watched him walk off in his drab Bertrand suit about which he had characteristically continued to lament and grumble even on this final occasion.

Kay Moore's account, also recently written, rounds out these London episodes:

> After Frank left us, quite apart from the varying degrees of love and affection which we had for him, I don't think any departure left three girls' hearts so miserable for themselves, but curiously so happy for him as he was doing what he wanted to do with all his being. He had left too in tremendous high spirits, relaxed and not nervous, not apprehensive, deeply content and sure of his mission and himself.

**

To MRS. SARA PICKERSGILL

Canada House, London,
Nov. 12, 1942

Dear Fambly,

Well everything is all set. I'm in the Canadian Army as a
lieutenant (already receiving pay but starting out with a bit of
leave, which is nice of them) – will be lent to the British
(toward the end of next week) then training, then job. I've
been approved by Colonel Simpson, Vincent Massey, Pierre
Dupuy, and General Montague (I mean my decision has been
approved by above). My medical examination revealed A-1
category health, which isn't bad after twenty months in a
concentration camp, *and* the rest – so you see no one need
worry about my health. But they gave me an intelligence test
and my rating there was very low!

I'm staying with Kay Moore, a Scotch girl named Mary
Mundle, and a Canadian girl (niece of Vincent Massey) named
Alison Grant whom I think you know, Jack. Alison is a
frightfully good thing and terribly amusing; and of course Kay
has been simply wonderful to me. If any of you see Major
Moore you might tell him how nice Kay has been to me. I pay
them a pound a week and up till now it has been one long
party.

Last night they had General Montague in to dinner (that
was where I met him) and we had an evening of reminiscing
about Ashern, which he knows well. He used to stay at the
hotel across from the station – who ran it? I've forgotten (all
this, I gather, before the last war) and he knew Bob Garson
very well. He's a dynamo of exuberance and we got on like a
house on fire; he is exactly what Tom will be like in twenty
years I imagine. I've also seen and had dinner with
Brockington but I had an uneasy, tracked feeling that he was
trying to pry information out of me and I was on my guard all
evening as I'm scared stiff of these news and radio blokes after
"stories." I still jump every time I see a policeman – why I
don't know as my experience with them, aside from the

Gestapo and the Portuguese police, has been all to the good – but I guess it's just a complex. J. B. McGeachy, who was there too, said I had all the earmarks of a captive anyway in the way I behaved – which was a bit disconcerting.

By the way, I should be terribly pleased to get a few of those duty-free cigarettes from home, now that I have a right to them. I think if they're sent: Lieut. Pickersgill, C.M.H.Q., London, that I'll get them O.K. – they will be forwarded to wherever I am. For one accustomed to French cigarettes Canadian ones seem the next strongest, which is rather queer. English are almost unsmokable. American are a bit better, but Sweet Caporals are the best – second best to Gauloises Bleues that I've discovered.

This period of quietly doing nothing is allowing me to catch up a bit on movies and plays. I saw a very good play of Lilian Hellman's called *The Watch on the Rhine* day before yesterday. She must be pretty good – an American writing about a Nazi Europe she doesn't know at first hand, yet it was sufficiently authentic that I found it very moving, and I guess I know what the score is. I shall now go to see *The Little Foxes*, by her also.

Did I tell you that in order to raise money for the escape I sold almost everything from your last parcel I received in St. Denis? I hope you don't mind, I think getting out of that hole was worth it. Anyway I couldn't have carried them away with me. However one thing I was sorry about was that the parcel with the boots in it didn't arrive before I had left. I had the most awful footwear problem until I got to Portugal; I was wearing shoes given me by the Secours National for about a month until they collapsed utterly, and I had to spend the last couple of months and the voyage to Lisbon in a pair of mouldy old borrowed sandals that tore what was left of my socks to pieces and raised some great callouses all over my feet. And now I suppose some lousy little Jerrie is wearing my boots.

I wanted to make a will leaving all parcels to a couple of friends in the camp, and post it to the Commandant just before leaving Occupied France – but the lads were afraid it might implicate them, and no notice probably would have been taken of it anyway: he would merely have been furious thinking I was pulling his leg.

Oh – if you can send razor blades they would be much appreciated, also a small quantity, some day, of maple syrup which I'd give anything to eat again!

The food here is marvellous. I can hardly believe my eyes, or my stomach, and as I said in my last letter I've got back nearly all my weight, and have never felt better in my life. I should be pleased to have a certain number of recent photos (small ones) of people. My nice picture of Mother I had to leave in the camp as it was too big to carry away.

I'm terribly anxious to hear from you all and hope you all write.

Love to all,
Frank

To J. W. PICKERSGILL
Canadian Military Headquarters, London,
Nov. 30, 1942

Dear Jack:

I've been rather long about replying to your letter which I got as I was moving about the country with – Mervyn Sprung! – visiting various regiments, and I didn't want to write until I had a permanent address. I was terribly pleased to get your letter and longed for it to be about twice as long. God how I had been starving for real news of home. . . .

I'm still having a wonderful time and enjoyed my sojourn with the Canadian Army immensely. Sprung has I think improved quite a lot: he smokes, drinks and swears, in fact is becoming almost human. And the Canadians, officers and men, warmed my heart terrifically. I hadn't realized what a pleasure compatriots en masse can give occasionally. Spent a very enjoyable day last week with the Régiment de Maisonneuve and we got along like a house on fire. I began to wonder if I hadn't been wrong about French Canadians.

Did you know Alison Grant? She is certainly one of the most amusing people I've ever met – and we have a riotous time making New Yorkerish surrealist jokes at one another.

If anything in the way of clothes or rare foods (orange juice, etc), *could* be sent in parcels to civilians, the following people have been pretty wonderful to me at some stage or other of my chequered career: Madeline Probert; Kay Moore, Mary Mundle, Alison Grant in London; and (what a joy to be able soon to do something for them); M. et Mme Henry Robillot, Bourse du Commerce, Casablanca, Morocco. Robillot is one of my best friends, and his wife is Fleurette Maurette. How marvellous is the news from North Africa. I'm sorry that rat Darlan has to be used, but Giraud has shown himself to be an even greater man than ever. Gosh what a guy! I feel something closely resembling hero-worship for Giraud.

Well, I can't go beyond this page without paying another threepence or something on stamps and anyway the dinner-gong is just about to sound. I'm just starting my instruction – and everything seems quite exciting.

My love to Margaret. I'm writing to Tom and his Margaret after supper. And my greetings to my small niece.

Love,
Frank

To THOMAS PICKERSGILL
C.M.H.Q., London
December 1, 1942

Dear Tom and Margaret:

I hope this letter brings forth a reply; I'm dying for letters from home. Jack's long one was certainly a joy but hasn't satisfied my long-standing hunger. Can't you get the Canadian Government Tom to send you and Jack over on some sort of half-ass mission or other for a week or two? What sort of work are you doing now? And since when? And how is my young namesake and does he talk yet?

I've now begun my instruction so I'm back to collective life – but God what a difference from a year ago! 1942 will have been an extremely full year for me, as far as varied experiences are concerned, and probably on the whole the best I've ever spent or could ever hope to spend – though I rather fancy I'll go on for a long time getting an abnormal kick out of life. After St. Denis, Paris seemed like heaven, then Unoccupied France seemed even better, then Portugal was another improvement, then here – it was positively delirious, and getting better all the time – except the climate which almost drives me nerts. Jack says youse peoples are thinking of sending me stuff. Thanks in advance, which means *please* send me *lots* of cigarettes (Sweet Caps), a certain amount of peanut butter & orange juice, woollen socks and the odd khaki shirt, size 15 collar preshrunk or 15½ not preshrunk. I've already said all this to Mother. I don't want to ruin everybody but I certainly would appreciate cigarettes in fairly constant flow and substantial quantities, as I detest English cigarettes.

I certainly enjoyed the time spent with the Canadian forces – it almost gave me the illusion of being back home for a while. They're certainly a nice lot of chaps – at least the ones I met are.

Well I must dash off a letter to Elizabeth before supper so cheerio and write.

Love,
Frank

To MRS. K. SEABORNE [Elizabeth Pickersgill]
C.M.H.Q., London,
December 1, 1942

Dear Ducky:

I want to dash this off before supper. . . . Do write, and often. I can't tell you what a thrill it was getting letters from home when I was in St. Denis, but I always felt a bit frustrated by their length and lack of detail and had a feeling people didn't want to hurt my feelings by telling me what they were doing, though in fact it would have had the opposite effect. Three things were good for our morale in that place, the letters from home, the Red Cross parcels and the R.A.F. raids.

Here I'm having a glorious time more or less learning how to behave like a military gent and in general enjoying myself. As I've just said to Tom, God what a change from this time last year. I sometimes find it difficult to believe I'm really awake, the whole of the year 1942 seems so incredible.

Is Ken in good form? Give him all the best from me, and is it true that Mother is going to spend the winter with you?

Love,
Frank

[The following is a fragment of a letter written in early December, 1942.]

To J. W. PICKERSGILL

I was interested in the reactions of the officers and NCO's of the Régiment de Maisonneuve, who were all Gaulliste, even the padre, while certain English Canadians I've met over here have been naive enough to be Petainiste, or, at any rate, to swallow the old line about Petain's 'doing all he could' – American influence, I suppose.

I believe whole-heartedly that the Fighting French are the only recognisable people. Unhappily I don't know much about them here in London – I think there are some good men and some very bad ones, and I hear some very nasty stories of intrigue and political plotting. But that is relatively unimportant as there isn't the slightest chance of the Fourth Republic turning into a dictatorship by De Gaulle's committee. The thing is that De Galle and his Fighting French movement have an importance as a *symbol* and a rallying point which I don't think can be imagined or realised unless one has been in France under the Nazis. De Gaulle is the flag and that's all there is to it. The appeal is patriotic and not political. The men who are resisting and risking their lives, or giving up their lives, are not doing it for their health and are certainly not going to let themselves be walked over when France is liberated.

The greatest problem in France when I left was the problem (in the Non Occupied zone) of Vichy groups who were beginning to doubt the possibility of ultimate German victory and were trying to get ready, not to drive the Germans out, but to seize power by force while the real patriots were occupied with getting rid of the Germans.

With a few notable exceptions, the real resisters were simple people – the working class (particularly railwaymen – what a marvellous lot of people!), the *poor* peasants (not the kulaks, who are Vichysois) and the very small bourgeoisie.

To GEORGE FORD (Nanaimo)

C.M.H.Q., London,
December 16, 1942

Dear George:

I can't tell you how pleased I was to get your letter and I've got my fingers crossed in the hopes that you make it over here and we can have a chat. What you said about writing to a ghost was good: I've been feeling like that too about letters written to Canada since my return to life. It's rather like shouting into a fog.

I got one of your letters in the camp and now I must congratulate you on your marriage. I take it I'll like your wife.

Give her my best wishes but you'd better warn her about me so she won't be too alarmed when we meet. The news of Angus MacDonald's marriage quite floored me. What is his wife like? Incidentally, it is vaguely in the cards that I also may get married before many moons. – I got a marvellous letter from Mlle Ballu in Winnipeg. She always rallies, doesn't she? It brought tears to my eyes. How she managed instinctively to guess my feelings – about staying here, doing something active and so on – before really hearing anything about me I don't know. She must know me pretty shrewdly.

I'm having a wonderful time. The Canadian Army received me with open arms and proceeded to commission me as a full-blown lieutenant. They have lent me to the British, however my address continues to be C.M.H.Q. – mainly for cigarette purposes! I'm now training for eventual liaison work and having an absolutely fascinating time. I agree with you about the difficulties of long-term political speculation while in the army – one's mind no longer runs along those channels – but a good many things remain at the back of my mind to act as dynamos. However, learning how to operate a Bren gun is not particularly conducive to deciding whether the political expediency of using Darlan in North Africa is worth throwing a lot of fundamental principles to the four winds. He's undoubtedly the worst swine of the lot – worse even then Laval – but there you are, these problems will take care of themselves, however incensed one may feel about some features of them.

Occasionally I get a few minutes to go on reading *For Whom the Bell Tolls* – which I find pretty impressive. I never thought he'd outdo *Farewell to Arms* but I think he has. Trying vaguely to catch up with current literary, political and film trends after two and a half years is difficult, but easier as far as literature goes, because apart from the Hemingway virtually nothing worth reading seems to have been written in the last two years.

This isn't much of a letter "after all these years" as the books say, but I also feel the need to get into the swing of things before letting myself go. One final thing: no more indy.

The enforced rest cure given my stomach must have done it good. For the rest, I haven't changed much physically – though rather sharply in certain ways.

Goomby,
Pick

To MRS. SARA PICKERSGILL (Calgary)

54A Walton St., London,
Dec. 30, 1942

Dear Mother and Elizabeth:

I just got your letters and was certainly bucked by them, and to see how everyone has seen my point about staying over here. I'm in town at the moment, on leave for a few days, at Kay's, Mary's and Alison's as usual – and will be pulling out again on New Year's Day. I'll be glad to get back – leave is very nice but runs furiously into money.

I had lunch yesterday with Nick and George Ignatieff. I knew Nick in Toronto (he's now a captain in the Royal Canadian Artillery) but hadn't known George, who is Vincent Massey's secretary and a very interesting chap indeed. We had an extremely pleasant world problem-solving session at what I had described as "a dump called Simpson's in the Strand"– which, it turns out, is one of the world's more famous restaurants. How travel broadens one! I told you in my last letter that I had got your parcel sent about Nov. 10. It certainly did please me.

I had Christmas dinner at the Massey's, which would have been very pleasant if I hadn't just got in on leave with an attack of what is called gastritis (stomach flu I think) which has rather spoiled my leave. They showed three National Film Board pictures about life in Canada which were very well done and made me homesick. One about the Peace River got me the most.

I can't imagine Ann Livingstone submitting to military

Some friends: Top left – Robert Lapassade; top right – John Macalister; bottom left – Alison Grant; bottom right – Kay Moore; top p. 233 – George Ford

discipline. But then I couldn't have imagined myself doing it –
though admittedly I got off with the easy end of the stick right
from the start. However, I even get up and do P.T. at 7.00 a.m.
without turning a hair – though I sometimes think my dead
past must be turning over in its grave.

I haven't been able to see this play *Arsenic and Old Lace* yet
and am afraid I won't get to it this leave. I'm sorry about that.
Oh – another thing that would be useful is one of those
woollen skull cap things that come down over the ears, as it's
beginning to get nippy.

Tell me, Elizabeth, have you still got a car? with tires? I see
such lurid jokes in the *New Yorker* from time to time that I
begin to wonder... They say there are no cars over here and I
guess as far as private cars are concerned it's true – but there
seem to be an awful lot on the street ready to mow you down,
in comparison with the continent! All the best to Ken –

Love,
Frank

To MLLE C. BALLU (Winnipeg)

C.M.H.Q., London,
Jan. 5, 1943

Dear Mademoiselle:

Excuse my being so long in answering your letters but I've been simply swamped in the welter of activity. I can't tell you how happy your letters made me. Aside from my own family I really think that you are the only person in Canada that I feel I have to live up to, if you see what I mean. That is – when I think of you I feel some muscles straining as I think "I must not let her down" or "I wonder if she would approve."

I am terribly pleased the family approved of my decision. I couldn't have gone back to Canada – much as I would have enjoyed seeing you all. I'm afraid I'm feeling too belligerent to be happy 4,000 miles away from the Nazis.

Do you remember Mervyn Sprung? He is over here, an Intelligence Officer in the Canadian army and has turned into an extremely good soldier. I used to think he was pretty terrible – but he's improved vastly – or I have! Another person who is doing absolutely marvellous work over here is Kay Moore. She's worth her weight in gold and deserves a V.C. or very nearly.

I'm still going through the business of training and finding it intensely interesting and not making quite such an ass of myself as I expected. How is Mrs. Jones?

Love,
Frank

P.S. Merci de m'avoir tutoyé. Ca m'a fait venir les larmes aux yeux.

F. H. D. P., 1942

To HELEN MAGILL

C.M.H.Q., London,
Jan. 12, 1943

Dear Helen:

I was terribly bucked to get your letter today (my God don't they take an infernal length of time to get here?).I hope you'll go on writing often. I'm so far from having reached the point of "ignoring my past" that the urgent necessity of my going back to Canada when the war is over becomes more apparent to me every day.

My work here hasn't started. I'm still being eddicated – that involves pretty strenuous work I can tell you, so much so that at times I realize with a shock that I'm not as young as I once was and that twenty months in the hoose-gow did have a slightly rusting effect on my iron constitution. (You needn't mention that little point to the family!)

But I'm enjoying it as I've never enjoyed anything in my life before. You know, Helen, I've been in a permanent state of exhilaration since March 8 last (the date on which I made my get-away) on the crest of a wave which kept getting higher and higher as each frontier was crossed, and which now, instead of subsiding, seems to be going on up. I don't know where it's going to land me, but it's damned good while it lasts.

I eagerly await a letter from Kay Sinclair, though won't know what to answer as I've forgotten how to write letters – being still inhibited by those twenty-five-line missives perused by the Nazi censors that I used to write.

If you see Margie Adams give her deux bons baisers de ma part. If not, write her a note. I've so little time I can't write much – but I wish people would write occasionally – even if I don't answer. I must stop.

Love,
Frank

To J. W. PICKERSGILL

C.M.H.Q., London,
Jan. 28, 1943

Dear Jack:

Just received 1,000 Sweet Caps from you, 500 Winchesters from Elizabeth and your letters of Xmas eve. I was delighted with all.

I'm just finishing off a month's course which has been about the most enjoyable piece of education I've ever received. In a sense it has been a real holiday as we've been parked in the nearest equivalent to the Lake of the Woods that could be imagined in Europe, and I have made the most of it. I've some excellent pals, and met some really splendid men in the last three months, among whom the C.O. here whom I'll be bloody sorry to leave.

The news is certainly cheering. Amid all the good war news the business of Giraud and De Gaulle meeting bucks me considerably. Perhaps the political "histoires" in North Africa will come to an end, though I wish somebody would do to Peyrouton what was done to Darlan.

I must get ready for dinner. Under the influence of good food, fresh air and strenuous exercise I'm turning into the picture of health. Love to Margaret, and to Tom and Margaret.

Frank

To J. W. PICKERSGILL

[The following is a fragment from a letter which was sent as a secret document. It seemed such excellent writing that extracts were made and held in safe-keeping until the end of the war.]
Feb. 16, 1943

Dear Jack:

.... Last week was quite the most exhilarating and exhausting of my life. We were at the paratroop school. I did four jumps, three day ones and one night one. It is absolutely marvellous. The training, which lasts a day and a half, is worse than the real thing.

But I can tell you that when we piled into the plane and the R.A.F. despatcher had hitched our static lines to the plane I felt pretty awful. We sat for about ten minutes while the plane took off and flew over to the landing park. I've never been so scared in my life. I was third to jump, and I sat there muttering to myself: "Head up, legs together, hands by your sides; head up, legs together, hands by your sides" which was about the only thing that kept me from rolling around and screaming with terror. Then the first pair went out and I had to move over right beside the hole while the plane circled round the field. Those were the worst two minutes as I was terrified that I would inadvertently glance through the hole and was sure if I did that I'd funk it. So I kept my eyes glued to the despatcher's hand. He yelled Action Stations and I got my feet into the hole and from then on I wasn't afraid any more, which is quite curious. I was conscious of absolutely nothing but the despatcher's hand. He brought it down yelling GooooOOOOO so loud it fairly blew me out of the plane, and my only feeling as I saw myself falling through the hole was one of complete relief to be rid of the god-damned plane. Then three seconds of absolute heaven. The displacement of air made by the plane causes a 100 m.p.h. wind all round the plane – this gale is called the slipstream – so that the parachutist, instead of dropping like lead until the chute opens, finds himself carried along on this wind, in a horizontal direction, absolutely riding on air. I came out beautifully from the plane and hit the slipstream in such a way that I found myself floating along on my back in the gale, 800 feet off the ground, as though I were lying on a feather bed, watching the plane drift off. Then a very slight tug all over the body and I looked still further up and saw the most incredibly beautiful sight in the world which is a 'chute opening. I swung my arms up to take hold of the rigging lines and suddenly the gale was no longer. Absolute peace and silence. I looked down and saw the ground gently approaching from a long way off, and suddenly out of this, a still, small voice saying, "All right No. I, a nice exit – now keep your legs together and take up a good position in the air" . . . then suddenly, "Careful No. 1, get ready to land" – and suddenly the ground was a few yards away and coming up at an uncomfortable speed. Then WHAM and I hit the ground, rolled over, and was on my feet without feeling even a bump, and this time it was the ground that felt vaguely unreal for a split second. Then about two hours of the most intense elation – an intensity of feeling such as I've never experienced. Then complete exhaustion for the rest of the day. Such a variety and intensity of emotion within such a short time is very tiring indeed.

With the other three jumps there was no more fear – just a certain nervousness in the pit of the stomach, but the elation was as great as ever.

But it is a tremendous experience – and has given me a lot of confidence. It does require a certain amount of guts to jump – and it requires quite a lot of discipline and self-control to jump well – i.e., not to fling the arms up wildly as one is going out of the plane, but to keep rigidly to attention.

I jumped well – and I must confess to feeling a bit pleased with myself, especially as I wasn't sure right up to the last minute whether I mightn't get cold feet and refuse. Some do. And it's marvellous, once you do get out of the bloody plane. It's the nearest thing to a perfect dream that could be imagined. I really feel deeply sorry for anyone who hasn't done it. . . .

Love,
Frank

To THOMAS PICKERSGILL

C.M.H.Q., London
February 22, 1943

Dear Tom:

I'm sorry to have been so infernally long about answering
yours of P.E.I. – and thanking you and everyone for all the
parcels, cigarettes and letters and the way everyone has been
rallying generally.

Your letter has bucked me up immensely. . . . You're right
Tom: I had a pretty unpleasant two years, though I'm glad
now to have had the experience – and I must say it has made
me terrifically appreciative of the pleasant things in existence.

Don't fail to write as often as you can find the time. Love to
all the family including my second nephew. Many congrats.

Frank

To MRS. SARA PICKERSGILL (Winnipeg)

C.M.H.Q.,
[March, 1943]

Dear Mother:

I just got your scarf which is lovely. The only thing is that
the winter is so warm I hardly need one – however, it'll
certainly be useful next winter if the war is still on.

And if it isn't I'll be back in Canada, I hope, as I certainly
intend rushing back home as soon as it's over if I can.

I'm still enjoying myself hugely and my morale is as good as
ever. It's now over a year since I said good-bye to my kind
keepers and left without their permission. I celebrated my re-
birthday on March 7 as a matter of fact. I hope I can spend
my second re-birthday at home!

240

Give Tante Céline my love if you write her and tell her I'll write again as soon as I have time and material to write about!

Love,
Frank

To GEORGE FORD

C.M.H.Q.,
April 29, 1943

Dear George:

As a letter writer I'm getting less and less successful in my old age. However, as you suggested, I've seen Andy Cowan (having just had a bit of leave, me I mean, not him) several times and consider him a hell of a good type. The first time I met him I wasn't much impressed – seemed like a nice fellow but a bit slow but *that* impression soon changed. I'm rather glad to find I agree with him about most things as he is fairly crushing in his disagreements.

Life is still rushing along at a pleasant sort of pace – what you say about army post-graduate courses certainly rings a responding bell in me, though I must admit to finding the material slightly more interesting than the nebulosities of the university world. I hope you manage to get overseas here and when you do drag old Jackson with you. I would certainly like to hear from him. Incidentally, there's a man from Winnipeg here that I've been avoiding like the plague as he apparently has an urge to discuss "my experiences" with me.

Did you hear that my marriage did not come off? I guess I'm just not the marrying type. Well, cheerio, and I hope to see you ere long.

Pick

To MLLE C. BALLU (University of Manitoba)

C.M.H.Q., London,
May 18, 1943

Dear Tante Céline:

I suppose your year will be finishing pretty soon, I
frequently wonder what sort of prodigies have taken our place
– if they are still as recalcitrant as we were. Who goes to
University these days? I'm so out of touch now that it's
positively frightening. And at the same time I feel more
Canadian – or North American – and more drawn than ever
back that way. I shall certainly take the first available boat
back when the war is over, if only for a short time.

After a pleasant week-end in London I'm back in the
country which is even pleasanter. I've certainly been living like
a king for the past seven months. I think my faculties for
enjoying life have been making up for lost time!

All the best to any old friends you may come across.

Love,
Frank

To J. W. PICKERSGILL

London,
June 13, 1943

Dear Jack:

I'm in town for the day. My training is completed.

I've just made a will which I deposit here, with a letter
attached containing a number of recommendations for you to
pay my various and sundry debts out of my assets, which, I
presume, include that insurance policy you have.

I'm in very good form and raring to go.

Will you pass on the gist of this letter to Mother? Kay owes
you a letter and will write regularly.

Love,
Frank

Part X

RETURN TO THE CONTINENT:
Romorantin, Blois, Fresnes, Rawicz:
June, 1943 – March 1944
(age 28)

*"The Nazi tyranny was a derangement so
complete and unprecedented, so irrevocably
beyond the premises of reason and decency, that
it is no wonder if historians have not known
quite how to handle it . . . [with its] fearful
qualities of singlemindedness and savagery."*
                    (Leon Wieseltier, TLS, 1977)

-i-

In the house in London where Pickersgill had been so thoroughly at home, there was a room known as "Frank's room." It had borne the same rather tousled marks of his occupancy as the many rooms he had lived in from Winnipeg to Warsaw, the usual scattered books, papers, and clothes – indications of an individualist asserting his independence from too much regimentation and order. After his departure, new visitors to the house sometimes enquired after him and were told simply that he was "away." It was hoped that he would be back "soon." In Canada also, his family had to discourage enquiries concerning his whereabouts. They had virtually no definite word of him for twenty months.

243

On the night of June 15-16, 1943, almost a year before Allied troops landed on the beaches of Normandy, Captain Frank Pickersgill, accompanied by Lieutenant John Macalister, parachuted successfully back into occupied Europe to set about the task for which he had been training so enthusiastically. The mission assigned to him was to establish a new resistance section north of Paris around Sedan, near the border between Lorraine and Belgium. The code name for his projected new section was ARCHDEACON. It had been prearranged that instead of being parachuted immediately into what was designated to become his own territory, he would be dropped in the valley of the river Cher in the Sologne district. The landing-field was in the vicinity of Romorantin-Valencay, about a hundred miles south of Paris, where there were experienced "F" section receptionists to meet him and his operator. His orders were to lie low for a few days before being driven by car to catch the train north to Paris for a rendezvous at the Gare d'Austerlitz, on June 21, with the chief organizer of the whole Paris region, Major Francis Suttill. It is of interest to note that Suttill's code name, PROSPER was derived from Prosper of Aquitaine, a fifth century disciple of St. Augustine, Pickersgill's favourite writer. Suttill had started organizing an extensive network after landing in France on October 1, 1942. A lawyer in civil life, with a clear head for planning, Suttill had so far been phenomenally successful. By the time of Pickersgill's landing there were 10,000 men in the PROSPER network, divided into some sixty sections extending far and wide outside Paris as well as within the city. ARCHDEACON was to be an additional strand to be attached to this rapidly expanding force. But the projected meeting at the Gare d'Austerlitz, at which Pickersgill would have received final instructions from his chief, never took place.

For it was unfortunately at this very time that the Germans set about smashing the whole PROSPER network, an operation which they carried out with devastating effectiveness. On June 22, they arrested the network's second-in-command, Gilbert Norman, who was imprisoned and later sent to Buchenwald in the same group as Pickersgill. On June 23, Suttill himself was captured. After severe interrogation by the Gestapo, he was sent to Germany where he was to be executed by hanging in March, 1945. Many other SOE agents were rounded up, and, it is estimated, about 1,500 French resistance persons, most of whom were to perish in concentration camps. Some 470 tons of the weapons and explosives parachuted from Britain were traced to their hiding places in the countryside and triumphantly confiscated by the Germans. The last two weeks of June, 1943, were, for SOE, a disaster, and one which took months to repair.

A whole bookshelf of histories has appeared purporting to account for what Jean Overton Fuller called *The German Penetration of SOE*. Allegations are launched that one important agent betrayed the whole PROSPER organisation by providing the Nazis with a list of its names and addresses. Even the Germans themselves are sometimes given credit for what happened. In Holland they had previously succeeded in virtually taking over the SOE network, and this success enabled them to acquire, by early May, 1943, some valuable leads as to what was going on in the Paris area. There have even been sinister hints that PROSPER became a pawn in an overall Allied strategy of deception, and that hence the network was deliberately allowed to be wiped out. The simplest and most incontestable explanation is provided by a homely saying cited in Fuller's book: that for the work of secret agents, four are weaker than three, three are weaker than two, and two are weaker than one. Clearly the PROSPER network, encouraged by premature rumours of an Allied invasion in 1943, rather than in 1944, was far too large and ever-extended. Penetration was inevitable.

In any event, these arguments about who or what was responsible for the disaster, are, however fascinating, somewhat peripheral to the Pickersgill story, and interested readers can consult the bookshelf dealing with this controversy. For although Pickersgill had been slated to join PROSPER, the events that happened to him developed separately from what happened to the organization as a whole. I recite this summary primarily to show that if he had not been captured near Romorantin, it is extremely likely that within a very short time he would have been captured in the Paris roundup.

If June 15 was an especially dangerous time for a PROSPER agent to land in France, the part of France selected for landing doubled the dangers. Indeed Colonel Buckmaster (as indicated to me in a recent letter) warned Pickersgill, in his final briefing in England, that he'd be landing in "a lion's den." And so it was.

By June, 1943, the "F" section-led group in Romorantin was a flourishing organization of some eighty members.[1] Its overall leader in the whole area of Sologne was Commandant Pierre Culioli, who was assisted by his courier and chief saboteur, Mme Yvonne Rudellat. It was with these two persons that Pickersgill and Macalister would share their last day as free men. Culioli, an officer in the French army, had been invalided out of a POW camp in late 1940. After the death of his wife in a bombing raid at Brest, Culioli moved to central France late in 1942, where he established contacts with "F" section agents. Early in 1943 he was appointed leader for the whole Sologne area. His chief assistant, Yvonne Rudellat, had arrived in France from England in July, 1942, the first trained woman agent to have been sent abroad. Of Anglo-French background, married to an Italian from whom she had separated, she had been working in London before enlisting. She was a remarkable and unusual agent. Although forty-six years of age, she had successfully graduated from "F" section training schools similar to those Pickersgill would attend. According to E.H. Cookridge's account, she was a cheerful person and a most resourceful agent. She was especially skilled in sabotaging troop trains, factories, and power lines, and her successes, on such missions, were said to have infuriated the Germans at their district headquarters in Blois.[2] She and Culioli worked

[1] See Paul Guillaume, *La Resistance en Sologne* (Orleans, 1945), p. 21.

[2] Cookridge, 129-30.

well together and had gained considerable experience in preparing landing fields for parachutists. It was they who received Pickersgill and Macalister on the night of June 15-16.

Three nights previous to the Canadians' arrival there had been a large drop of arms and explosives, supervised by Culioli, which had unfortunate repercussions. Two of the containers blew up on hitting the ground, and the Germans, alerted by the explosions, next day discovered the debris. To track down the now notorious resistance forces, a body of tanks and 2,000 soldiers from Blois were ordered to move into the densely-wooded areas around Romorantin. Check points were set up on roads in the vicinity, and soon many suspects were to be arrested.

Realizing that the Sologne had become a dangerously hot area, Culioli tried to send a message to London, via another agent, urging that parachute drops, scheduled for the next few days, be postponed. It is not known whether that message ever got to London. All that is known is that the drops continued. On June 13, Suttill himself was dropped and was received by Culioli (he had been on a short visit to London); on the 15th, the two Canadians arrived, and on the 17th, a young French officer, P.J.L. Raynaud. All four agents were en route to Paris. Suttill, driven part way by Culioli, reached Paris safely the day after landing, despite the check-points. So too did Raynaud, who left Romorantin on the 20th without a hitch. These two successes would have encouraged Culioli to believe that Pickersgill and Macalister could make it too, and preparations were therefore made for departure in the early morning of the 21st.

During the five days before leaving for Paris, the two Canadians had to find a safe hideout. They were taken by Culioli to an isolated summer house, with nine rooms, in a thickly wooded area some ten miles outside the town of Romorantin. This property, appropriately called "La Garde," was the country home of a mayor of Romorantin, a pharmacist, M. Charmaison. He and his then thirty year old son, Jean, had begun resistance work as early as 1940. At that date, as the son later said, it was considered sheer folly by most everyone in town, not to give up in despair. "But we preferred the blood, sweat, and tears offered by Churchill to the chains of the Boches." As a result, "La Garde" had been used many times as a shelter for British, French, and American airmen and others seeking to escape across the nearby border into Unoccupied France. Pickersgill and Macalister slept in the house, but in the daytime they generally stayed hidden in the shelter of the forest.

A touching recollection of their visit was sent to Jack Pickersgill, fourteen years later, by Jean Charmaison:

> Your brother Frank, in his late 20s, was a tall fair-haired man, not heavy, and pretty strong. He spoke correct French, absolutely without accent, but wasn't talkative. John Macalister was shorter and heavier, with dark, curly hair. He was more of a talker and had a rather deep voice. . . . He wore dark glasses. At that time he had a limp in his left leg, the limp having been caused by a sprain he suffered on landing by parachute a few days earlier.
>
> These two agents were well-informed and very cultivated persons. I remember an afternoon that we passed together under an oak tree where we talked over all sorts of matters: science, art, literature, Philosophy (even Plato's cave got mentioned!). All this discussion was combined with talk of ways of blowing up locomotives or other means of throwing a monkey-wrench into machinery. They had with them little radio sets for sending and receiving messages.
>
> They ate well and were comfortable on our estate. If the times had been ordinary ones, they would have been perfectly happy there. But incertitude and anxiety were in the very air around us; there were suspicious rumours floating round, and there were disturbing noises. Time and time again the German planes flew over at tree-top level and then slowly circled the fields. My father advised them not to take the boat out on our pond.
>
> One Monday morning in June, a warm and sunny day, they left us. My last word for them was 'Good Luck' (which was a strange thing to say, and I felt

embarrassed to have said that to them), but they had already disappeared into the woods.

That evening I was at Romorantin. A rumour was spreading like wildfire, and I learned that the Buckmaster circuit had just been blown. I was able to arrange it so that my father could escape and also a resistance man who had been staying at the summer house at the same time as Pickersgill and Macalister.

A few days later, however, at a time when I least expected it, I was myself arrested. The summer house was pillaged. Together with about forty of my friends we were deported by the Germans to Buchenwald, Mauthausen and other camps. It so happened that I was one of the seven or eight of the living dead who returned alive. What we did many others did also and suffered more for it. I regret nothing. And if it had to be done over, I'd do it.

In July, 1945, on my return, I learned of the fate of your unfortunate brother and of Macalister. I had seen so much myself behind those electrified barbed wire fences that I was not surprised.[tr].

Others in Romorantin beside Jean Charmaison remember the visit of the two Canadians – even those who never saw them in 1943. After Charmaison and his friends came back from the extermination camps, a monument was erected in the town honouring those who had died to overcome the Nazi tyranny. Prominently featured on one side of that monument are the names of Yvonne Rudellat, Frank Pickersgill, and John Macalister. In 1970, surviving members of the Romorantin resistance section held one of their reunions, which included a wreath-laying ceremony. This event was attended by Frank Pickersgill's brother, Jack, and Alan Pickersgill, Jack's son.

ii

At 7.00 A.M., Pickersgill and Macalister left their pleasant hiding-place at "La Garde" and piled into the back seats of an

Monument at Romorantin, 1970, Jack and Alan Pickersgill

old Citroën, in which Culioli was to drive them to Beaugency where they would pick up the morning train for Paris. In front, with Culioli, was Yvonne Rudellat who was also to accompany them to the rendezvous at Gare d'Austerlitz later that morning. The two small radio sets (latest models) had been sealed in packages so as to look like meat pies, and also, in the trunk, was a brown paper package, marked with a fictitious address, which, if they were questioned, could be said to be something being taken to be mailed at a post office. Inside the package were important messages from London for Suttill and other agents, which would be highly dangerous to "F" section if discovered by the Germans.

At first, the drive, covering about thirty-two miles, seemed to be going well. After some distance the car was stopped at an SS check-point, but their papers having been found in order, they were allowed to proceed. At the next check-point, however, on the outskirts of the village of Dhuizon, with two-thirds of the journey behind them, they were treated to a much more intensive scrutiny before an examining officer at the town hall. At the check-point the two Canadians had to get out of the car and walk to the town hall under SS escort. Two other SS men took over their places in the back seat, and Culioli drove on to the examining centre through a village swarming with troops. Upon entering the town hall he discovered why there had been all the military police activities and the extra security measures.

On the previous night the Germans had arrested sixteen sus-
pected resistance men who were lined up, that morning,
against the wall of the council chamber. When the four new-
comers arrived they were ordered to join the line of prisoners.
Once more their papers were found to be in order, and Culioli
effectively fended the questions put to him about his supposed
job in the agricultural department. Even a "meat pie" radio
package was returned to him without being examined, and a
safe-conduct pass was made out for him and for Yvonne Rudellat, who posed as his wife (they made a somewhat incongruous couple in view of the differences in their ages and their
heights – Culioli was a short young man, and she a tall middle-
aged woman). The couple were then told to wait outside in their
car, which they proceeded to do, while the other two passengers
were being questioned.

Hoping for the best, Culioli started his engine, but after an
agonizing wait, there emerged from the door of the building,
instead of Pickersgill and Macalister, an SS officer who
brusquely ordered them to return to the council chamber. Realizing that something had gone amiss for the Canadians, and
that this meant the whole game was up, Culioli floored his
accelerator and the Citroën took off down the village street
and around a corner without being hit by the shots fired after
it by the guards. Three cars, loaded with SS men, were driven
off in pursuit of the fugitives who were careening along country roads at a speed of eighty miles an hour. The SS cars were
more powerful than Culioli's old car, and after eight miles of
chase one of them got within range for the SS to open fire.
Yvonne Rudellat was hit in the head and slumped across the
seat bleeding profusely and presumably dead. Another bullet
went through Cullioli's hat. According to his own testimony, he
then made a desperate decision that instead of merely stopping
his car he would crash it into a wall in hopes that the car and
its passengers and documents would be destroyed by fire. Expecting suicide,[3] he drove at high speed across a ditch, through

---

[3] In *L'Epoque* (June 10, 1948) Culioli's testimony was cited: "Je me suis jeté
sur la façade d'une maison, esperant capoter, prendre feu, me suicider."

a fence, and crashed into the brick wall of a house. The car did not catch fire, and the two passengers were dragged away from it by the SS. Yvonne Rudellat had completely lost consciousness as a result of her wounds. Culioli, briefly unconscious himself from the crash, was brutally beaten and kicked by the SS. When he regained consciousness he tried to scuffle with his tormentors but was finally subdued when one of them shot him in the leg. The two agents were then loaded into the SS cars, together with the contents of their car, and driven back to Dhuizon town hall to confront the awaiting Gestapo officers in the company of their fellow prisoners, Pickersgill and Macalister.

iii

What had gone wrong at the town hall when the two Canadians were questioned? We really do not know. Some accounts of the incident (including one by Yeo-Thomas) contend that Pickersgill's command of French was hopelessly inadequate and it was this that gave them away. In view of the many testimonials already cited in this book concerning Pickersgill's extraordinary command of French, this explanation is nonsense. From other sources we do know that Macalister's command of spoken French was not on a par with Pickersgill's, and, that because of his accent, he had been provided in London with a plausible cover story to account for it (by 1943 in France it was not extraordinary to encounter unusual accents in a floating population). Whatever it was that prompted the suspicions of the examining officers, the result was that both men were stripped and their clothing meticulously searched. Macalister's money-belt, with its large store of francs, was discovered. When Culioli returned, the belt had been laid out on a display table to confront him.

The Germans decided that the four agents should be sent off to the town of Blois, fifteen miles away, for interrogation. Yvonne Rudellat's wounds were too serious to allow her to be questioned. Instead, in a semi-conscious state, she was taken to the hospital of St. Nicholas at Blois for treatment, where she lingered for some time on the brink of death. Pickersgill never saw her again. She was to be shuttled to other hospitals, and, when somewhat recovered, sent to Belsen where she died, reputedly in the gas chambers, in April, 1945, shortly before the British armies reached the camp and released it inmates.[4]

Culioli was taken to Blois in a different car from the Canadians. There he was installed in a German air force hospital to have his wounded leg treated. Despite his wound, he was interrogated by the Gestapo in his hospital room, where he was chained to his bed and beaten. Later he was interrogated in Paris and imprisoned there in various prisons. In one of these, less than a year later, he encountered Pickersgill again, and the two men also renewed their acquaintance at Buchenwald. Culioli was fortunate at Buchenwald in being transferred to another camp. In 1945 he escaped to the American lines and thus survived the war. After the war he was less fortunate for in 1948 and 1949 he had to face charges, in French courts, of having betrayed information to the Gestapo.[5] Happily, this brave man was eventually exonerated by the courts, but the trials did point up a difference between his response to interrogation and that of Pickersgill and Macalister. Under threats that there would be massive reprisals in the Sologne, Culioli eventually elected to play games with the Gestapo and to pretend to be giving information when, to his knowledge, the information was already in their hands. However adeptly played, this was a dangerous game and one in which the player's side is likely to be the ultimate loser.

Pickersgill and Macalister played no games throughout their long interrogation which began at the Gestapo headquarters in Blois on June 21, the day of their capture. To questions such as

[4]Most accounts of her death are as here presented. Cookridge, however, says she died on April 23, St. George's Day, as a result of her long incarceration, and not in the gas chambers (the Allies had taken over the camp earlier). A projected book about her by Stella King will presumably settle the point.

[5]See e.g., Jean Overton Fuller, *Double Webs* (London, 1958), p. 103; E. H. Cookridge, pp. 149-53; and Paul Guillaume.

where was the house in which they had been hidden since their arrival in France, and who was the owner, the answer was no answer. They were behaving as they had been trained to behave, and they never broke from what they had been taught to do and were resolved to do. About their exploits on this and later occasions, it is not hard to imagine their sense of frustration in realising that their mission itself, for which they had trained so hard, had been obliterated only six days after their arrival. Capture meant that there was to be no ARCHDEACON section in the north – at least under Pickersgill's direction. But secret agents have an alternative mission, for which their training also prepares them, which is, if captured, to betray no information under interrogation, and also – but this would come later – to sustain, as far as possible, the morale of one's fellow captives. Exploits behind bars do not have the glamorous cloak-and-dagger qualities of exploits in leading a section that is blowing up power lines and railway engines, but the exploits behind bars can have their honour, too.

The interrogation that began on the night of June 21 was under the direction of the awesome chief of the Blois Gestapo, Sturmbannführer Ludwig Bauer – "avec les procédés que l'on imagine" as a French historian comments about that night.[6] It is said that torture in Gestapo offices in the provinces, such as the one at Blois, was even more terrible than what went on at central headquarter prisons in Paris, although it is hard to conceive of treatment more savage than that meted out in Paris to a leading agent, Wing Commander Yeo-Thomas, as described in Bruce Marshall's book about him, The White Rabbit. Forty-five pages of that book recount the sickening succession of brutal beatings, whip-lashings, and near drownings, administered by the Paris Gestapo, day after day, until the victim's shoulder was dislocated and his face and body were a mass of welts, swellings, and cuts.[7] Nevertheless, Yeo-Thomas betrayed

[6]Henri Noguères et M. Degliame-Fouché, Histoire de la Resistance en France, vol. IV (Paris, 1976), p. 482.

[7]See Bruce Marshall, The White Rabbit: The Story of Wing Commander F.F.E. Yeo-Thomas (London, 1952), Evans Brothers Limited, pp. 100-45.

no information, and, in an interview after the war, he praised Pickersgill and Macalister for a similar feat: "Pick and Mac were given the usual beating up, rubber truncheons, electric shocks, kicks in the genitals and what have you. They were in possession of names, addresses and codes that the Germans badly wanted, but neither of them squealed." Even the Germans confirm what happened. In 1947, Allied investigators questioned S.D. personnel about what had gone on at Blois, and, as the report states, the Germans testified "to the outstanding fortitude and courage displayed by both these officers [Pickersgill and Macalister] under interrogation and have categorically stated that neither revealed a scrap of information that was the slightest use to the Germans."

An additional tribute to their endurance comes from a most unusual source. Present as a witness to their ordeal was Ludwig Bauer's mistress, Mona la Blonde as she was called, who, in addition to her other services, acted as the Commandant's secretary and interpreter. After the war she was sent to jail by the French, and indeed she seems the least savoury of witnesses. Nevertheless her testimony, in this instance, has corroborative value. Of Pickersgill and Macalister she asserted in court (August 8, 1946):

> These two officers took a most courageous stance. Refusing to make any other statements, they simply affirmed that they were officers who had been parachuted. One of them said: 'I know the fate that is in store for us. I demand that you notify my family the circumstances of my arrest and execution.' [tr]

Mona la Blonde, less credibly, liked to take credit for saving the two prisoners from summary execution by persuading her lover, the Commandant, that they should be treated as combatant officers rather than spies. The fact is, however, that her services were probably not needed to forestall execution, for it was common Gestapo procedure not to execute captured agents on the spot. Instead they were usually kept alive for a long time, just alive, in the event that they might later be of use for some unforeseen contingency. Frank Pickersgill's subsequent experiences will provide an illustration of their methods.

Having survived the interrogation, Pickersgill was transferred on June 26, 1943, five days after his capture, to Fresnes, a big prison on the outskirts of Paris. At Fresnes, "that black and forbidding fortress" as Buckmaster describes it, he was tried by the Germans and sentenced to be executed on July 7. The next day, however, he was still alive, and, like many prisoners, he contrived to record his existence by scratching an inscription on the wall of his cell[8]:

Pickersgill canadian army officer	26-6-43
trial and condemnation not	7-7-43
yet and see	8-7-43

The rest of the wall-scratchings, following these, cannot be deciphered, in this the last of the Pickersgill letters.

During July, August, and September, he remained in prison at Fresnes, except for a visit to the torture-rooms of a Gestapo prison in Paris on the Place des États-Unis. Here the Nazis tried unsuccessfully to persuade him and Macalister to send reassuring messages to London on their radio sets. In October Pickersgill was then sent to a prison in Poland located in Rawicz. It seems highly likely that Macalister was with him in Poland, although I have found no records of Macalister's whereabouts at this period.

At Rawicz he was imprisoned from October, 1943, until early March, 1944. These months are the period of his life about which least is known. In fact nothing about that period has subsequently come to light. When I visited the town (Rawicz) in 1977 I could gain no information whatever. In fact I was advised that the prison area was not to be seen let alone to be photographed. One can only make a guess about the appalling living conditions in the camp by the reports of Pickersgill's emaciated state when he was unexpectedly summoned back from Rawicz to one of the prisons in Paris.

[8]See Henry Calet, *Les Murs de Fresnes* (Paris, 1945, Editions des Quatre Vents) p. 102.

A possible clue as to what his state of mind during these months in Poland might have been like has been suggested in a letter of 1959 by his long-time friend in London, Kay Moore Gimpel, who had special reasons for her insights. In 1943, Kay Moore had herself married an agent who was en route to France, Charles Gimpel. Her husband, like Pickersgill, was also early captured by the Gestapo and similarly treated. Although permanently injured by this treatment, Charles Gimpel survived and eventually returned to peacetime life. About the state of mind of such captured agents, his wife writes with understanding:

> I always worried during the war about the sense of frustration that some of them must have had when caught, but I did have the comfort of finding that for many of them, like Charles, when the worst of the torture was over, and through the dreary long months of concentration camp, they often only felt, well – Others are carrying on. In Frank's case I worry about his having a sense of claustrophobia ... but Frank had become so much a man of action, so capable of deciding to live to fight another day, that the fact that he made such an effort to escape from his imprisonment means that his morale must have been basically good.

This reference to his "attempt to escape" and to "morale" calls for a separate chapter.

Part XI

THE CANADIAN CIRCUIT: 1943–1944
(age 28-29)

To explain why Frank Pickersgill was resurrected from Poland and flown back to Paris requires some consideration of what the Germans called *Funkspiel* – the Radio Game. Although the word *Game* may seem unduly playful in view of its sometimes deadly forfeits, all histories of agents use it extensively, and I shall therefore follow suit.

The Radio Game involved using the radio set of a captured agent to receive and send messages to his headquarters so as to deceive the opposing side in various and extremely profitable ways. There were several variations of the Game. Ideally, if a captured agent could be persuaded to change sides and become a double agent (usually a well-paid one), he would himself compose messages (under direction) and send them himself. British Intelligence excelled at this version of the Game. Every living German agent in Britain, according to J. C. Masterman, became a double agent. Masterman's book begins with his "staggering claim" that during World War II " we actively ran and controlled the German espionage system in this country."[1]

The German Intelligence services rarely had such good for-

[1]*The Double-Cross System in the War of 1939 to 1945* (New Haven, 1972), Yale University Press, p. 3.

tune when they played the Game with SOE. Being usually unable to persuade captured agents to establish communications with London, the Germans had a more difficult task. In their version of the Game, they themselves had to take over the circuit and assume the captured agent's identity.

The performance of the British in the arts of radio deception is now known to have been so stunningly brilliant that it seems to have put the Germans under a cloud. Yet by the time Frank Pickersgill was captured, the Germans had already become extremely adept masters of their version of radio deception. Their skills had been fully demonstrated in Holland, where they had gained control of most of the SOE sets from the time the first agent landed in that country in March, 1942.[2] In the summer of 1943 they were able to begin exercising the same expertise in France that they had been practising in Holland, and they soon had several sets communicating with "F" section in London.

One of the most successful circuits was called the Canadian Circuit. For this operation Macalister's radio set was used, and Pickersgill's identity was assumed by a German, Joseph Placke, who spoke good French and some English. Because Macalister's codes, security checks, and other papers had been discovered at Dhuizon, the German operators were in an ideal position to deceive the British. And the deception took in even more than the use of the Canadian's radio. Placke moved into the area in Lorraine where Pickersgill had been expected to start his resistance section. Posing as Pickersgill, Placke himself organized resistance groups (the unfortunate men in these groups were finally shot by the Germans after they had served their purposes in the Game). Through messages to London, Placke was able to request parachute drops and to provide instructions for landings. Fifteen large drops of arms were made during a ten month period. These supplies never got to be used by the resistance, for Placke contrived to have them sent to Paris in German trucks for safe-keeping. In September,

---

[2]See H. J. Giskes, *London Calling North Pole* (London, 1953).

1943, one agent was sent to join Pickersgill's supposed section and was of course captured. In February and early March, six more agents were parachuted into the trap and were captured by the waiting Germans.

The Canadian Circuit also served to provide information leading to the arrest of other "F" section agents in Paris. In August, 1943, the Germans proposed to London that a meeting take place in a café on the Champs Elysseés between "Pickersgill" and an "F" section radio-operator known as Madeleine, one of the most colourful of agents (she had been an Indian princess). Never having seen Pickersgill in person, and knowing only that he was Canadian, Madeleine was readily deceived, as might be expected, when she was met at the café by another one of Pickersgill's impersonators, Karl Holdorf, a German carefully chosen for the role. Having been a steward on an American boat, Holdorf spoke excellent English and with a North American accent that could readily pass as Canadian. Holdorf and his companion, Placke, did not try to arrest the young woman that day at the café; instead they simply concentrated on getting her to talk. And talk she did.[3] And so the chips from the Canadian Circuit continued to pile up on the German side of the game board for almost ten months.

That Colonel Buckmaster and his staff in London behaved like simple-minded credulous ninnies in falling for this cleverly contrived take-over of Pickersgill's identity by the Germans has been implied, if not openly alleged, but the allegation seems ill-considered. By midsummer, 1943, when the Game started, it was known in London that the established PROSPER network had been smashed, but they had no reason to think that the new-comers, Pickersgill and Macalister, had not been able to survive, and that their radio communications, coming from an entirely new circuit, were not genuine. Concerning the much more sinister allegations, that London *did* know of the German

[3]In Stevenson's *A Man Called Intrepid* (pp. 230-232), it is said that Pickersgill was in a Paris prison at the same time as Madeleine. This is a touching story but untrue. Madeleine had been sent to Germany six months before Pickersgill was installed in the prison she had been in.

take-over of the Canadian Circuit, and yet continued to send agents into Lorraine who would be doomed to certain capture, I must again send the interested reader to the bookshelves.[4]

For our purposes, what is relevant is how the developing situation brought Frank Pickersgill, the real Frank Pickersgill that is, back into the picture. On March 2, 1944, six agents were parachuted into the "Pickersgill" area of Lorraine, including two Americans and a young French Canadian, Guy Sabourin. These agents had been firmly instructed to notify London of their safe arrival. When no notifications were received, the operation's officer in London, Major Gerry Morel, at last had good grounds to be suspicious that the Germans might have been duping them. To verify whether or not they were still dealing with Pickersgill, he sent a message that a plane would fly to Lorraine in early May to talk with Pickersgill person-to-person. The talk would be by an S-phone, a kind of radio phone from plane to ground, by which voices could be identified. That Morel chose this safe method of testing the Canadian Circuit, instead of risking a landing by plane to meet with Pickersgill face-to-face, indicates that London was now aware of what might have been going on. Earlier there had been small-scale incidents that might have given them clues. As early as Christmas, 1943, Pickersgill's London friends at 54A Walton Street had arranged through Colonel Buckmaster to send him personal greetings by radio. Because of his insatiable tea-drinking habits in London, Kay Moore and the others contrived a witty message: "The samovar is still bubbling at 54A." What they had expected as a reply, via Buckmaster, would be something equivalently cryptographic and personal. Instead, the commonplace message they eventually received – "Happy Christmas to all" – was very distinctly not Pickersgillian, and these friends began to suspect, instinctively, that something had gone wrong in France. But it was not until March 2, 1944, that there was evidence more tangible for "F" section to go on.

[4]For a reasonable summary of these issues, see, e.g., Anthony Cave Brown *Bodyguard of Lies* (New York, 1975), part IV, chapter 10.

When the Germans received Morel's order from London about the plane, they realized that their Radio Game was now in serious jeopardy, and that the real Pickersgill must be located and brought back to Paris at once in order to be induced to talk on the phone to the British plane. They did not even know of his whereabouts at this date and had to have him tracked down via Berlin. Thus it was that he was flown from his prison in Poland to Paris and brought to 3 bis Place des États-Unis, a former villa which had been converted into a Gestapo prison. This was not the kind of establishment from which escape seemed possible. Unlike St. Denis, from which he and Hicks had escaped so neatly two years earlier, there was now no contact allowed with friends outside, and prisoners, whose cells were on the third floor, were under the rigid surveillance of a dozen SS guards, "les pires crapules de la création" as one of the inmates memorably described them.

What was to happen in March, 1944, the second anniversary of his escape from St. Denis, was much in character. If we look back over the letters Pickersgill wrote as a student and journalist, one trait predominates in them – vigour. Whether he was passing judgement upon Neville Chamberlain or St. Thomas Aquinas, Ernest Hemingway or the city of Toronto, his thinking was always full of energy and force. And his last letters from England indicated that as a soldier he would not only think vigorously but act vigorously – as he was to demonstrate on this occasion.

Upon Pickersgill's arrival in Paris the Gestapo chiefs turned on a very different reception for him from the brutal treatment he had received in this prison in 1943. Instead of beatings he was now cajoled with the soft treatment. The Germans intimated that if only he would provide minimal co-operation by conversing with the British on the S-phone, he would be guaranteed comfortable detention for the rest of the war, with adequate food and other privileges. And as if to illustrate these privileges, good food and drink were on hand during these interviews, and the interviewer would even deplore the inadvertence whereby a Canadian officer has been subjected to the indignities of the camp in Poland. For some prisoners flown in from the horrors of Rawicz, such assurances and blandishments must surely have been overwhelmingly persuasive, but the Nazis had misjudged what was going on in the mind behind the mild blue eyes of their prisoner. Seizing his opportunity during one of these seemingly friendly sessions in a third floor office, Pickersgill suddenly grabbed a bottle from the table and broke it off at the neck. So armed he rushed out into the hall to make his escape. When two SS guards tried to stop him he slashed and killed one of them with the bottle and the other he knocked unconscious. As a witness reported later: "Pickersgill's courage was extraordinary. He came within an inch of freeing the whole prison." From the hall he ran down a flight of stairs into a guard post in the next floor. Although these guards had been alerted by the noises upstairs, Pickersgill dashed into them, knocking them out of his way, and, after leaping out of a second storey window, started heading for the street.

Another agent, Bernard Guillot, who was to be with him in this Gestapo prison, tells about the finale of this episode:

> He was exhausted after such a long period of inactivity and imprisonment; he was unable to run very quickly. The SS opened fire from the windows with their sub-machine guns; he was hit four times, fell, tried to run again, but stopped from exhaustion and lost consciousness. Later he was taken to hospital, recovered, and returned to prison with us. [tr]

Guillot wondered afterwards why the Germans hadn't "massacred" Pickersgill then and there instead of rushing him off to hospital to have his bullet wounds treated and to set an arm that had been fractured when he hit the ground. One can only speculate that the Gestapo chiefs still hoped, upon his recovery, that he might reconsider their offer to help them with their S-phone problem. Evidently he remained unco-operative, for by mid-April they had decided to try someone else. A proposition was made to another imprisoned agent that it would be to his advantage to take over the job of talking to the British plane. This was John Starr, who played a game of his own with his captors by seemingly agreeing that he would perform for them. On the night in May when he was taken to Lorraine by a party of Germans, Starr unexpectedly announced that he too, like Pickersgill, would not co-operate. When the British plane began to fly over the ground station, the Germans were in a dilemma, for they had no one else on hand who could speak good English. They tried to make do with a German non-commissioned officer, Von Kapri, but his accent easily gave him away when he was heard by Major Morel in the British plane. Morel thereupon broke off the conversation and the plane returned to England. Thus ended the Canadian Circuit after its ten months of deceptions.

In the remaining six weeks before D Day, London was in a position to play the double version of the Radio Game by pretending that they had not guessed that the circuit was under German control. They also continued to test German responses by sending personal messages to "Pickersgill." During a visit to London in the spring of 1944 by Prime Minister King, his secretary, Jack Pickersgill, was invited by Buckmaster to send a personal message to his brother. It read: "Jack says mother is well." The reply, received in May, should have been a further give away: "Thank Uncle Jack for his message." Frank Pickersgill had no Uncle Jack.

On D Day, 1944, the last instalment in the Germans' Radio Game with "F" section took place. Hitler himself had taken a keen interest in it and even issued a special order on June 6 that a gloating message of thanks was to be radioed to Buckmaster. By that date, however, Buckmaster was no longer ill-informed about the Canadian and other circuits and could reply to the German message with ironic amusement.

Meanwhile back in the Place des États-Unis, the real Pickersgill had returned from hospital to his prison cell in early April. He was limping painfully and his arm was in a sling, but the example of his attempted escape inspired other agents to make plans to do likewise. In early June, one of them, Marcel

Rousset, seized the opportunity when he was sweeping a prison corridor. Knocking out an SS guard, he broke a window and jumped down into a garden. From there he made it to a nearby convent where he hid successfully. The Germans never found him.

Rousset's success, and Pickersgill's near success, may have led the Germans to seek even more secure quarters for their prisoners. Early in July they were all moved to the main Gestapo headquarters, at 84 Avenue Foch, where they were installed on the sixth floor. Here they were forced to wear handcuffs even while sleeping, and sometimes foot chains as well. Escape was no longer even a remote possibility, but, instead, there was now a new kind of hope. As the Allied armies started to close in on Paris in August, and the Gestapo began methodically burning its own records, the possibility of early liberation raised the expectations of the Avenue Foch prisoners to a high point. These hopes were frustrated on August 8, twelve days before Paris was liberated, when the whole group of captured agents was ordered to be sent to Buchenwald.

Part XII

JOURNEY TO BUCHENWALD

> *"Ne trouvez-vous pas d'une stupidité*
> *caractéristique de l'espèce humaine, (disait*
> *Ferral,) qu'un homme qui n'a qu'une vie puisse*
> *la perdre pour une idée?*
> *– Il est très rare qu'un homme puisse*
> *supporter, comment dirais-je? sa condition*
> *d'homme. . . .*
> *Gisors pensa à l'une des idées de Kyo: tout ce*
> *pour quoi les hommes acceptent de se faire tuer,*
> *au dela de l'intérêt, tend plus ou moins*
> *confusement à justifier cette condition en la*
> *fondant en dignité. . . . "*
> (Malraux, *La Condition Humaine*)

The journey to Buchenwald should have been covered in a day's train ride. Instead it took eight days to get the thirty-seven Allied officers from Paris to the camp. According to the handful of survivors who were alive at the war's end, those eight days included some of the most gruesome experiences that they endured in Hitler's Europe.

On the train itself, eighteen officers were crammed into one small compartment without seats, and nineteen into another. A third and smaller compartment was used for women agents, who were to be sent to other camps. All of them were handcuffed in pairs, and there was room for only two pairs to sleep on the floor of the carriage at one time. They were without food and water in the summer heat, and morale in the assorted crowd of British, French, Canadian, and Belgian agents was understandably variable. In the compartment in which Pickersgill was cooped up, the senior officer, Yeo-Thomas, took command. His comments on the two Canadians are worth citing: "The remarkable fortitude of the two Canadians, Pickersgill and Macalister, weaker than the rest because of a recent and heavy beating up from the Gestapo, also increased morale." Characteristically Pickersgill began making jokes. "They weren't particularly funny jokes," Yeo-Thomas recalled, "I can't remember one of them. At first they weren't appreciated. Then suddenly everyone realized that Pickersgill was only trying to keep them all from going crazy. They cheered up a bit and took a grip on themselves."

As a token of gratitude to Pickersgill for his performance, Yeo-Thomas offered him the only treat he had on his person, a cardboard box containing malt syrup. Pickersgill was touched and grateful and put the box in his pocket. The next morning there occurred one of those serio-comic incidents that recalls, with a new twist, the Pickersgill of Winnipeg and Toronto days to whom minor mishaps always seemed to happen. It was scorchingly hot in the crowded compartment, and the discomforts of the morning scene were not improved by what had happened to the carton of malt syrup. It had been crushed in Pickersgill's pocket while he was asleep, and so when he reached into his clothes to retrieve it, his hand, as Yeo-Thomas recalled,

> was covered with a gooey, sticky mess which soon covered not only his own clothes, but those of Macalister and his immediate neighbours as well. Trying to lick his hand clean Pickersgill succeeded only in smearing syrup all over his face, and all the time more syrup was oozing from his pocket. Macalister, attempting to help, spread the stickiness further. And when the guards refused requests that the two Cana-

dians be allowed to go to the lavatory and clean themselves the surly members of the party became vituperative.[1]

In the afternoon of the second day, the train, which had been rerouted several times because of SOE sabotage of railway tracks, was finally stalled near the German border after it had been hard hit in a strafing attack by R.A.F. planes firing 20 mm. cannon. All thirty-seven prisoners had then to be transferred to trucks which took them across the German border to a grisly transit camp at Saarbrücken. Here they were to wait another four or five days for another train to Buchenwald.

At Saarbrücken their trucks were received by a crowd of truncheon-wielding SS mobster-types who greeted each pair of prisoners, as they were unloaded from the vans, with beatings and savage kickings. Pickersgill came in for extra-special treatment, for one of the SS guards turned out to have been on the staff at the Place des États-Unis, the very guard whom Pickersgill had knocked out in his attempt to escape, and the guard remembered him. The whole party, for that matter, had a bad time of it. One of them, Bernard Guillot, has written of their experiences in a letter:

> All of us, already worn out after that infernal train journey, were locked up in one room of a tin-roofed hut, thirty-seven of us, that is. The room was nine feet long, eight feet wide, and about nine feet high. We were allowed out of it one hour of twenty four, but both our ankles were shackled, and there would be five of us all chained together. In this rig we were then forced to try to run around the edge of a small pond. Naturally every few steps we'd trip on the chains and fall down, and we'd then be beaten with clubs to make us stand back up. That was our hour's recreational promenade, and afterwards we'd be locked back up again in the hut for the rest of the day and night. We couldn't even sit in this inferno of a prison which was without windows and air. Certain

[1]Bruce Marshall, *The White Rabbit*, 169-170.

of the men in our group began to show signs of
going mad. [tr]

On August 16 they finally got away from this Black Hole of
Calcutta at Saarbrücken and were entrained for Buchenwald
near Weimar. The gracious world of Goethe and Schiller was
still perpetuated by the idyllic tree-lined avenue leading to the
extermination camp that the Nazis had built in 1937, in which
tens of thousands of men and women had been disposed of by
starvation or by gas chamber.

Buchenwald, even more than Avenue Foch in Paris, did not
inspire many illusions about likely escapes. The camp was
surrounded, as M.R.D. Foot notes, "by floodlit double electrified [barbed-wire] fences set in wide open spaces guarded by
alert sadists who were crack shots."[2] At the gateway which
Pickersgill and his thirty-six fellow-prisoners marched in, Bernard Guillot reflected on Dante's lines for the gates of Hell:
"Abandon hope, all ye who enter here." And their initial reception was indeed Dantesque, for they were advised not to
waste time in getting washed up inasmuch as orders had been
issued that they were to be sent immediately to the gas chambers.

This order was soon countermanded, and hope began slowly
to develop in the group that perhaps they might yet be classified as POW's and hence slated to survive rather than as state-
less "terrorists" (as the Germans called them) doomed for
death. Various signs pointed towards this happy eventuality.
Like all the rest of the prisoners they were at once shaved by
camp barbers after arrival; all hair from head, face, and body
was removed, and, like all the others, they wore wooden clogs
instead of shoes. But when clothing was issued to them it was
not the usual grey striped garb worn by other camp prisoners.
Instead they were to wear ordinary civilian clothes, which,
however shabby and ill-fitting, were a sign of their slightly
superior status. Nor were they required to work in labour
gangs. And the barracks to which they were assigned, Block 17,

2Foot, p. 425.

269

was a separate unit for Allied officers and resistance men. It was crowded and food was scanty, but it was certainly no Saarbrücken hell hole. Reinforcing these hopeful signs, the Gestapo let it be known (according to a Wehrmacht officer's testimony in 1945) that the thirty-seven agents were to be exchanged for some thirty-seven German officers captured by the Allies. The Gestapo, needless to say, were past masters of cat-and-mouse games.

Surrounded by the sights and smells of death and dying in the camp, the thirty-seven agents could hardly ignore altogether that their situation was still a precarious one. But reinforcing their sense of hope of survival by transfer, there was, in addition, the promise of possible liberation by the Allied armies. As Bernard Guillot, one of the few survivors, wrote: "Pickersgill was the best spirited of us all and was full of hope. The allied armies were advancing; we had a secret radio set in the camp and the good news spread quickly." Almost as a symbol of Allied power on its way to deliver them there was a massive air raid, on August 24, levelled against a munitions factory adjacent to the camp. Although several bombs fell on the camp itself, Pickersgill stood out in the open near their barracks, waving his arms to the sky and shouting with joy. Afterwards he jokingly offered Richard Rendl (an Australian prisoner who survived) a bet of a thousand pounds that they would all be home by Christmas. With Culioli, his fellow-prisoner from Romorantin, he had long talks about what he might do after the war. Culioli remembers that he had become interested in possibly going into documentary film-making in Canada instead of into journalism, or the Department of External Affairs, or academic life. Guillot remembers his talking of Canada itself: "He often spoke to us of Canada, his fine country. He was full of hope."

These descriptions of Pickersgill's feelings may recall the striking sentence in one of the letters written while he was in England in 1943 training to become an agent:

You know, Helen, I've been in a permanent state of

exhilaration since March 8 last (the date on which I
made my getaway) on the crest of a wave which kept
getting higher and higher as each frontier was
crossed, and which now, instead of subsiding, seems
to be going on up. I don't know where it's going to
land me, but it's damned good while it lasts.

The wave finally broke at Buchenwald. On the morning of
September 9, 1944, sixteen names (including Pickersgill's and
Macalister's) were posted at their barracks with instructions for
those named to report to the main watch tower of the camp in
the afternoon. Almost everyone listed assumed that they were
being called up for some routine inspection, and they had no
anxieties that anything unusual was to be expected. The one
exception was a little Corsican, Marcel Laccia, who cried out:
"We shall be hanged!" The little Corsican was, it turned out, a
true prophet, for orders emanating from Hitler himself had
recently been sent out that all captured SOE agents were to be
disposed of.

In the mid-afternoon, the sixteen doomed men marched off
in good spirits with Pickersgill cheerfully leading the singing of
"Madelon" and "Alouette" and "Tipperary." When the singing
columns of marchers arrived at the gate of their Dark Tower,
however, their good spirits soon evaporated as the SS suddenly
disclosed their hand. Each man was shackled and handcuffed;
death sentences were read to them in pairs, and they were then
escorted off to a bunker for a final thirty hours of treatment.
Because of the suddenness of their being seized, there was no
opportunity for a Catholic priest in the camp. Father Georges
Stanger, to get to the prisoners in time to offer a last commun-
ion to those who sought it. (Stanger, a camp inmate, came
from Lorraine, site of the Canadian Circuit).

Bernard Guillot's letter to Jack Pickersgill, in 1946, unflinch-
ingly states how the incident ended:

I suggest that it wouldn't be a good idea to say
anything to your Mother about the exact details of
his execution, for a mother shouldn't know about
such sufferings of her son. But I do want you, his

brother, to understand what went on right to the end. The special report I've read says this: 'The prisoners were brought into a basement of the crematorium on the night of September 11th. There they were beaten atrociously by a half dozen SS. They were then hanged on butcher hooks that had been cemented into the walls, until death came to them. Their bodies were immediately cremated in the furnaces.' This is the sad truth, and the record can be verified.[3] [tr]

A month later, fifteen more of the group of agents were also summoned for execution; this time, instead of being hanged, they were shot, in pairs, on the SS pistol range.

Of the five or six out of the thirty-seven who contrived miraculously to survive, the one who has contributed the most vivid account of how Pickersgill carried on during the last month of his life was Yeo-Thomas. In 1951 he was interviewed in Paris by McKenzie Porter for *Maclean's* (although the interview was not published until 1961). Parts of Porter's summary of that interview deserve citing at some length:

> In this nightmare, according to Yeo-Thomas, Pickersgill seemed to become possessed of 'superhuman spirit.' The student who had once laughed affectionately at a group of French *poilus* straggling along with their tunics undone and flowers in their caps now became a zealot for military bearing.
>
> Yeo-Thomas had given orders that members of the group should march about like the soldiers they were and not creep as they had been trained to do in the underground. Pickersgill was the first to approve of this. He recognized it as a last effort to bolster morale against the suck and drag of the Stygian conditions.
>
> When a ragged section went off to draw its rations Pickersgill would march at its head, chin up, shoulders back, singing. For a moment or two his follow-

[3]Speaking of these execution procedures, Foot notes (page 425) that the Nazis had devised special nooses for such hangings which were made of loops of piano wire "to make their deaths as slow and as degrading as could be."

ers would be too miserable to fall into step or take up the refrain. Then the poignant loneliness of Pickersgill's bearing and voice would shame them and they too would start marching and singing.

The camp rules laid down that every military prisoner, no matter what his rank, should salute all German officers. On sighting an officer in the distance Pickersgill would halt his section and order it to disperse behind huts. Then, when the officer had passed, he would reform the section and march on. Yeo-Thomas says: 'In avoiding the according of military honors to human rattlesnakes, Pick helped our men to hang on to the last shreds of their pride.'

It was Pickersgill who laboriously collected the bits of pasteboard and drops of paint that enabled the thirty-seven to manufacture a set of playing cards and stage bridge drives. Desmond Hubble, one of the English officers, had contrived to save a set of portable chessmen. Pickersgill not only gave the accomplished players a good match but spent time teaching chess to those who didn't know how to play, a tedious task at the best of times.

When a brooding silence fell upon the hut Pickersgill would utter a challenging statement, then fan the tiny grudging sparks of response until he had a widespread discussion crackling. Any subject under the sun, from movie cartoons to Picasso, from ragtime to Mozart and from westerns to Shakespeare, was sufficient to bring forth from his brain the sprout of an idea that stimulated the others to thought and self-expression.[4]

When this Buchenwald story was published in *Maclean's* it was read by an old friend of Pickersgill's in Winnipeg, Lloyd Wheeler, with whom he used to spend summers, as an undergraduate, working on a road for a summer cottage at Lake of the Woods. The small incident of Pickersgill's using bits of cardboard and drops of paint to manufacture cards to play

[4]McKenzie Porter, "The Last Days of Frank Pickersgill." *Maclean's*, December 2, 1961, page 48.

bridge with seemed to Wheeler especially typical of his young friend, and he was moved to write some lines of verse about it:

One of his companions who escaped remembered
Frank's voice cajoling, wheedling, commanding,
Urging his companions to complete the task,
From the first tiny patch of paper to the finished
    playing card –
The pitifully improbable, trivial means to a noble
    end.
The disciplined scholar's mind,
The strength of the lumbering, wounded giant's
    body,
The love,
All devoted to one object:
To keep his companions' faces,
Lit by the oven's glow,
Recognizably human.

More prosaically, Yeo-Thomas, at the end of his 1951 interview, summed up his estimate of his fellow-inmate at Buchenwald:

Frank Pickersgill was a man who knew how to live and how to die. You don't come across many of them who can do both quite so well. You should not forget him in Canada.

Part XIII

EPILOGUE

The following are extracts from four of the many letters received by the Pickersgill family. The first pays tribute to Frank Pickersgill's army record; the second recalls his early student days in Canada; the third deals with his knowledge of France and the fourth with his last months in England.

Also included, as a fifth and final item, is a translation of a statement made by the French Ambassador to Canada, His Excellency Hubert Guerin, on the occasion of the award of the Cross of a Chevalier of the Legion of Honour (posthumous) to Frank Pickersgill. At the awarding ceremony in Ottawa, the Cross was received by his brother, Jack Pickersgill, on behalf of their mother, on December 12, 1950.

- 1 -

From Lt. Col. R. O. Macfarlane, May 12, 1945:
".... Last night's *Free Press* carried Frank's picture on the front page and the story of his execution last September. I thought that you ... would like one more assurance, even from one on the fringes of Intelligence work, of the splendid job he did.... Frank knew, too well, from his 1940–1942 experiences, what he was going back to – if anything slipped. He didn't go in for heroes and I can only say to you what his chief told me on this point: 'Frank is the bravest boy I know.' That from the

man who handled everyone who went into Frank's branch of Intelligence. . . .

As you well know, he had changed a lot from 1938, matured tremendously, and felt almost as intently on the war as anyone I ever came across. And he had every reason so to feel. It is a far cry from the morning he held on to the bumper of the car and was dragged into the Park when the Chevrolet fired in reverse, or the morning when in his usual degenerate appearance at 7.45 he came out with 'Re this Azalea' which was reposing in the wash basin.

I should like you to know that . . . those of us who knew the job he was doing in the service regard him as the bravest man we met."

$$-2-$$

From Brock King, May 5, 1945:
". . . . In a sense it seems strange that it was Frank who made his contribution to a better life in the manner that required the greatest personal bravery, for superficially he was the mildest-looking guy among all those who sought truth and life and fun in the rickety classrooms at Wesley and over at the University Library where we'd run into old Horace and be waylaid for half an hour, and up at your house where it was ping pong and games like Quotations and lots of good talking. That's where I first ran into Frank. . . .

As in the deep past I remember our doings together. The long walks at night, sitting in Moore's till all hours, a midnight snack at your place or mine, rolling all over Frank Jones' bed as we roared over the humor of J. B. Morton . . . I recall our visit one night to an auction where Frank bought a pen for about a quarter – it wouldn't write, of course – and we also startled the place by purchasing a couple of chamber pots with which we regaled Donald Street, eventually placing them on top of a car which swerved onto Portage, dumping its load with a great clatter. There was the night we three went to a late movie and had the place in an uproar because we couldn't stop howling at a short featuring a little bear called Itchy Scratchy. And the other night Frank and I were walking up Portage from a play and we saw some men working on a store front; there were some long planks by the curb, we asked them if they needed these, one of them mumbled a sort of okay, we took up the planks and held them across the sidewalk for some moments so that the passers-by couldn't get across except by taking to the street. And the night we discovered a discarded toilet in a back yard of a place near yours and we roused the neighbourhood dogs with our laughter. . . .

Our serious times were many, though they don't stand out as vignettes in the memory, of course. Though I remember when I had Frank up to our cottage at Matlock and each of us came up with a suitcase of books to read. We each read one book a day, because we thought that would be a good gesture to culture. . . .

We can't tell now whether Frank would have found a place in the literary world . . . or what. What he was always best at was being a companion, the liveliest in the group, the one to boom out first round your piano and get the others singing. . . .

There are so many other memories, things about Frank which he may never have mentioned. They comprise a picture of a person who in many ways was not of this world – yet it is he, Frank, who has played his role now in the very centre of our present life. While we live out our lives at the edges of it."

— 3 —

From Jean Varille of Lyons, France, June 24, 1945:
" . . . . J'ai connu votre frère en 1938, depuis nous étions extrêmement amis. . . . Je suis dans un grand désespoir à la pensée de ne plus jamais le revoir avec sa claire amitié, sa gentillesse, ses colères naives et ses yeux bleus. Ce garçon avait une grande valeur. Je croix que bien peu d'Anglo-Saxons avaient une telle comprehension, une telle culture et une telle participation à la vie française. Je l'estimais beaucoup, car il pouvait

rendre de grands services à la cause alliée, et à la cause occidentale.

La mort est venue comme un bandit de grand chemin, le saisir dans le sinistre camp de Buchenwald.

Puisse sa mort avoir été soutenue par les amitiés qu'il savait faire naître. Puisse-t-il ne pas avoir été seul.

Veuillez présenter à sa mere tout le profond chagrin de ses amis français."

—4—

From Alison Grant, April 1945:
"I do know he was happy in England – his time was very full, and consequently to those of us who were drawn into that circle of unbounded affection, love and happiness, which he created, the loss cannot be counted.

He bound the household together with his humour, his embracing interest and love of mankind. He set a standard we try to follow. I also know that nothing would have stopped him going – nothing anyone could say or do. He knew clearly and definitely to the day of his departure – he must go. His death is not only a personal loss to a few like myself who know his place will never be filled. His brand of courage – his courage coupled with his imagination – are not only needed in war, but needed so badly when the war is over, needed by everyone.

But his life wasn't wasted. I feel, as so many of his friends have here said to me, he left us his spirit and faith and uncompromising belief in what was right. That is the legacy he left us. He showed us a way of life and I for one won't forget it ever."

—5—

Statement of the French Ambassador, December 12, 1950:

"My country, in awarding the Cross of the Legion of Honour to the memory of Frank Pickersgill, has performed an obligation of gratitude for one of its best friends.

The letters of Frank Pickersgill are profoundly touching. These lively letters that he wrote to those close to him reveal clearly his fine spirit, always preoccupied with philosophical, literary, artistic and political problems which seemed ever-present to a clear intelligence which was already prematurely developed. The reading of the letters is singularly moving for Frenchmen for the light which it throws on the way in which France came to occupy an ever-growing place in the heart and spirit of Frank Pickersgill. Thoroughly Canadian though he was, he seemed to have reached the point where he could not detach himself from the French soil and from the many friends he counted among my compatriots.

The effort, at times uncertain and uneasy, that he made to find his real destiny led him finally to choose for the accomplishment of his patriotic duty, at a time of testing, the most dangerous and most secret course and it is for us a striking symbol that he landed in Touraine in the very heart of France to undertake the series of dangerous missions which were to lead him to his supreme sacrifice.

I hope you will allow me to say that if France is today honouring a heroic Canadian she is also rendering homage to one of her own adopted sons. I am particularly grateful to the Prime Minister of Canada for the honour he had done us in emphasising, by his distinguished presence, the real significance of this honour on our part. Our thoughts at this moment go also with respectful sympathy to the mother of Frank Pickersgill to whom I ask you, dear Mr. Pickersgill, to be good enough to transmit this Cross of a Chevalier of the Legion of Honour as a symbol of our admiration and our gratitude to her son."